THE ROBINSON CRUSOE STORY

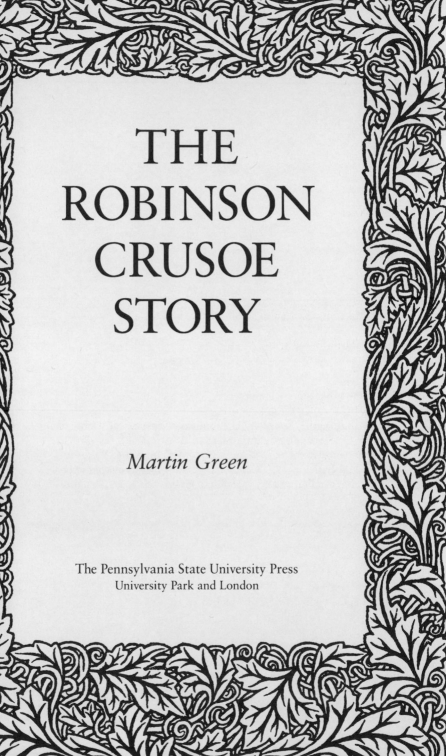

THE
ROBINSON
CRUSOE
STORY

Martin Green

The Pennsylvania State University Press
University Park and London

Library of Congress Cataloging-in-Publication Data

Green, Martin Burgess, 1927–
  The Robinson Crusoe story / Martin Green.

     p.   cm.
  Includes bibliographical references.
  ISBN 0-271-00705-2 (alk. paper)
    1. Defoe, Daniel, 1661?–1731. Robinson Crusoe.   2. Defoe, Daniel,
  1661?–1731—Parodies, imitations, etc.   3. Survival (after airplane
  accidents, shipwrecks, etc.) in literature.   4. Literature, Modern—
  History and criticism.   5. Crusoe, Robinson (Fictitious character)
  6. Castaways in literature.   7. Solitude in literature.   8. Islands
  in literature.   I. Title.
  PR3403.Z5G7   1990
  809'.93355—dc20   90–30687

It is the policy of The Pennsylvania State University Press to use acid-free paper for
the first printing of all clothbound books. Publications on uncoated stock satisfy
the minimum requirements of American National Standard for Information
Sciences—Permanence of Paper for Printed Library Materials, ANSI Z39.48–1984.

Contents

1

Introduction

D aniel Defoe's novel *Robinson Crusoe* tells the story of how a solitary castaway makes a desert island into a happy home. This story has also been told by other writers, a few before him, and many after him, but embodying differences: French and German versions differ from English, 1880s versions differ from 1840s. And the sequence of those tellings, recurrent over two hundred and fifty years, and moving from one European literature to another, constitutes another story. In this the main character is the Robinson Crusoe story, which grows and changes, responding to new national settings, to events like Great Wars, and to ideas, like Marxism. It is sometimes happy, sometimes bitter, sometimes funny. It changes character, sometimes being children's literature, sometimes satire, sometimes romantic idyll. But all this constitutes one continuous story, full of meaning for our past and our present. This second story is the one I want to tell here.

Its significance extends beyond literature, to culture, even to politics. *Robinson Crusoe* is one of the most important genres of that huge literary form, the adventure tale, historically speaking the most important of all our literary forms. For adventure in this sense was the literary reflection (and to some extent the inspiration, intensification, communication) of the expansive imperialist thrust of the white race, the nations of Europe, which started around 1600 and which has not ended yet. That imperialism has been more than a matter of overseas colonies and conquests. It has involved technological invention, economic expansion, religious change, and political institutions. Adventure has been the main form within literature (and literature was in these two hundred and fifty years unusually powerful within culture) that inspired that thrust—inspired nationalism and imperialism and cultural chauvinism. Adventure has also, or therefore, been the liturgy—the series of cultic texts—of masculinism. This word I use to mean that intensification of male pride that began in the seventeenth century, along with modern science, and capitalism, and other great sources of contemporary culture.

So much is true of adventure in general. The Crusoe story in particular differs from the other types in various ways. (In another book I shall try to divide the mass of adventures into seven genres.) One such way is that it seems so pure a type, so persistent—so many writers, from 1719 on, have retold the same story (the plot, as well as the themes and settings) and have made so many powerful meanings out of it. In the other genres (for instance, what I call the Three Musketeers story), each telling differs much more from its precursors.

The Crusoe story remained so much the same partly because, for at least two hundred years, almost every boy read it in his boyhood, and many girls in their girlhood, across most of northern Europe and North America. It became a literary archetype, at the back of every reader's mind, that writers could play upon. It won that special status because it was recognized as the most edifying and improving kind of adventure, the one that had the most to do with work and the least to do with war, and so was the one most recommended by teachers and preachers and incorporated into moral culture.

It was also a realistic story, in its original form and so more respectable than other adventures in that way too. In his essay "Boys' Weeklies," George Orwell says, "Of course no one in his senses would want to turn the so-called penny-dreadful into a realistic novel or a Socialist tract. An adventure story must of its nature be more or less remote from real life."[1] That passage opens up more than one line of thought for us, but for the moment let us just note that what may apply to penny dreadfuls

1. *Collected Essays*, 113.

(and to their apotheoses like *Treasure Island*) certainly does not apply to *Robinson Crusoe*. At least it does not apply to the story as Defoe wrote it and as it was retold by those faithful to him. This is a story that seems as close to real life as the author could make it seem. And partly for that reason it was taught in schools and given as a prize, whereas penny dreadfuls were not.

The result of that continuity in the story's status is that one can study the sequence of versions, interpreting the way they differ from each other in various lights. Even more important, one can interpret the way they do not differ but remain the same, which shows us both the persistence of the appetite for that story in the book-buying public and the fascination it exerted over the book writers. We citizens of the white countries wanted to hear the story told over and over again, because it fed an appetite deep in us. It was the mythic fuel of our cultural engine.

Of course some of those retellings were satiric, anti-adventurous, designed to arouse moral anxiety and inhibit triumphal action—to check our instinctive egotism, political or personal. We might call these anti-Robinsons; a famous example is *Lord of the Flies*. But satire in its own way pays tribute to the pressure it reacts against. Men and women of letters have often rewritten this story against its grain. But that too makes it interesting.

This book therefore studies the Robinson Crusoe story structurally, in two senses of that ambiguous word. First of all, it analyzes the story into a number of motifs, or narrative elements, which the writers have varied and recombined in fairly demonstrable ways. This analytic technique allows us to show economically how the story changes or stays the same. We notice, for instance, that three major motifs of this story—shipwreck, the island, solitude—differ from each other in the degree of their variability. Shipwreck is *usually* the means by which the castaway arrives on the island (but he may be marooned there, or have jumped overboard). The scene is nearly *always* an island (the two exceptions studied here are the comparatively obscure *The Desert Home* and *Die Hoehlenkinder*), while the solitary castaway is *often* replaced by a pair, a family, or a group.

This way of studying narrative, by analysis into recurrent motifs, has been much practiced in recent times; a famous early example is Vladimir Propp's work on Russian folktales. Later critics have tried to apply it to novels, but with less success, because the novel is such a different kind of narrative. Novels are so long, so full of details, so complex in plot, and most of them aim some of the time at being "realistic." But adventure tales are in some ways the folktales of white nationalism and empire; the different versions of a story are so like each other, so simple and easy to read, so obvious in their political morals. (The German fairy tales collected and edited by the brothers Grimm at the beginning of the nineteenth century are another body of literature into which a moral-political tendency has been built, this time in the service of German nationalism.) And of all adventures the Robinson Crusoe story is the simplest to study, by virtue of the number of its retellings.

"Folktale of white empire" is an exaggeration and a paradox, of course, because a folktale cannot be a long printed book. In Defoe's *Robinson Crusoe,* for instance, one has to speak of *categories* of motif because there are so many incidents. But the phrase does point us to the important truth that Propp's model works better on adventures than it does on ordinary novels, and that it can serve us here better than ordinary fiction criticism would.

The other sense in which this study is structuralist is that it takes an interest in the system of literature; the invisible forces that act upon writers and readers, like electromagnets, and assign to a given topic in one generation a given literary form and a given cultural prestige. Adventure has rarely been assigned high literary prestige; and so writers have rarely been recommended to write the Crusoe story carefully, with artistic scruple, despite the high pressure of reader demand. (Because educationists took the story seriously, however, there was, in some times and places, a rather different—a nonliterary—pressure to write it carefully.) Men of literary talent did write the story, and did so seriously. They produced most of the texts we shall study here, for literary quality is one of the criteria I have consulted. But few of their tellings have any of the polish and "perfection," the depth and "interiority," that literary art can give to a book when the writer is aiming at greatness. Those seemingly inherent qualities are of course also partly the result of the interpretations and perspectives established by critics when they have decided that a text deserves them: this is another way in which these qualities are in the gift of literature—of the men and women of letters. Writers with those ultimately spiritual ambitions that are suggested by the word "art" did not choose to write the Robinson Crusoe story, except to subvert it.

This is because one of the severest laws of the literary system is that writers must not yield to the seductions of the larger culture. Literature must maintain a set of values different from and higher than those of the marketplace, the hustings, and even the popular pulpit; it must be a center of spiritual resistance. (This law varies in force with time, but here I shall ignore those variations and concentrate on the way it persists.) The effect this law has on writers is often complicated, paradoxical, and oblique. I mean they rebel against it in a number of ways. But the law is nonetheless deeply felt. And one fairly straightforward and demonstrable effect has been the relegation of adventure to the periphery of the literary system.

Adventure is reading for men, not for readers. Here we see the difference between true masculinism (recalcitrant to the laws of literature) and the gender-linked androgyny of literature in a patriarchal society. The literature taught by English departments may be said to be masculinist in this second sense, but it is very unlike the rank masculinism of adventure. Usually adventure lives in the Siberia of literature—unvisited by either traditional scholars or radical feminists—far removed from respectability, though romantically attractive to male literary rebels for that reason.

There are exceptions. The period 1880–1910 in England was a time when Stevenson and Kipling, and the critics who loved them, tried to combine adventure subject matter with high literary ambitions. So was the period 1945–70 in America. But both attempts were short-lived because they went against the grain of literature, fighting the literary system.

Behind this severe prejudice lies a good deal of bitter experience and keen insight, which many of us are still unwilling to turn away from. Adventure in literature has been the ally of adventure in the national life. It has been a myth of risk and movement and expansion, material as well as moral. It is a liturgy for the cult of potency and potestas—the social management of force, the exertion of power, material and moral. (I suggest we use the concept of potestas as the equivalent in the world of the adventure tale for eros in the world of the novel of love.) No state can exist without some cult of potestas; and no elaborate hierarchical state, no empire, can function without a strong cult of that kind. Thus the spirit of adventure makes itself felt in the army and navy, in covert operations, in giant industries and aggressive trading, in schools—for instance, the public schools of Victorian England, which produced administrators for the empire—in education books (both history and geography were imperialist subjects), and even in the churches, in the work of missionaries.

Moreover, adventure has also been, as I said, the liturgy of masculinism. It has identified power with violence for men, and has told stories about men acquiring power by relating to other men, in loyalty or feud, while women are either absent or play small roles. *Robinson Crusoe,* for instance, has no women characters, and its men feel nothing for women. The first appearance of a woman in one of our texts occurs in *The Swiss Family Robinson,* which does have a wife and mother, but she is quite peripheral. In other kinds of adventure, for instance, the Three Musketeers story, women are more vivid presences, but still rather provide occasions for men to act than act themselves.

There are exceptions to this generalization. For instance, several eighteenth-century German versions of the Robinson story put women in central roles. A woman survives alone on an island; she may be joined by another woman, who may be pregnant, and they raise the child together.[2] These stories must be of great interest to feminists. But from the historical point of view, they are exceptional; and this book takes a historical point of view. We are studying adventure as it has been—as a masculinist imaginative form.

To this masculinism and imperialism, serious literature has traditionally offered a resistance that was surely honorable. To follow a different policy, as I now propose, and to take the adventure seriously, is not to repudiate that tradition as a mistake. Men of letters are no doubt properly contemplatives rather than men of action in most times and places. They extend alliance and protection to other resisters of empire. Some of the latter can be defined in race, class, or gender terms—the Welsh within Great Britain, women in general, the low-church middle class. These groups, quite distinct from the men and women of letters, were nevertheless like them in their aversion from, or distance from, adventure.

The case of women is particularly interesting. Adventure tales were written about, and for, boys, but they were *read* by girls. For a girl to identify with boys was always, within certain limits, acknowledged as an advantage. The reverse was true for boys. The tomboy was always, at least in books, to be admired; the sissy was to be despised. Adventure

2. Jeanine Blackwell, "An Island of Her Own: Heroines of the German *Robinsonaden* from 1720–1800," *German Quarterly* (Winter 1985): 5–26.

reading for girls was closely linked to tomboyishness. Women, the mothers of adventurous boys, could look back on an adventurous past of their own, complacently. This extended adventure's circle of influence. But it probably accentuated the idealizing tendency of adventure writing and reading. In their *Practical Education*, Richard and Maria Edgeworth, being moralists, even said that adventure tales were especially suited to girls because they understood better than boys that adventure tales are fantasies (p. 215).

Other resisters of adventure we might think of in more temperamental terms: the ascetics, those nay-sayers who distrust the expansion of the appetites; the morally anxious, those with a sense of sin, or a need for laws and controls; and the humanist conservatives, those who value above all what civilization has built up, of material and moral culture, and do not want to exchange it for grandeur or excitement. All these groups have been hostile to adventure.

Tales of adventure, including the Crusoe story, were recommended by, and in some sense written for, the others—for men of action, for masculinists who needed a reinforcement of their values, or a clarification of their purposes, and for those we can perhaps call the pharisees of culture. This could be a useful term for our argument, if we let it combine a nineteenth-century sense, which blends into "philistine," of the pharisee as the quintessential enemy of "the artist" (enemy of the free imagination, of the pure spirit) with the biblical sense of the righteous, those who embody the respectable energies of the culture, who legislate its sense of practical moral standards. The pharisees of adventure reading would then be a group-alliance between some of the teachers and preachers and some of the civic, political, and business leaders. In his *Lay Morals*, Robert Louis Stevenson said that most of his contemporaries did not really believe in what Christ taught but in what Benjamin Franklin taught.[3] This is a neat definition of the pharisaic by example, especially appropriate because of the close relation between Franklin and Defoe, both being celebrators of prudence and the respectable virtues, but also celebrators of practical adventure.

We may call many such writers themselves pharisees, in their adventures and in their essays. Defoe, for instance, built up his readers' pride in average Englishness. Scott did the same for Scotsmen. Cooper did the same for Americans. But being pharisees or being in alliance with the

3. *Works of Robert Louis Stevenson*, vol. 15, 422.

pharisees meant that such writers were *not* in alliance with the aesthetes of their time, or the world of letters insofar as that was ruled by aesthetes. (*Aesthete* is of course a word we use more comfortably about people after 1880, but there were before then people who cared enough about art to make it a medium of spiritual values, and it is to them I want to point.) The combative careers of two of our Crusoe writers, Defoe and Cooper, are enough to demonstrate that split among writers. Kipling and Hemingway, who wrote a different sort of adventure, were also literary loners.

Scott was not so combative, but he had, in his later years, like Defoe, a large circle of nonliterary admirers, and a small band of committed critical enemies. What marks off the pharisee as writer is that he does *not* belong to the inner literary circle of his time, the circle that gathers to protect and appropriate the values of literature (and therefore of culture, in opposition to those of civilization). The pharisaical writer usually lets his civilization (i.e., its dominant class) speak through him quite freely, as Defoe did, and defends it against ideals and idealism used to attack it. Rider Haggard used to speak scornfully of England's "children of light," those idealists who disapproved of the adventurer heroes in his tales. Cooper attacked those who wanted to abolish flogging in the American navy. In *Mr Standfast,* John Buchan attacked those who resisted war in 1914.

Such a writer speaks on behalf of gentlemen rather than artists. Other examples are Sir Richard Burton in England and Francis Parkman in America, both excellent adventure writers, incidentally. More typically the man or woman of letters is a liberal, who takes society's tenderest conscience for granted and extends it outward, or inward, detecting new abuses where things had seemed to be all right. When they attack their civilization, they speak for the spirit, and in the name of an ideal consensus.

I said before that the teachers and preachers recommended Crusoe but not other adventurers. Now I seem to have implied that in the nineteenth century they—insofar as they were pharisees—recommended adventure as a whole. That is an exaggeration, for the other forms were seen to be much less edifying than *Robinson Crusoe.* But it is true that in eighteenth- and even more in nineteenth-century Protestant Europe—in marked contrast with the world of letters today—adventure was often regarded as morally healthy.

Today of course we have moral enterprises like the Peace Corps and

Outward Bound, which involve elements of adventure. And there is a cult of the memory of the Freedom Summer in America, when white students risked danger to go south and help in the civil rights movement. Generally speaking, the world of education includes many who believe, quite idealistically, in adventure, which they try to divorce from its imperialist history. But after 1918, and even more after 1945, intellectual opinion even among Marxist radicals turned against it. At best, the excitement of adventure *can* still seem palatable (in literature) if it is linked to feelings of outrage or disgust, as in the work of Norman Mailer.

One or two cases survive of the old attitude, the enthusiasm for respectable adventure, and help us, by their feeling of abnormality, to see what our sense of the normal is. One such case is E. J. Pratt, whom Northrop Frye has described as the "unofficial poet laureate" of Canada. Pratt was born in 1882 and did not die until 1964, and he wrote long narrative poems, nonmodernist and in various senses adventurous, on public and national themes. For instance, *The Titanic,* in 1935; *Breboeuf,* on the martyrdom of a missionary, in 1940; *Dunkirk,* on the war, in 1941; and *Towards the Last Spike,* on the building of the Canadian Pacific Railway, in 1952.

Pratt became a Methodist minister in 1913 and a professor of literature in 1920, and spoke for his culture in a nineteenth-century style. He led the privileged classes, the men of leisure and position, in a sentimental reverence for the men of labor and the men of action. He believed in his country morally, even in its military actions, saying, "This country went through two World Wars with sterling moral credit."[4] He remembered fondly how "all of us have gone through periods of hero-worship in the manner of *Tom Brown's Schooldays.* Strong men, men of action, men of emergency, have been our demi-gods" (p. 15). In 1945 he was invited to go to sea with the Canadian navy, an invitation extended to Kipling in his day, and to Scott in his, but to hardly any other writers. Kipling was of course another of those rare cases of pharisaic writing in the twentieth century.

Pratt, therefore, was an adventure writer, and as such was very unlike most modern poets. Frye, in his essay on Pratt, says he was like a much earlier kind of writer, the oral poet, who remembered and recorded his country's legends, science, philosophy, etc. Such writers (like Homer and

4. *E. J. Pratt on His Life and Poetry,* 4.

Shakespeare) are "symbols of a remote past in which the poet had a central social function from which he has since been dispossessed."[5] Between such a poet and his audience there is no break. He speaks for them; his values are theirs (p. 187). (I might interject that this assumes that the literary audience too identifies with their country and its public image.) Shakespeare had a similar identification with his audience's assumptions (ibid). But in the nineteenth century, Frye says, only Long-fellow and Kipling were popular in this sense; such poetry became a submerged tradition after the Romantic movement.

Speaking of the poet's recording of knowledge, let us note that Pratt researched both the historical and the natural-history facts of his poems. Poetry like his and Kipling's has to seem to know more about such things than the average person knows. (Modernist authors need not do that; they can offer fantasy.) The same is true of writers of respectable adventure in prose, and especially of the Crusoe kind. That is why our quotation from Orwell reminds us how unlike the penny dreadful is to Defoe's story.

This factual imagination is different from, and opposed to, the fanciful imagination we associate with more literary writers, those opposed to one meaning of poetry. *The Tempest*'s version of castaways on an island is fantastic and not factual. The opposition between the two kinds of imagination preoccupied the Romantics. Thus Lamb wrote to Coleridge: "Think what you would have been now, if instead of being fed with old wives' tales in childhood, you had been fed with geography and natural history."[6]

In the last part of the eighteenth century educationists did in fact try to substitute that more rational mental diet, and often they used the Crusoe story for that purpose, as we shall see. Many Romantic writers rebelled against that enterprise, and much modern criticism has remained romantic in this matter. Thus C. S. Lewis says, "The dangerous fantasy is always superficially realistic. The real victim of wishful reverie does not batten on *The Odyssey, The Tempest,* or *The Worm Ouroboros:* he (or she) prefers stories about millionaires, irresistible beauties, posh hotels . . . [or, we might add, desert islands]. . . . There are two kinds of longing. The one is an askesis, a spiritual exercise, and the other

---

5. Frye, *The Bush Garden*, 184.
6. Eggoff, Ashley, and Stubbs, *Only Connect*, 423.

is a disease."[7] *The Tempest* treats more or less the same subject as *Robinson Crusoe,* but it is not "superficially realistic," and so no one imagines himself or herself as living on Shakespeare's island. The images of the fanciful imagination carry on them the sign of unreality; though whether we, like Lewis, should regard that as being to their advantage is another matter. (Surely it would be just as plausible to say that the unrealistic imagination is a diminished thing, enfeebled by its sophistication?)

Literature, however, in the sense of its critics, scholars, and theoreticians, has often prided itself on its unrealism, its sense of the gap between words and things, the gap between stories and events, and so on. At the moment, with the enthusiasm for poststructuralism and deconstruction, that pride is at a very high pitch. The men and women of letters feel they have a professional knowledge of these uncertainties that is as esoteric as the particle physicists' knowledge of particles. Thus in the literary world what I call the naive or factual imagination, which is so important in adventure, goes at a heavy discount.

To put the point another way, the fanciful imagination, in the ordinary sense, does not lead on to action. The other kind, being linked to what Lewis called "dangerous fantasy," does. They thus seem linked to opposite ideas of the function of education, one fostering engagement and action, the other fostering doubt and disillusion. This does not mean that the facts of adventure may not seem fantastic in the loose sense. They have often done so. Defoe's precursor as an adventure writer, Richard Hakluyt, certainly dealt in such facts; for instance, in his stories about El Dorado, which certainly have some character of fantasy. But those tales are parts of a collection dominated by factual reports on real voyages and were designed both to inspire and guide readers on other real voyages.

Thus many adventures, and notably most of the Crusoe story versions, have recommended themselves to their readers as real. They have been read in sequence with, side by side with, narratives of real-life exploration, of feats of courage and strength and force, of sailing around the world alone, of flying across the Atlantic when that was dangerous, and so on. This is not naive reading any more than those are naive actions. It is not necessarily self-deceptive. It is certainly not unimportant. And it is time we learned how to focus critical attention upon it again.

7. Ibid., 215.

Perspective and Method

Perhaps, since we live in an age of theory, I should say that I regard myself as a cultural studies critic: that is, my comments on books are designed to have a bearing on issues outside literature, and to situate literature as a whole in a larger context. (I am not thinking, of course, of those books of mine that are biographical or historical.) This cultural criticism was one aspect of the work of F. R. Leavis, my principal teacher, and though it is not quite what "cultural studies" most fashionably means today, it is not totally different.

The quarrel betweeen adventure and literature is a topic to which my argument will have to recur, because this is a literary argument, about form as well as content, and yet adventure scarcely counts as a literary fact with most people, and so at a dozen points it will be necessary to justify what I am doing. I should perhaps sketch the larger map of the adventures written by gifted writers and deserving critical attention. Besides the Crusoe story itself, and the Three Musketeers story (the romantic-historical novel that derives from Scott and Dumas), I recognize five other categories. (These seven are not exhaustive, but they cover an enormous mass of writing, and they include what interests me most.)

Of these five, one is the frontier story, such as James Fenimore Cooper wrote around the figure of Natty Bumppo; I have discussed this, in its American versions, in *The Great American Adventure*. Another is the wanderer or picaro story, which traverses a geographical or societal panorama, as in Kipling's *Kim* or in Jules Verne's geographical romances. Then there is the avenger story, especially popular in the nineteenth century, such as *The Count of Monte Cristo* and *Twenty Thousand Leagues Under the Sea*. Finally, there are two stories somewhat more tied to a time and place. One is the Icelandic saga, which became so popular in England and Germany in the later nineteenth century; and the other is about a man fighting alone against an organization, which seems to be the form most popular in the twentieth century. But this larger subject will be addressed in another book.

As for the Robinson Crusoe story itself, it has long been agreed, or at least often declared, that it deserves study. A German scholar named Hermann Ullrich embraced the subject as his lifework in the last years of the nineteenth century and produced an annotated bibliography entitled *Robinson und Robinsonaden* in 1898, which he offered as volume one of a large enterprise. He also produced a new translation of Defoe's version in 1905, and in 1908 a supplement to his bibliography which, for instance, listed new translations (new since 1898) into French, Dutch, German, Italian, Serbian, Welsh, Maori, Hungarian, Czech, Icelandic, Russian, Romanian, and Spanish.[8]

But World War I both interrupted Ullrich's enterprise and dispersed his collections and he could not complete his scheme, though he did produce a sketch of what he had intended, in 1924, entitled *Robinson Crusoe: Geschichte eines Weltbuchs*—the story of a world-book, a phrase that is in itself a contribution to the subject. Dying echoes of his project continued to sound for some time. A Dutch scholar, Werner A. Staverman, produced *Robinson Crusoe in Nederland* in Groningen in 1907, and wrote in 1926 that the world still needed "an enquiry into the significance of *Robinson Crusoe* and the development of the *Robinsonade* in the 18th and 19th centuries."[9] And Philip Babcock Gove, an American, wrote in 1941 that such a work had been anticipated for already several decades.[10] But the major energies of literary scholarship were given to very different ideas in the decades after 1918. It seems clear that the project fell victim to the reaction against adventure in general, and *Robinson Crusoe* in particular, left behind by World War I.

My own project is significantly unlike Ullrich's. It is less massive in its scholarship and more tendentious in its argument. Each of my chapters is at core an essay on the nature of adventure and the function of literature, as well as being, more obviously, a continuation of the Robinson Crusoe story and of the intellectual history it belongs to.

Perhaps this is the place to point out that in a study like this, one deals with stories, not with texts. That is to say, what concerns us is a sequence of imaginary events, a recombination of literary motifs, with the ideas carried by them, rather than that unbreakable and unsubstitutable sequence of words that forms the originary unit, the text, the sacred object for traditional literary studies. The various versions of the Robinson story exist in a number of different wordings, in abridgments and adaptations and modernizations, changes in form that do not matter to us unless they constitute changes in the story. The most striking case is *The Swiss Family Robinson,* for which there is not and never was any

---

8. Ullrich, *Zeitschrift fuer Buecherfreunde,* vol. 11, 444–56 and 489–98.
9. *English Studies* 8 (1926): 193.
10. *The Imaginary Voyage in Prose Fiction,* 152.

definitive text, for English- and French-reading audiences. It always existed in a number of slightly different versions, which are from our point of view the same.

Such a study cannot of course even mention all the retellings of the Crusoe story. To do that would be the virtue of a scholar like Ullrich. I discuss what seem to me the most interesting among those I have read— which means in effect those published in English, French, and German and recommended by some earlier critic. Luckily, German scholars have done a good deal of work on this subject; German scholarship has its category, *die Robinsonade,* which covers all the books I will discuss. The French also speak of *la robinsonnade,* but they have put more of their intellectual energy into *le voyage imaginaire,* a category that includes *Gulliver's Travels* as well as *Robinson Crusoe;* of which, indeed, Swift's book is a better example than Defoe's. To study *Robinson Crusoe* in that context is to see it as a variant on *Gulliver's Travels.* My point of view has the opposite effect.

But it is the English-language literatures that are worst equipped to help any fruitful study of the Crusoe story. They have no category like *die Robinsonade,* and to track even *Robinson Crusoe* itself through the bibliographies, one must follow the trail of the author's name; and since Defoe was so prolific, that trail splits up into dozens more, most of which are quite unprofitable.

It is paradoxical that it should be the Anglo-Saxon literatures, to which the Crusoe story belongs and where it played its most important part in history, that avert their eyes from that myth. But the paradox is probably self-explanatory. Just because that myth blazed so powerfully in Anglo-Saxon culture, literature had to defend itself by turning its eyes away. Now, however, men of letters must turn back toward adventure and reconsider the nearly three centuries of empire and the books that were written to inspire and reflect it, as well as those in which the Robinson Crusoe story is used simply to reflect upon that history. (This last category includes such books as J. M. Coetzee's *Foe* and Jane Gardam's *Crusoe's Daughter.*)

From the cultural studies point of view, the most challenging implication of this argument and method is that it is stultifying to concentrate on English-language adventures and on the British Empire to the exclusion of the other white nations, all of which engaged in the same imperial adventure. Holland, France, Germany, Scandinavia, all northwest Europe took part in that immense thrust that characterizes, that in a sense

constitutes, modern history. Their literatures are similarly intercon-
nected. In terms of literal colonial power there was all the difference in
the world between England and, say, Switzerland; but in imaginative
terms it is the likeness that is striking. *The Swiss Family Robinson* was
immensely popular reading in all Europe and North America.

Thus the Crusoe story is a continental, not a national, one. Its versions
reflected (to some degree inspired) the conquest by one continent,
Europe, of the four others, Asia, Africa, America, and Australasia. It
was easy and exciting—by the testimony of many writers—for Danes,
Swiss, Frenchmen, perhaps above all Germans, to take part in the great
adventure, both literally and literarily, whether the flag flown from the
fort was their own or British. It mattered, at least at first, that all those
on the winning side should be Christian, preferably Protestant, but
doctrine was rarely important. What mattered most—at first it seemed
a mere common denominator, but it proved to be of tragic importance—
was that all should have white skins.

The Robinson Crusoe story, and the adventure story as a whole, has
been racist. But the virulence of that racism has differed from case to
case so much that some can be called comparatively innocent. And in
such cases that racism must be taken for granted (perhaps we could call
it racialism) and adventure is a priori a phenomenon of racial action and
racial consciousness. The word *racist* must be reserved for the really
virulent cases. In other words, I shall call this or that version of the story
racist, even though of course all of them are racial. The adventure tale
would not be half so important—would scarcely deserve study—if it
were not a racial phenomenon, using that word neutrally. That is not
something one need discover or point out.

2

Robinson Crusoe (1719)

A s everyone knows, Defoe's story of a castaway and how he survived follows (at a distance) the facts of Alexander Selkirk's four and a half years of solitude on Juan Fernández, from 1704 to 1709. It is likely that Defoe met Selkirk, but he could also have read about Selkirk's experiences in at least three publications: E. Cook's *Voyage to the South Seas* and Captain Woodes Rogers's *A Cruising Voyage Round the World*, both of 1712, and Richard Steele's essay in *The Englishman*, Number 26, for 1–3 December 1713.

In this Robinson Crusoe story of ours, Selkirk remains a shadowy presence behind Defoe even now, because so many writers about *Robinson Crusoe* or retellers of the story have gone back to Selkirk to use him against Defoe, or to put themselves on an equal footing with their great precursor. A notable modern case of this is Michel Tournier in *Vendredi*. He develops at some length Selkirk's anecdote, which Defoe does not use, about chasing a goat and falling off the edge of a precipice in its embrace.

Crusoe also had several other precursors, in the form of tales about solitary survivors on a desert island. Famous literary examples are the

Sinbad story in *The Arabian Nights,* the Hagan story in the *Gudruns-saga,* and the Philoctetes story in the *Iliad.* There were also several less literary stories of shipwrecked sailors, answering to the interest in the new geographical spread of European commerce, in the century before Defoe wrote.

The Author

The Crusoe story belongs to Defoe, and the most important context into which to put his book is his life, his other books, and his ideas. Daniel Defoe was born in London in 1660 into a Dissenting tradesman's family, and attended a Dissenting academy. He thus belonged to that commercial and entrepreneurial class that was outside the Establishment, outside the established Church of England, the aristocracy, the squirearchy, the top levels of the army and navy, which yet was, in his time, taking a national lead, building up its own and the nation's wealth.

Because of his personal endowment, Defoe's views were broader than most tradesmen's, his information was immense, and he claimed, not implausibly, to have been consulted by the king, William III. But nowhere in his voluminous writings, which seem to touch on every conceivable topic of the day, do we meet ideas sharply at variance with those of his class. He was their spokesman, Crusoe was their hero, and his story was the entrepreneurial myth.

Defoe's other books can be seen to serve his class interests, and some even complement this most famous title. His *Complete English Gentleman,* for instance, defines gentleman so as to make that title applicable to successful tradesmen, and defines education with a stress on modern subjects like geography and mathematics (rather than classical literature). Thus Crusoe could be called an English gentleman. Defoe's *Essay Upon Projects,* which proposes a great variety of ways to improve England's social arrangements, is like Crusoe's work on his island, with a whole society replacing the solitary individual. His *Tour of the Whole Island of Great Britain* describes in explicit detail the England against which, in *Robinson Crusoe,* Defoe implicitly measures the destitution in which Crusoe begins and the savagery with which Friday is content. In this book Defoe's stress is on Britain's improved technology and new wealth; he tells of the famous past of each place he comes to, but his real excitement is reserved for its present and future. And in his other novels, like *Moll Flanders* and *Captain Singleton,* part of the interest is seeing emerge, through the mask of the adventuress or the pirate, the solid tradesman look of Crusoe/Defoe.

As for Defoe's ideas, they belong to the Enlightenment. He stands in time between Bacon and Locke, the first spokesmen of that movement toward tolerance and reason and practical work (and all that such values imply). He was not so much the intellectual as either of that pair; nor was he so much the man of letters as Pope and Swift; and though he was closer to Addison and Steele, they were more polished teachers of the new manners and the new morality than he. Yet Defoe was more many-sided than any of them and he opened his mind more enthusiastically to the ideas of his time; through him *all* its voices seem to speak. It is appropriate that he should have created this ubiquitous and immortal myth.

There are of course signs that now, in the second half of the twentieth century, that myth has died, has proven mortal, just as there are signs that its "ubiquitousness" was always limited to the white races. But it would be unwise to believe those signs implicitly. They are what we, the men and women of letters, would like to believe, and what is largely true within our circle of influence. But just as it has always been easy for black and brown readers to identify with Crusoe and not with Friday, so it is still easy (in some sense natural) for naive readers to love the story and believe its teaching.

The Book Itself

Robinson Crusoe has been above all else an extremely popular story. In the National Union Catalog, fifty-four pages are given up to listing different editions, whereas only four pages go to perhaps the most famous literary novel of eighteenth-century England, Samuel Richardson's *Clarissa Harlowe,* and the same to the most famous nineteenth-century novel, George Eliot's *Middlemarch.* Moreover, another fourteen pages are given to Wyss's later Robinson story, *The Swiss Family Robinson.* So, if you add together all the pages given to all the versions of the Crusoe story, you will get a number that will contrast with the four for *Middlemarch* the way a genre or subgenre contrasts with an individual title.

The success of *Robinson Crusoe* was immediate. There were seven reprints in London in seven years; it was serialized within the first year and pirated, abridged, adapted, and dramatized endlessly. It was translated into French in 1720, and the translation was reprinted in 1721, 1722, and 1726; the Dutch translation was reprinted in 1721, 1736, 1752, and 1791. The greatest interest was shown in Germany, where a great number of books were issued with "Robinson Crusoe" in their titles. Some of them had been written and even published before 1719, but were reissued to cash in on the enthusiasm for Defoe's book. Some were famous and important in their own right. Both *Gil Blas* and *Don Quixote* appeared in German as, respectively, the Spanish and the Schwaebische Robinson.

One feature of these German titles was that they claimed the Robinson image for specific parts of Germany (the Prussian Robinson, the Saxon Robinson, the Westphalian Robinson, and so on) and also for specific professions (the doctor Robinson, the baker Robinson, the minister Robinson). Such titles show, among other things, how fast the middle classes everywhere claimed the title as their own. Or perhaps one should rather say that those classes acknowledged Crusoe's claim to represent them.

There is some culture-history significance to the story of the book's translations even. There was, for instance, no translation into Spanish in Spain until almost the mid-nineteenth century, *much* later than anywhere else in Europe. The book had been placed on the Index of forbidden reading in 1756, but this silencing was more than a Church phenomenon. Robinson was unwelcome in Spain because the Enlightenment as a whole was unwelcome; official Spanish culture by and large refused to participate in Europe's secularized-Protestant adventure.

Russia, on the other hand, though its intellectuals often saw their country as a twin to Spain in its retarded and peripheral relation to Europe, and for the same reasons of governmental obscurantism, nevertheless had a translation of *Robinson Crusoe* a hundred years earlier, in the early 1760s. Indeed, twenty years before that and only a decade or so after publication, *Robinson Crusoe* in the original English was one of the books the explorer Vitus Bering took with him when he was sent out by Peter the Great to look for a Northwest Passage for Russian ships. It was recognized, there in St. Petersburg, as a good book for explorers to read.

From the point of view of Russian men of letters, the Russian state was hostile to the new ideas that came from Europe. But that was above all true of the liberty-equality-fraternity ideas that interested men of letters. The Robinson story carried those ideas implicitly, but also some of a different kind, those useful to an autocratic state. The Tsarist government wanted to harness for its own purposes the entrepreneurial and technological energies that were serving England so well. This continued to be true during the nineteenth century.

Indeed, in the twentieth century, the Bolshevik regime continued to protect the story, and Defoe in general, as recommended reading. In 1933 Defoe, Swift, and Jules Verne were officially declared the foreign authors most deserving translation into Russian. Marx himself had, after all, vigorously applauded entrepreneurial capitalism in its triumph over feudalism; and then Communist criticism has never been afraid of being pharisaical. It is typical that it would be the Communist critic Ralph Fox, who, in his *The Novel and the People* of 1937, called *Robinson Crusoe* and *The Odyssey* the two greatest stories in the world.

But what do *we* see when we look at Defoe's story from this book's vantage point? I want to sum up Defoe's novel in terms of seven of its motifs; or rather, since it is a novel rather than a folktale, in terms of seven categories of motif. These categories are designed to have one surface of literary form but another that suggests cultural meaning.

First of all, most of the story's events take place on a desert island. From high points Crusoe can see the ocean all around him. No human beings live there, though primitive savages use it for occasional cannibal feasts. When Crusoe finds a footprint, he is overwhelmed with shock, because he has grown used to complete solitude. Moreover, the climate of the island, therefore its animal and vegetable life, belongs to the tropics. He has to adjust to, and learn to survive in, a new world.

Second, Crusoe arrives on his island during the night and in a terrible storm. The ship on which he was sailing was wrecked, and he alone survives. He gets his first sight of his future home when he awakens from sleep on a brilliant morning on a sandy beach. His past, and even his transition from that past to this present, is totally blotted out. He begins a new life. This is a single moment, but it echoes through the rest of the story, and so provides a category of motifs.

Third, Crusoe survives by means of work—this story is an epic of intelligent work—but that does not mean sheer slog or phenomenal muscles. It means cunning and luck, and skills and tools—skills that have to be learned and tools that have to be made. Some things he finds in the wreck of his ship, but others are shadowy presences in his brain, half-remembered from half-observed workmen at home. One of the hidden subjects of the book is Defoe's England seen as a gigantic storehouse of skills and tools, a Crystal Palace Exhibition. (An even more hidden subject is the status of the gun as Crusoe's ultimate tool, the ultimate Western tool, on which the structure of Western cultural superiority is reared.) The way things are seen, what is seen, expresses a workman's viewpoint; this is a do-it-yourself sensibility. Crusoe swims around the wreck and finds no way to climb aboard, but the second time around, for no good reason, he does find a rope. This untidy process, which rarely finds expression in poetry or high drama, is the way things happen to a workman engaged in a practical enterprise.

Fourth, Crusoe does more than survive. He prospers, and succeeds. Long before he leaves the island, he is the object of the reader's envy, not anxiety. His island is a plantation, and he is a planter, a proto-Nabob. He has accumulated wealth, which is stored in excellent order, and a number of estates. More than that, he is the island's king or governor, with subjects. All this is said jocularly, but the jokes conceal, or ensure against, hubris, a swelling excitement. The narrative curve of the book is strongly upward; it is a success story, and Crusoe is lucky—not unbelievably, and no more than he deserves to be, but lucky. This is a modern (and eighteenth-century) version of Dick Whittington, played out on a desert island, not in London, and in total social mobility. (This is Dick Whittington, it may be worth pointing out, as opposed to, say, Robin Hood.) All the limits of guild and apprenticeship are burst, and Crusoe gets to be butcher, baker, and candlestick-maker, in the spirit of the modern world. He even does the work that women do and bursts the bonds of gender.

Fifth, Crusoe, embodying white civilization, encounters people of a different color, culture, religion, technology. The reader, through an identification with Crusoe, feels put to the test. Can he survive without the protections of his homeland culture? Then, has he the right to survive by killing or enslaving others? And how can he imagine living with them, doing both them and himself good? Crucial to answering these questions is the central place assigned to cannibalism within savage culture, for cannibalism finally justifies the white man's violence.

Sixth, the central representative of that other culture, Friday, is a willing slave. (This version of our story is certainly racist.) The moment when Crusoe fires his musket at Friday's assailant, and the following moment, when Friday puts Crusoe's foot on his own neck, together form the supreme sign of white imperialism. In the first case, the white man speaks in thunder and lightning, with the voice of a god, and the black man falls down dead. In the second, the good native approaches the white man on his stomach and makes himself his willing slave. This category of motif is concentrated in the last part of the story, but it had premonitions in Crusoe's own experience of slavery, and his dealings with Xury, so it is far from being a single event.

Robinson's exaltation of spirit facing Friday, which the reader shares with him, is developed in later adventures, and comes to a sort of climax in Kipling's story "The Man Who Would Be King." We meet the same idea in Rider Haggard, in Conrad's *Lord Jim,* and in Rolvaag's *Giants in the Earth.* In these stories, too, the idea of king blends into the idea of god, both ideas being officially disinfected by the jocular ambivalence of tone Kipling and Defoe and the others maintain. In actual history, one of the striking cases of divinization—and of consequent punishment—was that of Captain Cook. The adventure, fictional and nonfictional, carried that secret excitement at its core.

Last, this is a story of *morally justified* imperialism. Crusoe starts with a desert island and a wrecked ship, two things of no use to anybody. But after a while, swimming to and fro between the two, he has sewn them together to make a valuable property. By the time he leaves it has become a colony, fit to belong to the British Empire. But Crusoe's titles of ruler or governor are always semimocking, partly because this is also an anti-imperialist story, on the side of self-help, not hierarchy, of the adventurous individual, not official authority. The idea of empire is attached to the Spaniards, with their silver mines, their cruelty to the Indians, and their Inquisition. Crusoe represents the opposite of all that.

Indeed, most adventures carry signs of anti-imperialism as a way to enlist readers' sympathies. Imperialism is in most times and places a concept that is self-described as evil, or at least hubristic; moreover, we normally—or while reading—sympathize with acts of violence only when they are performed on the side of an underdog. But few adventures carry anti-imperialist signs that are as convincing as *Robinson Crusoe*'s. In stories of the Three Musketeers type, for instance, the young men's attachment to the king (or the queen) and against the cardinal (who

represents power) is not much more than a grace of quixotic chivalry. As
the plot makes clear, the cardinal is France, and the Musketeers cannot
but serve him, finally. But *Robinson Crusoe* clearly speaks for cultural
forces (such as the Protestant conscience and the democracy of labor)
that powerfully opposed empire.

The novel spoke, as we saw, for entrepreneurial hard work and social
mobility. Such ideas were associated with later democratic moralists,
like Benjamin Franklin in the eighteenth century and Samuel Smiles in
the nineteenth—both of them direct heirs to Defoe in various ways.
Those ideas have been largely discredited, in intellectual circles, since
1918. But they remained powerful for two hundred years; indeed, they
are so still, in the ordinary world—the intellectual underground.

The Persistence of Robinson

We may take some examples of how long these ideas persisted from
modern America. The first one is Floyd Dell's autobiography of 1926,
Intellectual Vagabondage. Chapter 2 is entitled "Robinson Crusoe."
Everyone, Dell says, reads Defoe's story as a child, and our adult
enjoyment of it is very like our enjoyment as children. "We lived in
imagination Crusoe's life, and our cramped egotism found free scope in
the creation of a world after our own fancy. . . . We learned in such play
to believe that we were self-sufficient and all-conquering. We learned
that the individual is by right the master of his environment, and not its
helpless victim."[1]

Dell connects that experience to the history of America in particular.
After they had taken its gold, the Spanish conquistadores found no use
for America; but other Europeans saw a great possibility there. "The
people who were at odds with feudal institutions and traditions. . . . It
was the Protestant English who now became foremost in settling the
new continent" (p. 29). They had a new idea of society. Dell gives the
example of Captain John Smith saying that in his colony the man who
would not work should not eat. "It was early in the 18th century when
this idea was first expressed in a realistic prose fantasy by a capable man
of letters" (p. 31). That was, of course, *Robinson Crusoe.*

---

1. *Intellectual Vagabondage,* 27.

A second example shows how other aspects of the idea still operated for immigrants into America in the twentieth century. This is an immigrant autobiography published in 1923 entitled *From Immigrant to Inventor: An Example for Young Americans*. It was often reprinted, up to 1949. The author, Michael Pupin, was born in Idvor, a highly traditional ("feudal") village in the Austro-Hungarian Empire. Pupin came to America young and eventually became an inventor and a teacher of electromechanics.

Pupin reflects on the cultural inferiority of Idvor to the United States thus: "We had a blacksmith, a wheelwright, and a barber in Idvor"; men of skill, like Robinson. But they came from elsewhere, and "there was not one respectable Serb peasant in Idvor, no matter how poor, who did not think that he was superior to these people who had only a transient existence in our historic village." These men of skill, who were, again like Robinson, wanderers, did not belong in the village's tradition. "The knowledge of our historical traditions and our implicit belief in them made us feel superior to people who wandered about like gypsies with no traditions, and with nothing to anchor them to a particular place. A newcomer to our village was closely scrutinized, and he was judged not so much by his skill in a craft . . . but by . . . the traditions of the people to whom he belonged."[2] The author is clearly writing from Defoe's point of view; life begins when one breaks free from the rootedness of tradition.

Pupin tells us he had trouble when he first reached his Promised Land in America because he had no skills and was even unready to learn them; he had more muscular power but less manual dexterity than American boys (p. 86). This is the Robinson idea translated into somatic terms. As for the sociology of work, his American friend, Christian, had several trades at his fingertips and yet had served apprentice to none of them. "My description of a European apprenticeship amused him very much, and he called it worse than slavery" (p. 76). And finally Pupin becomes an inventor, the perfect American calling. He never mentions *Robinson Crusoe,* but there is a clear correspondence between his book and Defoe's. His theory of American social psychology, and its difference from the Old World's, finds its perfect narrative expression in the Robinson Crusoe story.

Yet another book by an American, and published in the same decade,

2. Pupin, *From Immigrant to Inventor*, 439.

made the allusion to Defoe explicit. It was entitled *Robinson Crusoe: Social Engineer,* and it promised that readers could find solutions to the worst social and political problems of the period by turning to Defoe's book. The author, Henry E. Jackson, had some connections with the Technocracy movement of that decade.

The Original Appeal and Imitations

Of course, this ideological character to *Robinson Crusoe* was not apparent to its first readers; neither did they conceptualize it. They apparently saw the book simply as an exciting narrative. Its appeal was surely in part a matter of the contemporaneity of its themes and all the Hakluyt-like anecdotes it recalled. Selkirk's story is the supreme example. And then there were certain traditional or mythical elements in the story.

There had always been tales of men left alone on desert islands, but it does not seem likely that Defoe was indebted to them. For instance, the most interesting of these predecessors, the one with some imaginative power, occurs in the German *Simplicissimus.* But that book's main scheme of ideas is mystically religious, and so almost the opposite of *Robinson Crusoe*'s. The coincidence of the two island settings is not much more than a narrative pun. Defoe's meaning was quite unlike these precursors' and was allied to the drives of secular modern Europe.

Besides the reprints and translations of *Robinson Crusoe,* there were the retellings. For instance, forty German *Robinsonaden* appeared between 1722 and 1769. Nevertheless, this was mere popularity, so far as the first half of the eighteenth century went. Nobody, it seems, was taking the book seriously, or at least not consciously. Among the English imitations, or comparable cases, the best known are *Ashton's Memorial* of 1726, F. Dorrington's *The Hermit* of 1727 (ascribed to Philip Quarll), *Peter Wilkins* of 1751, and Ralph Morris's *John Daniel* of the same year. Such books have more in common with Swift (or with Poe) than with Defoe. Not because they have any literary brilliance, but because they have passages of comic fantasy, which quite destroy any illusion of reality. Insofar as they remind us of *Robinson Crusoe,* it is of the parts before and after Crusoe's life on the island, his picaresque wanderings.

A title typical of such books, which sets out the menu of reading pleasures ahead, runs thus: "The Voyages, Dangerous Adventures, and Imminent Escapes of Captain Richard Falconer: Containing, the Laws, Customs, and Manner of the Indians in America: his Shipwrecks, his marrying an Indian wife; his narrow escape from the island of Dominico, etc . . ." The title of Defoe's book is comparable, but, as we shall see, the Robinson Crusoe story soon came to mean something quite different from that. It came to mean simply the island episode and the work done there.

The only interesting book from a literary point of view among the first-generation progeny of Robinson was German. This was J. G. Schnabel's *Die Insel Felsenburg,* published between 1731 and 1743, which will be discussed later. This book had a considerable impact on writers of the German Romantic movement, though largely because of the non-Robinson elements in the story. However, there is a general likeness between Schnabel and Defoe, for instance, in their shaky literary status. Schnabel was no better esteemed by the men of letters of his country and century than the Englishman was.

Resistance to the Story

Defoe's story of course occupies a prominent position in the panorama of English literature. Its author is one of the dozen names everyone knows, and hundreds of scholarly studies have been devoted to him, with a large proportion focusing on *Robinson Crusoe.* Nevertheless, it is my impression that the Crusoe story—at least in its adventure aspect—has been disliked by men and women of letters, if we set them off from the pharisees, the direct spokesmen for the ruling class. (Historically speaking, these two groups are not always so distinct, but in relation to this story they can be treated as separate.) Indeed, even taking Defoe as a whole, the warm love so often expressed in books about Pope, or Swift, or Johnson—the strong suggestion that the scholar writing the book has defined himself in terms of his subject—is rarely given to him.

The only large exception, where men of letters were enthusiastic for Defoe, was the case of the English Romantics. That is largely to be explained by the reaction of the Romantics against Pope and Swift. Defoe could seem "natural" to readers disgusted by the severity and snobbery of the Augustans. Wordsworth and Coleridge, moreover, made considerable use of explorers' and travelers' tales of adventure and descriptions of faraway places, though mainly for metaphorical or ornamental purposes. Coleridge even drew an interesting critical comparison between Defoe and Swift, to the advantage of the former, but that is quite exceptional among men of letters. A general literary judgment on *Robinson Crusoe* is represented by Henry James's remark to H. G. Wells, reproving his looseness of form; James said that Defoe's story, which Wells seemed to be imitating, was not a novel at all.

James's judgment is, moreover, irrefutable if one has in mind some severe and self-conscious ideal of fictional art. *Robinson Crusoe* is not, in the full sense of the word, a work of literature. There have been many attempts to read patterns of irony or symbol into Defoe's text, but they derive from littérateurs' restless need to appropriate any well-known book as a work of "literature." To use a modern term, *Robinson Crusoe* is only a semiconstructed narrative; it offers small reward to analysts with either deconstructionist ideas or those more traditional ideas we might call reconstructionist. (James told Wells he always rewrote novels in his head as he read them, testingly, and that is a good metaphor for traditional criticism.) Literature is that set of books which deserves and rewards such analysis. Defoe, one might say, deconstructs himself; or rather, he never really constructed a book, in the mystical sense of that term.

Nor does *Robinson Crusoe* reward that interest in personality that novels normally foster, using "personality" to cover both the field of personal relations between characters and any one character's play of tone about himself. Crusoe is not a fully created character, as unfriendly critics have often pointed out. Not only is Defoe careless about consistency and continuity, but whole aspects of the man and his experience, like his sexuality, are omitted. The range of our transactions with him is very limited. Dickens said that the book had never made anyone either laugh or cry—the crucial criteria as far as Dickens's own work was concerned.

However, to admit the justice of these comments is not to say that the book is trivial, or even that Crusoe is unlifelike. He is unnovelistic, unliterary, which is a different matter. A historical figure with whom he has much in common, Captain Cook, was also usually called dry—which was Dickens's word for Crusoe. Cook's biographers have not "brought him to life" in the novelistic sense because, as they themselves have said, aspects of "human nature" seem to have been left out of him. But if, from a novelistic point of view, Cook and Crusoe are uninteresting or unengaging, that indicates a limitation in novels rather than in them. To anyone with an alert mind, they are of the greatest interest. James Joyce says (in one of the best general essays on Defoe) that Crusoe's personal dourness and apathy are just what make him a convincing hero of British imperialism, for those interested in the making of the empire.

Irish writers like Joyce, who stand at a little distance from England, have often been the ones to see the powerful way Crusoe represents his country—the way he, rather than John Bull, should be its symbol. George Moore, another Irishman, in his *Avowals,* talks of the prosaic, unimaginative, *terre à terre* quality of English culture, and says, "Nobody was more terre à terre than Crusoe. England seems to have expressed herself in her first narrative uncommonly well" (p. 8). And it is of course the implicit distaste or disgust of the man of letters that gives such remarks half their flavor.

In France, Paul Dottin made much of the strong affinity between Defoe and Franklin, one of the great American pharisees. Dottin called *Robinson Crusoe* "la Bible du self-made man," and also credits the story with creating many vocations to a life at sea, and in the service of the empire. There is of course no way to demonstrate how many such careers were inspired by Defoe, but the assertion is made in dozens of autobiographies and biographies. And the fact that such declarations seem plausible *is* a demonstrable fact, and an important one.

To those who care primarily about the values of personality, as opposed to those who care about the formal pleasures of literature (and those two classes contain between them most men of letters), Defoe has often seemed a comparatively unattractive writer. We might take Dr. Johnson as a symbol of both attitudes: for what he wrote, for what he was socially, and for the strong moral sense he made out of the literary life. Then we might use Boswell as an opposite figure, remembering his enthusiastic resolve to sail with Cook—in other words, to become a temporary Crusoe. Johnson quickly dissuaded Boswell, saying how soon he would be bored, and making his enthusiasm seem adolescent excitement. Boswell stayed with Johnson and the Club and justified his life by writing his great biography. (When Cook's journals were published, Johnson said, "Sir, if you talk of it as a subject of commerce, it will be gainful, if as a book that is to increase human knowledge, I believe there will not be much of that."[3]) And later men of letters have usually agreed that staying at home is the option of moral maturity.

Contemporary Explorers

We shall return to Cook because he is so like Robinson, but he belonged to a later generation, and so we shall consider him in relation to Campe's version of the story rather than Defoe's. The contemporary explorer best suited to stand beside Defoe and to extend our understanding of the writer is William Dampier, who was only nine years Defoe's senior. He was a geographer as well as an explorer. Defoe was a sort of geographer himself; he edited an atlas, called himself a Master of Geography, and volume two of *Robinson Crusoe* is a world tour, heavily indebted in fact to Dampier's writings. Dampier, moreover, was involved in the story of Alexander Selkirk, since he sailed on both the expedition that marooned Selkirk and the one that picked him up. His *New Voyage Round the World* of 1697 was a best-seller in the terms of seventeenth-century publication. Seven editions appeared before 1727. And the book has been credited with reviving the whole genre of travel literature, which had lapsed in popularity after 1627.

Dampier had first sailed in 1679 and did not return to England for twelve years. His temperament, at least as expressed in his books, was practical, sober, and scientific. In fact in temperament, he has often been said to be a precursor for Cook. Though he was one of a band of buccaneers who marched across the isthmus of Darien to attack that city, his account of these places and people is informative rather than excited. One of his companions wrote, " 'Twas gold that tempted a pack of merry boys of us, near three hundred in number, being all soldiers of fortune."[4] This sounds like the pirate legends of the Spanish Main, but Dampier's voice is utterly different—sober and responsible, practical and prudent. Yet he was one of those three hundred.

The paradox—perhaps a transition from an earlier to a later style of adventurer—is summed up in the legend under his portrait in the National Portrait Gallery in London, "Pirate and Hydrographer." It is

3. Beaglehole, *The Journals of Captain James Cook,* vol. 1, ccxliv.
4. Lloyd, *William Dampier,* 11.

the second identity, as scientist, that he most nearly shares with Defoe and Crusoe, though critics of the latter pair not unfairly see a suppressed and self-righteous pirate in several of Defoe's heroes. Dampier's "Discourse" on winds and meteorology was cited by scientists for a century to come, and the members of the Royal Society sought him out and consulted him.

As a writer, Dampier is, we are told, "pre-eminent in satisfying the mind that studied for delight, the imagination that fed itself on strange birds and beasts and peoples. . . . The calculation that dwelled more on rare commodities than on bloodshed and battle smoke . . . a pen of gold, which imparted to the materialism of empire-building a gleam of humane and scientific enlightenment."[5]

Humane and scientific enlightenment versus bloodshed and battle smoke: these are the terms in which the English compared their own empire-building with other people's, at least before Kipling. It is praise that could well be applied to Cook after Dampier, and—more metaphorically—to Crusoe and Defoe. Dampier's book is said to be halfway in style, as it is halfway in date, between Hakluyt and the official narratives of Cook and Anson later in the century.

Thus the Robinson Crusoe story, the fictional equivalent of these others, gave a new voice to powerful tendencies in the imaginative life of the eighteenth century. Defoe gave those tendencies the special fluency and multivalency of fiction, which seems to carry cultural ideas into more minds, or to make them ferment in more mental recesses, than other forms, narrative or analytic. But Defoe's book was only the first step in the Robinson story's career. Had not certain other *foreign* writers (independently responsive to their civilization's needs and drives) taken up the story idea that Defoe sketched in, his initiative would have petered out—as it seemed to have done among the English writers of the late eighteenth century.

5. Dampier, *A Voyage to New Holland*, lvi.

3

Emile (1762)

The second event in the Robinson Crusoe story occurred in 1762, when Jean-Jacques Rousseau reinterpreted Defoe's book in his educational tract, *Emile*. His discussion of *Robinson Crusoe* established it as a major textbook of the Enlightenment. Of course Rousseau had his opponents, and the immediate reaction to his argument included a good deal of disagreement and controversy; but its effectiveness is shown by the fact that over the next quarter of a century several writers, in both French and German, began to create versions of the story that followed Rousseau's interpretation, and that some were adapted, as Defoe's was not, to the young reader.

A few of these, plus *Emile* itself, were translated into English and renewed England's interest in Defoe. But Rousseau's education theories in general, and his enthusiasm for *Robinson Crusoe* in particular, had perhaps more effect in Europe. All the famous pedagogical reformers of his own and the next generation, like the Swiss Pestalozzi, owed a great deal to Rousseau. And what he said about *Robinson Crusoe* was undeniably true. It did set forth, in vivid narrative form, the ideas about labor, production, and value, about religion, nature, and conscience, which Enlightened people believed.

Rousseau's Ideas

Rousseau's ideas were expansive and optimistic and democratic, about history and about psychology; in a sense, they were egotistic ideas. (We have seen Floyd Dell use the word *egotism* in discussing *Robinson Crusoe*.) For instance, in Book 2 Rousseau says there is no original perversity in the human heart, and our first duties are not to others, but to ourselves. While as far as democracy goes, we should begin the educational process with the training of the senses, proceed to learning-by-doing, and go on to the learning of trades, *métiers*. Rousseau's ideal pupil is to learn various *métiers:* first agriculture, then the forge, then carpentry. The relation of both these ideas to *Robinson Crusoe* is obvious. That story shows us someone learning without books, practicing several trades, and acting—far outside traditional guidelines—without sin.

Throughout his multivolumed work, Rousseau represents an ideal student through the image of an individual alone on a desert island in order to stress our need to learn from things, to obey the law of necessity, and to value the principle of utility. And then, in Book 3, he offers us *Robinson Crusoe,* the literal story of a desert island, as the book—the one book—for Emile to read. For the rest, the *métiers* will teach Emile what he needs to know; not only mechanical skills but, as a natural consequence, manhood. "Before his parents chose a calling for him, nature called him to be a man. Life is the trade I would teach him. When he leaves me, I grant you, he will be neither a magistrate, a soldier, nor a priest; he will be a man."[1] This is the voice of the Enlightenment, which still sounds in our ears like the promise of freedom.

On the other hand, Rousseau's "man" turns out to include or represent "woman" only in a reduced form. *Emile* has often been the object of feminist indignation, not only because Rousseau's scheme was devised

1. *Emile,* 9. "Avant la vocation des parents, la nature l'appèle à la vie humaine. Vivre est le métier que je lui veux apprendre. En sortant de mes mains il ne sera, j'en conviens, ni magistrat, ni soldat, ni prêtre; il sera premièrement homme . . ." *Emile,* 16.

for men and not for women, but because, when his attention was called to this lack, the education he outlined for Sophie, Emile's bride-to-be, was an education in obedience, in subordination. Thus in periods of feminist protest, like today, *Emile* is often cited as a classic text of masculinism.

In this character too, *Emile* forms a natural twin with *Robinson Crusoe*. As was noted, there is no place on Crusoe's island for a woman. Not that either author was indifferent to or uneasy with women. Rousseau was, after all, the author of *La nouvelle Héloïse*, an immensely popular book about and for women. But then Defoe was the author of *Moll Flanders* and *Roxana,* also important books in the history of women's fiction. Both men were unusually able to imagine women's experience, and both were ready to give it a voice. But when they came to imagine survival-adventure (and they ascribed to that topic a quite mythic political importance), they either omitted women or allotted them subordinate roles. In the Enlightenment as a whole, the liberation of men entailed the limitation of women.

This new masculinism was not a result of indifference to women. Nor was it a calculated exploitation. It seems to be simply the dark or shadow side of a gender myth—the founding myth of both adventure and the Enlightenment, which summoned men to stand together against all their enemies—feudal tyrants, false priests, tax farmers—and spoke of lordship over women and children as their natural reward. Men were to be the sturdy yeoman class of the human race, each with his little kingdom of a home behind him, including his consort and his subjects.

Huguenots and Philosophes

Paul Dottin says that the first readers of *Robinson Crusoe* in France were the enlightened or the anglophile. The two categories were closely related, as witness the alternative titles to Voltaire's seminal text of 1734, *Lettres philosophiques* or *Lettres anglaises*. The two were related via a third category, Protestant. Louis XIV's revocation of the Edict of Nantes, which had proclaimed tolerance for France's Protestants, sent 400,000 Huguenots abroad, to settle in England or other Protestant countries (Switzerland, Holland, or Brandenburg). There they became critics of France and Catholicism and enthusiasts for England and the ideas of Newton and Locke. One theory of Defoe's family origins is that they were Huguenot. Certainly among the Huguenot community were the first translators of *Robinson Crusoe* into French.

The Huguenots were skilled artisans, tradesmen, professionals, and journalists. The journalists interpreted England to the rest of Europe by essays in journals and thus set the precedent for Prévost, Voltaire, and the *encyclopédistes,* the most famous spreaders of Enlightenment ideology. (The *Encyclopédie* itself had an English-language precedent, in Chambers's *Encyclopaedia.*) Theirs was, among other things, an emigration of intellectuals. The Huguenots translated the work of Locke, Shaftesbury, and Temple into French and published them in Holland, whence they flowed into France. For them, England seems to have stood for two large ideas—science and freedom. In the year of publication of *Robinson Crusoe, Nouvelles littéraires* said that the tag "Translated from the English" on the title page of a book, no matter what the subject, promised readers a taste of freedom.

At the Rainbow coffeehouse on Fleet Street, among the wits of the day one could see Huguenot Fellows of the Royal Society, like de Moivre and des Maizeaux, editors of the first complete edition of Beyle's *Dictionnaire,* and Thémiseul de Saint-Hyacinthe, another member of the Royal Society, but also the translator of *Robinson Crusoe.* According to Joseph Texte, seventy to eighty thousand Huguenots lived in England, and mostly in London, from 1688 to 1730, the years of Defoe's adult life.[2] They told the world about Bacon and Locke, the Royal Society and Parliament, and English literature. Rousseau's praise for *Robinson Crusoe* was a rather eccentric part of that enterprise—eccentric just in that Defoe was not one of the prestigious names. When Voltaire and other Enlightenment luminaries visited England, they made sure to meet notables like Locke and Newton, Pope and Swift. But Defoe was not a name they asked after. Even Rousseau was not interested in his author; he treated *Robinson Crusoe* as an anonymous work.

But what Rousseau saw in the book was what he and the other philosophes saw in England as a whole: freedom and common sense, just the qualities needed to awaken French society from its feudal dream or nightmare. L.-C. F. de Montbron, in his *Préservatif contre l'Anglomanie* (1757), said Voltaire had transformed England from France's national enemy to her national model, at least for Anglo-maniacs. The

2. *Jean Jacques Rousseau and the Cosmopolitan Spirit in Literature,* 1.

abbé Prévost, counted as the first Anglo-maniac, spoke of England, in 1728, thus: "The love of the commonweal, the taste for the solid sciences, the horror of slavery and flattery, are virtues that come almost naturally to this happy people."[3] Thus the average Englishman was supposed to be a Robinson Crusoe.

These writers were the spiritual heirs of the Huguenot exiles, and Rousseau was so more directly than the others. Protestantism was his civic heritage. Many people said, including Rousseau himself, that the people of his home city, Geneva, were more like the English than like the French. While living with Madame de Warens, he had read Locke and Addison, models of the new civility of mind, and later Milton, Richardson, and Defoe.

Emile was, like the translated *Robinson Crusoe,* published in Amsterdam, a city of French Huguenots and freethinkers living in exile. It has been said that Crusoe entered France via Holland, and the same is true of Emile. And inside France it was the Huguenots who were associated with this adventure type, even before Defoe published his story. Thus *Le voyage et aventures de François Lequat,* of 1708, which was later translated into German as *Der franzoesische Robinson,* was about a company of Huguenots wrecked on an island in the Indian Ocean. Such adventures were already felt to belong to Protestants, not to Catholics. And then came Defoe's book, which strengthened the Protestant-Enlightenment link greatly.

Moreover, Rousseau's readers, or some of them, had been prepared to share his enthusiasm for the Robinson story. Defoe's book had had partial predecessors in France, like Marivaux's *Les effets surprenants de la sympathie,* of 1713, which also presents a white man living among natives. But it is, as the title suggests, a sentimental story, in which the savages call the hero Father, and when they want soup, he makes them a pot from dried mud, baking it in the sun, just for the occasion. This is quite unlike Defoe's realism about work.

The first translators of *Robinson Crusoe,* however, took a condescending attitude toward just that realism that we (and Rousseau) take to be Defoe's great literary virtue. Saint-Hyacinthe and his collaborator, Van Effen (who translated Swift also), took a superior tone about Defoe's style. "The style smells of the sailor a bit too much to please French politeness."[4] He also apologized for the *longueurs* of the central narra-

---

3. Green, *Eighteenth-Century France,* 35.
4. Dottin, *Daniel Defoe et ses romans,* 399.

tive of volume one about events on the island. We see how necessary was Rousseau's commentary.

After *Emile* the French came to see Defoe's profusion of detail and looseness of syntax as so characteristically English and Protestant as to be almost virtues. They found something comparable in Richardson, whose novels of sentiment became very popular in France at the same time. They compared both the English writers with the great Dutch painters; these were the great achievements of Protestant realism and middle-class moralism in the arts.[5]

Desfontaines, in his *Lettres d'une dame anglaise,* and du Resnel, introducing Pope's *Essay on Man,* contrasted this English style with the much more noble, classical, selective French style. There was plenty of reason for some Frenchmen to prefer their own tradition in the arts. But the new spirit breathed by Voltaire, among others, Texte describes as "contemptuous of questions of art, critical, eager for reform, combative and practical, which concerned itself rather with politics and natural science than with poetry and eloquence, and was interested, before all things, in literature dealing with the active side of life and the diffusion of knowledge" (pp. 55–56). Obviously such a spirit would find Defoe congenial.

Thus Rousseau saw that just that central part of *Robinson Crusoe,* volume one, which Saint-Hyacinthe apologized for, was a story to delight true philosophes. Henry Steele Commager defines that key eighteenth-century concept by distinguishing philosophes from philosophers. Philosophers were interested in truths that might be useful here and now.[6] Philosophes were men of the world, eager to reform, to change, to enlighten; and they wrote, typically, about education. This immediately reminds us of *Emile,* and of Defoe, and indeed of *Robinson Crusoe.*

Commager's first chapter, "The Enlightenment as an Age of Discovery," explains how important literal voyages of exploration and narratives of survival like *Robinson Crusoe* were for the Enlightened thinkers. "They sailed the seven seas and others that no-one had charted before; they mapped unknown islands and unveiled hidden continents . . ." (p. 1). And they used the images of travel for philosophic purposes. Liberty, equality, and fraternity were first defined by describing innocent savages.

For a contemporary definition of the philosophe, Commager takes an

5. Texte, *Jean-Jacques Rousseau,* 174.
6. Commager, *The Empire of Reason,* 236.

article by César Dumarsais, which was included in the *Encyclopédie.*
"Your Philosophe does not think that he lives in exile in this world. He
does not believe himself to live in enemy territory. He is kneaded, so to
speak, with the leaven of rule and of order. . . . He is suffused with
concern for the good of civil society, and he understands its principles
better than other men" (p. 239). This of course reminds us of Rousseau's
(and Defoe's) interest in the social contract, the memory of which should
free men from the political and religious superstitions of feudal tradition—of throne and altar. But it is above all the emphasis on practicality
that connects *Robinson Crusoe* with the *Encyclopédie* and with Rousseau and his disciples, like Madame de Genlis, with their armory of
practical skills. The Enlightenment saw itself as a triumph of the practical
over the theoretical.

Emile and Crusoe

Rousseau said that *Emile* was inseparable from *Le contrat social* and *Le
deuxième discours sur l'inegalité,* two of his most important works in
social philosophy. And *Emile* itself contains, in Book 4, the most famous
summary expression of enlightened deism, "La Profession de foi d'un
Vicaire Savoyard." *Emile* was thus a very important book; one that was
put on the Church Index, publicly burned, and nearly caused its author
to be arrested. The French national bibliography, which stops in 1939,
lists nearly a hundred editions of the book, and the National Union
Catalogue gives it nine pages. And so this interpretation and recommendation of the Robinson story, which was a part of *Emile,* was one of the
most powerful of all editings, and reshapings, of a myth.

It was a ruthless act of editing. Rousseau's discussion of the story
radically, though nonchalantly, changed the text Defoe had written. He
dismissed as nonsense ("tout ce fatras") everything in the story—in
volume one, never mind the other two volumes—that happens either
before Crusoe arrives on the island or after he leaves it. This makes a big
change in terms of quantity (about fifty percent of what Defoe wrote is
lopped off) as well as in character. All Crusoe's wanderings disappear,
and with them go the descriptions of other countries, the parade of
minor characters, and the sequence of small adventures—everything that
fitted *Robinson Crusoe* into the genre of the picaresque. That was the

more ordinary and entertaining, the less serious, part of the book. The French translators had apologized for the island part and promised the readers better things to come in volume two. What Rousseau preserved was the original part, both intellectually and literarily original, dominated by the themes of survival and work. Academic critics often base their discussions of the book on the complete text published in 1719, and sometimes they include the sequels. But the rest of the world, since 1762, has taken *Robinson Crusoe* to be what Rousseau made of it. He therefore deserves a place in this narrative, comparable with that of the literal rewriters.

Rousseau's editing also minimizes the wreck, and all that Crusoe took from it to start his new life. He put his stress on self-help. And later versions of the story by Rousseau disciples like Campe make that explicit and extreme. He also, in the same negative, silent way, eliminates Friday, the noble savage. And he eliminates the pious reflections; not only the whole third volume of what Defoe wrote, but the passages of Protestant piety in the first volume. The book emerges from Rousseau's hands radically secularized and modernized.

For the text he has thus created, Rousseau then makes very high claims, as a "treatise on natural philosophy." His ideal pupil is to have an ideal education by discovering for himself all of science, culture, and morality that is worth knowing; not via books in preconceived categories, but by original dealings with nature. He will learn geology from the stones around him, botany from the flowers he picks and presses, and so on. His moral character will be formed when his desires are frustrated by unbribable fact, when he meets the awful powers of nature and adores her beauty. Truth will come to him in the form of facts, not words. He will read only one book, and that will be Defoe's:

I hate books . . . [but] . . . since we must have books, there is one book which, to my thinking, supplies the best treatise on an education according to nature. This is the first book Emile will read; for a long time it will form his whole library, and it will always retain an honoured place. It will be the text to which all our talks about natural science are but the commentary. It will serve to test our progress towards a right judgment, and it will always be read with delight, so long as our taste is unspoiled.

What is this wonderful book? Is it Aristotle? Pliny? Buffon? No; it is *Robinson Crusoe.*[7]

This simple book contains a complete education, says Rousseau, leading from individual to social values. "The exercise of the natural arts, which may be carried on by one man alone, leads on to the industrial arts which call for the cooperation of many hands."[8]

The reading of *Robinson Crusoe* is to take place at a definite age in a definite sequence of learning processes; *Emile* contains a theory of pedagogy. Some things come before reading Defoe, other things come after. Here too, many later pedagogues have followed Rousseau, especially in Germany, though they have not agreed about exactly which years should be called the "Robinsonalter," the Robinson Age. Rousseau made it the third stage of Emile's development, between twelve and fifteen. Charlotte Buhler in 1905 made it ten to twelve; Busse, in 1927, made it eleven to thirteen. Most definitions agree that the "Robinsonalter" comes when the boy is interested in technology and skills, in strength and conquest, in social relations and heroes—in reality as opposed to fantasy.

Of course Rousseau's stress on this one book is a rhetorical device. *Robinson Crusoe* could be said to stand in for many others; for instance, descriptions by travelers and sailors, which were in fact used this way by Rousseauist educators. Essentially, Rousseau was challenging older and more scholastic ideas of education in the name of his own and his contemporaries' ideas. His unqualified praise for, and singling out of, Defoe's book in particular may even be in part accidental. Another book might replace that one in a pinch. But however that may be, *Robinson Crusoe* was what he named, and that naming had a remarkable effect; it transferred Defoe's book from one (very humble) niche in the literary system, marked "pastime reading for the nonliterary," to a different and

---

7. *Emile,* 147. "Je hais les livres . . . [mais] . . . puisqu'il nous faut absolument des livres, il en existe un qui fournit, à mon gré, le plus heureux traité d'éducation naturelle. Ce livre sera le premier que lira mon Emile, seul il composera durant longtemps toute sa bibliothèque, et il y tiendra toujours une place distinguée. Il sera le texte auquel tous nos entretiens sur les sciences naturelles ne serviront que de commentaire. Il servira d'épreuve, durant notre progrès, à l'état de notre jugement; et, tant que notre goût ne sera pas gâté, sa lecture nous plaira toujours. Quel est donc ce merveilleux livre? Est-ce Aristote? est-ce Pliny? est-ce Buffon? Non, c'est Robinson Crusoe" (232–33).

8. Ibid., 148. "La pratique des arts naturels, auxquels peut suffire un seul homme, mène à la recherche d'industries, qui ont besoin du concours de plusieurs mains" (233).

exalted niche, marked "the one book needful" or "the textbook of our times." And other intellectuals followed his lead. There have been few such dizzying changes of intellectual fortune for a single book.

For one result of Rousseau's recommendation of this one book (out of the dozens he had written) was that Defoe entered into literary immortality, some thirty years after his literal death. After *Emile,* literary critics talked about *Robinson Crusoe.* Among the French, we can cite Grimm in his *Correspondance littéraire* in 1768, Fréron in *Année littéraire* in 1766, 1767, and 1768, and La Harpe in *Cours de littérature* in 1799; and in Great Britain, Hugh Blair and Beattie, both in 1783, and Scott soon after.[9]

Blair and Scott agreed with Rousseau about *Robinson Crusoe,* different as their views were in general. Blair stresses the story's universal appeal, to young and old, to educated and uneducated. Scott agrees about the superiority of the island episode. In 1778–80 C. G. T. Garnier published a thirty-six-volume collection of *Voyages imaginaires,* which included seventy-one narratives in seven languages, and *Robinson Crusoe* was placed first (as best) in the "romanesque" division, while *Gulliver's Travels* came in the "merveilleux" division.

The Romantic Robinson

Better than becoming immortal, Defoe became a father. Several French *robinsonnades* were published in the quarter century after *Emile.* The best known were *L'Elève de la nature* of 1763, by Guillard de Beaurieu (for several years attributed to Rousseau himself), about a child who grew up entirely isolated from people, and *L'Ile inconnue* of 1784, by Guillaume Grivel.

L'Ile inconnue is a long work with an elaborate plot and formal rhetoric, owing much more to Rousseau's *Rêveries* and his *Nouvelle Héloïse* than to *Emile* or *Robinson Crusoe.* Indeed, in the preface the author criticizes Defoe's book quite loftily, as "a spoiled work; small designs, small powers, small effects."[10] Grivel had high literary ambitions, and though he makes allusions to Captain Cook, his real interest

9. Dottin, *Daniel Defoe et ses romans,* 404.
10. P. x. "Un ouvrage manqué; petites vues, petits moyens, petits effets."

is sentimental rather than adventurous. The chief "large power" and "large effect" he employs is to give his shipwrecked sailor a "tender companion." Once you, the writer, have a pair of lovers on your island, "Oh, what a career opens before you."[11]

Grivel's work clearly is a romantic, idyllic Robinson. We see this subgenre developed further in the work of the German Rousseauist "Jean-Paul" Richter. He began to talk longingly of Robinson's island in 1783. His *Vorschule der Aesthetik* of 1812 says that the lake-island life described by Rousseau in *Rêveries* fills us with the charm of the idyllic, and we gather that that island and Robinson's are much the same to Jean-Paul. In his *Selbsterlebensbeschreibung* he says that no book gives so much *pleasure*—one comparable with physical intoxication—as *Robinson Crusoe*. It is a pleasure that seems to come from the imagining of Paradise. That sort of extravagance is certainly not something we can associate with Defoe, but as we shall see, Jean-Paul was not the only writer to interpret the Crusoe story that way.

Robinson's island, Rousseau's lake-island, the legendary Arkadien, and the real Otaheite or Tahiti, as described by the explorers Cook and Bougainville, all merged into one for Jean-Paul. All were retreats or compensations for grief and disappointment in the world. In France, Bernardin de Saint-Pierre's *Paul et Virginie,* set in the Caribbean, was another famous development of the romantic *Robinsonade*. And Jean-Paul's *Hesperus* described its author living on an island in the East Indies; though this turns out to be (this writer is essentially playful and ironic) also an island in a pond near home. Rousseau himself, in 1782, had written that way about islands in his fifth *Rêverie,* and in the twelfth book of his *Confessions,* where he makes Robinson a sentimental symbol of himself and a model of his personal philosophy, not a pedagogic example this time, but a wounded poet with complex feelings.

Behind Jean-Paul (and behind Rousseau too, as far as date goes) stood J. G. Schnabel. His four-volume *Robinsonade* called *Wunderliche Fata* (but usually referred to as *Die Insel Felsenburg*) was published between 1731 and 1743. This was widely read but not taken seriously as adult reading. Only recently, for instance, in a contemporary dictionary of literature, is it called the first significant novel of the eighteenth century— significant for its psychology and its value structure.[12]

11. P. xi. "O, quelle carrière s'ouvre devant vous!"
12. *Reallexikon der deutschen Literaturgeschichte,* vol. 3, 478.

Schnabel, the son of a preacher, probably served under Prince Eugene in the War of the Spanish Succession, and then became court surgeon and editor in Stolberg. He wrote other novels, but they are, by report, less interesting. (It is, however, another reminder of Defoe that, in contrast with the Puritan piety of *Die Insel Felsenburg,* another of Schnabel's books is described—as one might describe *Roxana*—as a "galante Pornoroman." He seems to have been as much the literary handyman as Defoe.)

Schnabel drew on *Robinson Crusoe* and a dozen early *Robinsonaden,* according to Ullrich, in writing *Wunderliche Fata.* The book is long and has a complicated plot, covering generations, but the beginning is about a young pious Protestant, Albert Julius, who gets wrecked on a Dutch ship, in the company of M. van Leuven and his young bride, Concordia, and a wicked aristocratic and Catholic Captain Lemelie. The captain belongs to an old French family, famous for its haughtiness and brutality. (The likeness to *Pamela* and *Clarissa* will be obvious.) Wanting the young woman, the captain kills her husband. He is then himself killed, though honorably, by the young Julius, who, after a prolonged and highly scrupulous courtship, wins Concordia's heart and hand.

All this may be said to derive from the sentimental Puritanism that inspired other of Defoe's novels—and Richardson's. But at the same time the novel tells another story, about the characters' struggle to survive on this island, and its dangerous animals, and the crops they grow there, and so on. This is clearly derived from Defoe's story. In fact, Schnabel's characters read *Robinson Crusoe* as a religious book. In the later volumes, a whole society is described, descended from Julius and Concordia, as well as from others who join them on their island. All these people are in flight from corrupt, intrigue-ridden, wartorn Europe. They engage in praying, hymn-singing, and Bible-reading together, and form a new and nobler community (like Crusoe's colony, but more idyllic).

Thus Schnabel brought together the two main lines of middle-class Protestant writing as no English or French writer did. Defoe wrote examples of both kinds, but no book that partook of both. *Die Insel Felsenburg* had considerable influence in Germany and also in Scandinavia. In Denmark O. G. Oelenschlaeger developed the story into a two-volume *Inseln im Sudemeer* in 1824, as well as writing *Robinson i England.* And the German Romantics discovered Schnabel; Ludwig Tieck brought out a new edition of *Die Insel Felsenburg* in 1828.

We can put together Grivel and Saint-Pierre and Jean-Paul, and perhaps Schnabel and Oelenschlaeger, and align them with the Rousseau of the *Rêveries* and the *Confessions*. This grouping defines the romantic *Robinsonade,* which has perhaps been more important to purely literary people than the pedagogic *Robinsonade* derived from *Emile.* But if we are interested in the broader career of the Robinson story, its broader scope of significance, we must pay attention to its pharisee readers and writers; and if we do that, clearly the *Emile*-styled *Robinsonade* deserves more attention. And one of the intellectual fields in which the Robinson story is referred to most often is economics.

The Economic Robinson

Here we take leave of the romantic idyll of Robinson's island, but not of Rousseau, who was not always a Romantic. The man who wrote *Emile* made nothing of the landscape of Crusoe's island and little of his romantic solitude there—of that deliverance from the falsities of civilization that Schnabel, for instance, made so much of. All of *this* Rousseau's attention was focused on Crusoe the exemplary learner, worker, inventor, reasoner. In other words, this was Rousseau the colleague of Voltaire, d'Alembert, Turgot, Diderot, and d'Holbach, not their opponent. The *Encyclopédie* itself was Defoe-like or Crusoe-like in its painstaking descriptions of trades and techniques. Those descriptions were what distinguished this encyclopedia from earlier summations of knowledge. And it should perhaps also be counted a sign of the *encyclopédiste* in Rousseau that he paid no attention to the violence implicit in the adventure—both the loud violence that Crusoe directs at the cannibals and the quiet violence of his masterful relationship to Friday.

Rousseau's interest, in this phase of his development, was in economic matters rather than in sensibility, like a good *encyclopédiste*. And it was from the *encyclopédistes* that the German philosophers—including Hegel and even Marx—learned to rate economics so high. Though we might note that Hegel was able to take account of other sides of the Crusoe story. At least he cites the story in the passage in which he puts forward his influential theory of Master and Slave.

But Hegel was extremely attentive to the questions of production and labor, and later Hegelians have seen a connection between his remarks on those themes and *Robinson Crusoe*. In discussing the Greek epic, that ideal literary form, Hegel remarks enviously on how Homer could bring to life his hero's "tent, chair, bed, sword and spear, the chariot which carries him into battle, boiling and roasting, slaughtering, eating and drinking . . ." In Homer these things are not merely a means to an end; the Greek hero "feels alive in all these with his whole sense and self . . . [whereas] . . . our present machinery and factories, together with the products they turn out, and in general our means of satisfying our external needs" prevent the modern novelist from achieving anything comparable. Georg Lukács quotes this in his *Studies in European Realism* (p. 115) and goes on to say that Defoe alone solved the problem of giving life to the objects and background of modern life. Defoe alone has the kind of epic vision appropriate to the modern capitalist economy.

Marx and Engels, Hegelians in their way, said that man was crucially distinguished from animals by his tools and tool-making, which is what Defoe implied. On the other hand, of course, Marx quarreled bitterly with the Robinson myth of individualism, which idealized the entrepreneur. By name he attacked not Defoe but Adam Smith and the Physiocrats, who expressed Defoe's economic views in a more authoritative way. Physiocracy, Marx said, dissolved the idea of feudal property into political economy, but then restored that idea in a new form.[13] Bourgeois property is as much an expropriation as the feudal kind, and the entrepreneurial qualities mythified in Crusoe created a hidden injustice worse than the open kind they had gotten rid of. But, in thus quarreling with the Physiocrats and Defoe, it is nonetheless clear that Marx is their rebellious child.

Marx attacks the capitalist idea that "the *subjective essence* of private property is . . . labor" (p. 93). Defoe, for instance, makes Crusoe's property seem to be directly the product of his labor, his creation. Marx calls this a mystification that justifies owning property: "Engels was therefore right to call Adam Smith *the Luther of Political Economy*. Just as Luther recognized religion—*faith*—as the substance of the external *world* and in consequence stood opposed to Catholic paganism—just as he superseded *external* religiosity by making religiosity the inner substance of man—just as he negated the priests outside the layman, because he transplanted the priest into laymen's hearts, just so with wealth" (ibid.). Adam Smith has given wealth a subjective and spiritual character and made the capitalist a culture-hero. In *Robinson Crusoe,* to make a

13. *Economic and Philosophical Manuscripts*, 95–96.

connection Marx himself does not make, ". . . *this external, mindless objectivity* of wealth is done away with, with private property being incorporated in man himself and with man himself being recognized as its essence" (p. 94). This surely applies irrefutably to *Robinson Crusoe.* What does Defoe's novel show but a man incorporating property in this sense, and what other novel shows it so eloquently?

Marx makes bitter fun of the actual character and story of Robinson, in volume one of *Capital,* because of the way the island story was used by political economists of the capitalist school. But perhaps more interesting than an example of his invective is an example of what aroused it. Harriet Martineau wrote a tale called *Dawn Island,* published in Manchester in 1845, for the Bazaar of the National Anti-Corn Law League as her contribution to the cause of Free Trade. This does not in fact include a Robinson character, but it includes most of the story's other categories of motif. It is a fable of the impact of Western culture on a South Seas island when an English ship arrives there. The captain shows the inhabitants knives, scissors, axes, hammers, nails, and teaches them the principles of honest trade. He also teaches them morality—to give up human sacrifice, and to serve God with their lives, not with their deaths. Above all, he exhorts them to work. And they listen, because they want the material things he brings; commerce and Christianity work hand in hand. Thus Martineau's *Robinsonade* is the kind of capitalist fable that Marx attacks.

Talking so much of Marx, we seem to have strayed a long way from Rousseau. But both were important crossroads of ideas, especially in this field of economics, and both paid significant tribute to *Robinson Crusoe,* even if, in Marx's case, the tribute was hostile. Now, however, we must leave both the Romantic and the Economic Robinson behind, and move on toward the actual rewritings of the story.

4

Robinson der Juengere
(1779)

A fter Rousseau had given his new stimulus to the Robinson Crusoe story, several people began to rewrite it. The story especially struck the German imagination. And for the first time the retellers included intellectuals. Two of them, both Rousseauists, indeed Emilists, completed their versions in the same year, 1779, and in conscious competition with each other. These were Johann Karl Wezel and Johann Heinrich Campe, of whom the second will concern us. It is said by some German scholars that Wezel's version is the better, if judged by narrowly literary standards. That is to say, it is more like a serious novel. But Campe's version, which was meant for children and for pedagogical purposes, had the greater social impact.

The title page of the English translation, in two volumes, which appeared less than ten years after the German, gives a good idea of how Campe's work was seen abroad: *The New Robinson Crusoe; an instructive and entertaining history, for the use of children of both sexes, embellished with thirty-two beautiful cuts.* The frontispiece shows Robinson with parasol, spear, and bow and arrows, but no gun, unlike the frontispiece to Defoe's book—a typical difference. And the reader is told that he or she will find nothing in the *New Robinson Crusoe* but "things that are useful, introduced in an unaffected manner, clearly expressed and demonstrated without pedantry . . . children speak like children, and their instructor assumes the simple language of child-hood."

Wezel's version too, *Robinson Krusoe, neu arbeitet,* was aimed at a young audience (up to the age of eighteen), but it was less pious in tone than Campe's. Wezel, like Rousseau himself, did not believe that children should be given religious or moral training. He thought their instructors should focus on teaching practical skills and leave the rest to nature. He also gave Friday more equality with Robinson, being less interested in Robinson's status as hero and model.[1]

It was Campe's version, however, that became and remained so popular that it forms a chapter in the Robinson Crusoe story. It stayed in print in Germany for a hundred years without interruption and was reprinted two hundred times. Defoe's version itself was reprinted only ten times during that period in Germany.[2] Indeed, Gustav A. Graebner's reworking of Campe, which eliminated the dialogue form used in the original, was popular in Germany into the 1930s. Abroad Campe had quite a career, too. Translated into Spanish in 1789, *Robinson der Juengere* became the "Trojan Horse" inside which the forbidden ideas of *Robinson Crusoe* and *Emile* first reached Spain. Both books were still prohibited there.[3]

Campe's was the most widely distributed version of the story in Germany throughout the nineteenth century, and internationally had 724 editions by 1900, counting continuations and adaptations and translations. An excellent English translation appeared in 1788, within a decade of the German publication. By 1900 there had been seventeen French versions and five English, and thirty-five adaptations. Meanwhile the flow of other German *Robinsonaden* continued. In 1778, when H. A. O. Reichard published his *Bibliothek der Romane,* he remarked that if England had her one Robinson story, Germany had a hundred. And between 1805 and 1808 J. C. L. Haken published *Bibliothek der Robinsonaden,* which included thirty-four works: *Robinson Crusoe,* six adaptations from it, one adaptation of *Die Insel Felsenburg,* and twenty-

1. Liebs, *Die Paedagogische Insel,* 99.
2. Dottin, *Daniel Defoe et ses romans,* 444.
3. Heidenreich, "Der spanische Crusoe," in *Pikarische Welt,* 265.

six *Robinsonaden* proper. (Schnabel seems to have been the first person to use the word *Robinsonade* in print. It came into general use as a category, as opposed to a sneer, sometime after Haken's publication.)

Changes in the Story

The story Campe told was significantly different from Defoe's. His Robinson, a German from Hamburg, is only eighteen when he is wrecked on his island (Defoe's hero is thirty-five), and he has nothing in the way of tools and provisions to get him started. All he can dispose of are things found on his desert island: shells, stones, fish bones, and strings made from plant filaments. Campe pressed the themes of "starting from scratch" and "necessity is the mother of invention" more rigorously than Defoe did. He made things harder for Crusoe to begin with, so that his success would be greater in the end. The logic of his general scheme is therefore clearer, but the plausibility of the narrative moment, the way the hero finds the solution to the practical problems, by the use of skill and effort and persistence and luck, is much greater in Defoe. When Campe's Crusoe needs a tool, the reader knows that by the bottom of the page he will have it. Thus the categories of motif are significantly different.

In general, Campe makes his points more emphatically. When his Crusoe finds a lump of gold, it is worth ten thousand pounds, and he *immediately* cries "O for a lump of iron" instead to make a knife, or a hatchet, or nails.[4] The point is later developed by telling us that southern, warm lands contain gold, whereas northern, cold lands contain iron. Thus northerners must work harder, but by doing so acquire more power, and geography and geology conspire to enforce the superiority of white races over black and of use over luxury.

In the matter of form, Campe is just as innovative. He shows us only the skeleton of the Crusoe story, and we see it over the shoulders of an attentive child audience listening to a narrator. A teacher (someone just like Campe himself) tells an installment of the story every day to a group of children, his pupils, who live in his house, with the participation of a few family friends. The listeners express feelings and opinions about the

4. *The New Robinson Crusoe*, vol. 1, 170–71.

hero and his plight and are asked many questions. They are given assignments: for instance, to write Crusoe a letter, or to each make an umbrella like Crusoe's. Prizes are offered to stimulate competition. Moreover, as Rousseau had suggested, they are taught geography, botany, natural history, and seamanship, apropos of the story they are hearing.

Campe's version thus becomes unmistakably a pedagogical tool, and further away from ordinary fiction than Defoe's version. However, the dialogue is fresh and credible, the children are clearly characterized, and the whole enterprise makes interesting reading. (Campe's part of it, the teacher's interactions with his pupils, is better than Crusoe's part.) Campe writes a better, in the sense of more classical, prose than Defoe, and the structure of his book is clearer and more satisfying. He was a late eighteenth-century intellectual, a friend of Lessing, and he had benefited from the disciplines invented by the classical writers of France and the *encyclopédistes*.

In his preface Campe names his intentions as to instruct, to entertain, and even more to teach values or—to use the word of his day—the virtues. He thought Defoe had been careless about the virtues in his version. As for the instruction, Campe, like Rousseau, wanted schools to give "ground knowledge," *Grunderkenntnissen:* not the preliminaries to scholarship but "the first concepts of things that belong to daily life, to Nature, and to the broad-spreading circles of common human reality." ("Vorbegriffe von Dingen aus dem haeuslichen Leben, aus der Natur, und aus dem weitlaeufigen Kreise der gemeinen menschlichen Wirksamkeit.") All the things around the children, not just the remote doings of classical or biblical heroes, should be charged with imagination and intelligibility. Campe also wanted to create a model for the relations between a father and his children, without which, he said, no education is possible. Family virtue and household instruction went hand in hand.

In thus setting virtue above learning as the aim of education, Campe exemplified the Enlightenment model. He followed Rousseau, and before him, Locke. (The Renaissance model of education put more stress on classical learning.) Like his teachers, Campe stressed the value of spartan severity, and a secular asceticism, expressed through physical work. For instance, as part of their response to the story of Robinson, the children in his book ask to go on a fast, and the father gives up (permanently) alcohol, snuff, and tobacco. (Campe's education, like Rousseau's, is designed primarily for males.) Defoe's story attracted Campe, he says in his preface, especially because it could be an antidote to the contemporary disease of *Empfindsamkeitsfieber*. This was the epidemic of sensibility, deriving from contemporary novels of "feeling," which was weakening the moral fiber of his countrymen.

This spartan strain in the Crusoe story, which distinguishes it among adventures, has continued to recommend it to pedagogues and moralists. It is a pervasive part of the book's image. The main character's steadfast stoicism seems reflected in the minimal equipment the author allowed him, and even in the cheap bindings in which so many have read about him. Ruskin, for instance, remarks on how powerfully the cheap woodcuts of *his* copy of *Robinson Crusoe* acted on his imagination. Their crudity was part of their power. This was a *humble* story, like the story of the Gospel.

In this matter of morality Campe was even more severe than his great teacher. He praised Rousseau as a genius, who had enlarged everyone's ideas about education. But he reproached him for setting too great store by youth and its ardors, and too little by age and maturity. In other words, Rousseau was too Romantic for him.

According to J. Merkel and D. Richter, who edited Campe's story again in 1977, his Crusoe is unlike Defoe's in that he is trying to *escape* from capitalism. This Crusoe returns home at the end of his adventures, not wealthy like Defoe's, but ready to be a useful member of society, ready to work humbly, alongside Friday, as a carpenter. Certainly the experience of work was of the greatest educational importance to this writer.

Campe's Background

Pedagogy was at the time a new science and carried with it many of the best hopes of the Enlightenment. Since feudal tradition was so blind, so unreasonable, education could improve human behavior quite radically just by teaching people to reason—to analyze their problems. Campe has been described as the world's first professional educationist. At the time of writing his Robinson story he was in fact conducting his own school, which he founded in 1777. It was just outside Hamburg, and his pupils, to whom he did tell the Robinson story, were the children of well-to-do Hamburg merchants. Hamburg was the busiest commercial port in Germany, with close ties to England and was also, not incidentally, where the first German translation of Defoe's story had been published. It is worth noting how the geography of Crusoe's popularity corresponded to the sectarian geography of Germany. As in France, his story was read by Protestants. In southern and Catholic Germany the book was less influential than in the Protestant northwest, while within the Austro-Hungarian Empire this kind of moral adventure was quite alien.

Before that, in 1776, Campe had taught at a famous experimental school, the Philanthropinum, run by Johannes Basedow. Basedow (1724–90) was another Rousseauist, though more eager than Rousseau himself to invest the responsibility for education in the secular state. Campe took from the Philanthropinum the doctrine of the importance of practical work. Other teachers of Basedow's group, like Guts Muths, invented school sports and school gymnastics, other ways to save education from its academic-idealistic bias.

Campe's school became well known, and starting in 1786 he was also *Educationrat,* or Minister for Education, to the Duke of Brunswick, the most famous enlightened despot of the Germany of his day. This meant that the schools of Brunswick fell under secular control. The duke's and Campe's aim was like that of other Enlightenment pedagogues: to wrest education from the control of the churches and open it up to the liberal ideas and the self-liberating spirit of the day. The Robinson story suited his purposes because it so unobtrusively breathed the spirit of self-reliance and antifeudalism into all who read it.

Duke Karl Wilhelm Ferdinand of Brunswick (1735–1806) was Frederick the Great's favorite nephew and disciple. Like his uncle, he cultivated the friendship of leading intellectuals. He knew Voltaire and Winckelmann, and brought Lessing to his court to be his librarian. When Lessing died, the duke made Campe his successor, to maintain the tradition of intellectual distinction. He wanted to make Brunswick another Weimar.

Campe was so well known for his liberal sympathies that when the French Revolution broke out and the revolutionaries set up a republic, which was attacked by the European monarchies, he was offered, or nearly offered, the command of the revolutionary armies. However, under the pressure of circumstance he refused, and in fact later commanded the allied forces that attacked France. This change of sides of course was forced on many moderates in those days. In step with that change, the duke imposed censorship upon Campe's educational journal, and in 1790 gave the administration of schools back to the clergy.

Campe, however, survived these storms and in his last years regained his former prestige as a liberal educationist.

Campe was born in 1746 in Deenen, a small Brunswick village of about five hundred people, much overshadowed by its feudal lord. The landowner's will was law in all but matters of life and death. Campe's father was the village innkeeper, a position he held partly because he was an illegitimate son of the Schloss. The village children were sent to work in the fields as early as three in the morning, and their education was at the mercy of the parents' or the landlord's whim. This was feudalism at its grimmest, and the experience inspired Campe with a deep drive toward political change. The rigidity of the caste structure and the tradition remind us, much later, of Pupin's village of Idvor. The Robinson idea appealed to both writers as a way to escape from that prison.

Campe himself escaped the hard physical labor imposed on the peasant's sons by grace of his mental precocity. But he was drafted into the severe intellectual disciplines of the German university of that time, where he studied theology and philology, and his health and nerves seem to have been permanently affected. No doubt this too contributed something to his love for the Robinson story, as an outdoors and natural model of learning, free from marks and grades and answering by rote, as well as from exclusively classical or religious texts. (Campe declared that Homer was a less important figure in history than the anonymous inventor of the spinning wheel.) But more important was the inspiration the story offered to people like his fellow villagers to build a new life for themselves in a free society. In literal fact, Campe's Hamburg pupils were middle class, not peasants. But the logical culmination of Campe's efforts would have been to change the whole structure of German education.

Like the French, the Germans saw eighteenth-century England as a model of freedom in many ways, and the Englishness of the Robinson story was one of its attractions. The fact that Germany was not a united nation until the last quarter of the nineteenth century, and so was not a naval or imperial power, did not prevent Germans from being interested in English-style adventures. Rather, it seems to have made them the keenest of all readers about modern colonies. Indeed, many of them went to explore and settle in the British Empire or the United States, where they wrote about the frontiers. The German Karl May was the writer about the American West with the largest world readership at the end of the nineteenth century.

When the French Revolution broke out in 1789, Campe went to Paris to witness the events firsthand, and wrote back to Germany some widely read and enthusiastic reports that caused great scandal to conservatives. He went in the company of his former pupil, Wilhelm von Humboldt, whose response to the Revolution was more cautious than his ex-tutor's. While in France, Campe was made an honorary citizen, visited Rousseau's grave, and acquired his snuffbox, which he treasured as a sacred relic. He translated *Emile* into German, with a commentary, in 1792.

As the Revolution developed into the Terror, the number of its sympathizers in Germany dropped away, and those who remained loyal, like Campe, were fiercely attacked by reactionaries. His experience was like that of many German intellectuals then, for instance, Kant, Hegel, and Fichte, and his pedagogy paralleled their philosophy. He never recanted, but for a number of years he had to fall largely silent.

This Robinson's Relation to Other Ideas

Campe's pedagogical schemes imply a clear philosophy of history. He wrote a three-volume work entitled *The Discovery of America*, published in 1799, 1800, and 1801, which was as much designed for young people's reading as *Robinson der Juengere*. Indeed all these books were closely aligned. Campe wanted children to read *Robinson der Juengere* at the age of twelve and the other three volumes in the three succeeding years.

Campe's trilogy comprised a life of Columbus, a life of Cortés, and a life of Pizarro. These books also, like the Robinson story, are told by a father/teacher to his children; and as before, he says, he has tried to conceal the dark side of human nature, which might depress the young man's eagerness for virtue, or rather to reveal it little by little.[5] Such stories, the introduction tells us, both form character (defend it from the habits of romantic reverie) and give the reader a "salutary contempt for the affected jargon of frivolity, or sentiment, and of false delicacy." These stories offer "chaste and profitable amusements" (p. xii). And this

5. *Columbus or the Discovery of America,* xv.

is a *virile* chastity; that is to say, a by-product of gender dominance or, to use its own terms, of moral and political manliness.

Thus Columbus was a moral hero, who disdained to pamper his appetite with dainties and persisted in his purpose when everyone else scorned it and him, and treated the omens that scared other sailors quite rationally (pp. 4–5). We should all imitate Columbus as we imitate Robinson. On the other hand, the later parts of his story, and much more the volumes on Cortés and Pizarro, cause the narrator distress. The stories mount upward, progressively, both in subject matter and treatment—from innocence toward guilt, from idyll toward tragedy—in the picture they give of the modern adventure, Europe's conquest of the New World.

Columbus was not a conquistador but an explorer, in his way a scientist, and an underdog who suffered before he triumphed. Cortés, on the other hand, was a charismatic military leader who showed how a few Christian soldiers could defeat a pagan horde; but his success was stained with blood and power-lust. While all Pizarro's triumphs could not disguise his appalling cruelty and greed. Even while hearing about Columbus, Campe's children (Protestants, of course) cry out, "What dreadful monsters were the Spaniards" (p. 178). They continue to participate imaginatively in the conquest of the New World, but with a sobered and perplexed commitment.

Campe's trilogy thus offered its readers an education in the moral character of Europe's great historical adventure, to which the Robinson story gave a fictional and idyllic introduction. These three volumes also were quickly translated into English, so the British and the Americans were able to read about the white conquest of that continent from a German's point of view. Sometimes bound with these volumes was another story by Campe, about some Russian sailors who survived some years in Crusoe fashion after shipwreck in the Arctic. This was Campe's most direct imitation of Defoe, and interesting also for showing Russians involved in modern adventure.

The Edgeworths' *Practical Education* cites this "Three Russian Sailors," together with *Robinson Crusoe* and *Gulliver's Travels,* as general favorites. "There is a class of books which amuse the imagination of children without acting upon their feelings. We do not allude to fairy tales, for we apprehend that these are not now much read; but we mean voyages and travels; these interest young people universally" (p. 250). This shows a close dependence on or harmony with Campe's ideas. But the Edgeworths were more cautious. "Will it be thought to proceed from a spirit of contradiction if we remark, that this species of reading should not early be chosen for boys of an enterprising temper, unless they are intended for a seafaring life, or for the army? The taste for adventure is absolutely incompatible with the sober perseverance necessary to success in any other liberal professions" (p. 251). Whether or not Campe would have agreed with this, it bears witness, in its own way, to their sense of the power within adventure that he too valued.

The idea of a series of graduated readings over a period of years (and the related idea of building a year-long curriculum around one book) was taken up by later German educationists and was often associated with the Robinson story. Most notable among them was J. F. Herbart (1776–1841), whose work was immensely influential in Europe and Japan in the second half of the nineteenth century. Herbart began as a Fichtean and believed that the aim of education was the formation of character by the means of an enlightened will. It is easy to see how Campe and Crusoe's story could illustrate such a philosophy. Herbart's disciple, Tuiskon Ziller, who founded the *Verein fuer Wissenschaftliche Paedagogik,* designed closely integrated curricula, with the sequence of topics following the cultural evolution of man. The Robinson story played an important part in those curricula.

Campe became the most important publicist of pedagogy in the late Enlightenment. When he lost control over the educational system in Brunswick, he turned instead to writing and publishing children's literature. His magnum opus was the thirty-seven volume *Bibliothek der Jugendalter,* largely composed of travel literature, ending with his own verse history of the world. It also included his *Robinson der Juengere* and his *Discovery of America.*

Campe taught an enlightened Christianity and deplored the habit of giving children legends, superstitions, and folktales to read. (He was one of those rationalists Charles Lamb referred to in his letter to Coleridge.) And despite his conflict with churchmen, his moral teaching was emphatic enough for his works to be read aloud, in some pious circles, as semireligious edification. He saw the relations of the father to his children (mirrored in his Robinson story) as parallel to that of the prince to his subjects, and that of God to his creation. Liberal though Campe was in many ways, Frederick the Great remained one of his idols.

Before becoming an educationist, indeed Campe served as a military chaplain in the Prussian army. This was in the days when Prussia was a shining example of enlightened despotism, and a home of advanced ideas, but clearly was still a military state. Campe's political conscience and his enthusiasm for self-determination somehow accommodated that; as of course did Fichte's conscience and that of other German intellectuals.

Campe was also for a time tutor to both Alexander and Wilhelm von Humboldt, and the brilliant careers of these two brothers in nineteenth-century Germany make them striking representatives of Campe's teaching. Alexander was, perhaps after David Livingstone, the most famous European explorer of the nineteenth century, and much more the scientist than Livingstone. He spent many years in South America, made large natural history collections, and was also a spokesman for liberal nationalist sympathies in the politics of that continent. He also played an important part in Europe in his later years, as a statesman of science and culture.

Wilhelm became a philosopher of education, like his old tutor, but his most famous idea was to transfer the classicism of Goethe and Schiller into the curriculum of Prussia's state schools; whence it permeated the educational systems of other German states. Campe, as we know, was hostile to the cult of the classical languages and literatures, preferring the modern subjects that go naturally with the Robinson story. However, there was a consonance between the two. Humboldt's classicism embodied a liberal ideology, at least originally. He maintained that the aim of education was the cultivation of the individual, and not the service of the state. And he, like Campe, was concerned with "the creation of a Nation [in a special German sense] and the education of the men who were to constitute it."[6] This special sense could be called a nonstate nationalism. As Peter Jelavich says, "The desired Nation was not a politically unified German state, but rather a body of educated citizens who would employ a common [German] language to maintain a constant public discourse" (p. 16). Campe and Humboldt both did a lot of work in German philology, with the aim of creating a national language.

The liberal and national tendency of Humboldt's classicism was clearly like that of Campe's Crusoeism. "Significantly, the creation of such a Nation would have been meaningless without a fundamental change in the sociopolitical system as well. The petty aristocratic potentates of central Europe would have to abandon their belief that subordi-

6. Peter Jelavich, *Munich and Theatrical Modernism*, 15.

nate classes existed for their personal benefit" (p. 16). Moreover, Jelavich points to an ambiguity in classicism, which we can also find in Crusoeism. They both "hover between enlightened monarchy and democracy." When Humboldt installed the classical curriculum in schools, its liberalism soon became conservative (p. 17). The same thing happened when the Crusoe story was applied pedagogically.

Another connection links Alexander von Humboldt with both Campe and Captain Cook, the greatest sea adventurer of the later eighteenth century. The German father-and-son scientists, Johann and George Forster, who sailed with Cook and subsequently wrote about the voyage, were friends of Campe, and they helped determine Humboldt's choice of a scientist's career. In 1790–91 Humboldt traveled with George Forster to France, Holland, and England.

Johann Reinhold Forster was born in 1729 and had been employed in Russia by Catherine the Great as a pastor and a scholar. He was one of those wandering scholars of the eighteenth century who carried the seeds of the Enlightenment wherever they could be planted. He has been compared, for instance, with Joseph Priestley. After Russia, Forster went to England, where he taught at the Dissenting Academy at Warrington (replacing Priestley) and became a member of the Royal Society. And then he and his son sailed with Cook to the South Seas. Both wrote about that adventure, and George's *Voyage Round the World* is considered the most readable of all contemporary accounts of the journey.

Captain Cook

Via the Forsters, therefore, Cook was a presence to Campe, who refers to him in *Robinson der Juengere*. Indeed he was a presence to everyone in those years. His voyages were acknowledged, while they were occurring and in their preparation, as great cultural events. The importance of Columbus's voyages was only appreciated long afterward; Cook's were a chance for Europe to recoup what it had failed to prize and celebrate at the time. It was of course a triumph for Protestantism over Catholicism, and for England over other countries; but all Europe shared in it to some extent. Representatives of the arts and the sciences sailed with Cook. And it was an adventure, fraught with danger and uncertainty, penetrating into the unknown, calling for courage, leadership, long endurance.

All enthusiasts for the Enlightenment heroized Cook, in poems, paintings, Academy exercises, and ceremonies. He was one of the stars of English culture for the Anglo-maniacs in France, along with Newton and Locke. His journals were published and then abridged and edited for reading by children. Between 1770 and 1780 there were a hundred printings of them. He was the first hero of European expansion into the Pacific. "To put it bluntly," says Bernard Smith, "[he was] the prototypical hero of European imperialism."[7] But of course imperialism was not the word used at the time. In Italy he was explicitly contrasted with Cortés and Pizarro; in France he was praised for taking not cannon but agriculture to the Pacific. Pierre Lemontey described him as "the personification of Europe, which is to say of free movement" (p. 164). This refers to both the literal movement of his journeys and the larger freedom they seemed to symbolize.

Bernard Smith also calls Cook a global agent for Adam Smith and mercantilism (and all that Marx inveighed against). But he seemed to his admirers like a moral hero. The names of his ships carry the adventure-ideology of eighteenth-century Europe: the "Endeavour," the "Resolution," and the "Adventure" on the 1772–75 voyage and the "Resolution" and the "Discovery" on the 1776–80 voyage. (They were renamed for these voyages, having before been called things like "The Earl of Pembroke.")

Cook came from Yorkshire, like Crusoe, and he consciously embodied the dour, dry virtues of his place and vocation. Before he joined the Royal Navy he sailed out of Whitby for a Quaker shipowner. He apologized for his "plain style" in writing, but it was in fact much appreciated. Diderot called Cook's style "le ton de la chose," the tone or style of facts. It expressed what I have called, in reference to Defoe, the imagination of fact.

And if the two writing styles were similar, so were important aspects of the two personalities. Cook's biographer, J. C. Beaglehole, says, "He is an exceptionally difficult man to get inside" because he was a "genius of the matter-of-fact."[8] At the same time, we get flashes of impersonal

7. "Cook's Posthumous Reputation," in Fisher and Johnston, *Captain James Cook and His Times*, 160.

8. *The Journals of Captain James Cook*, 698.

ambition, even hubris, in Cook's account of himself, which explains his and his country's achievements. Thus in 1772 he wrote, "I whose ambition leads me not only further than any other man has been before me, but as far as I think it is possible for men to go" (p. 39). This has, in context, a specific and practical reference, but its ulterior, Manfred-like ring is also not to be ignored. Or again, "the world will hardly admit of an excuse for a man leaving a Coast unexplored he has once discovered" (p. 25).

This combination of dry impersonality with limit-breaking ambition—and achievement—was just what the world admired in the British empire-builders. It is what Joyce saw in Crusoe. Cook was not a literal solitary, but that is just the difference between fact and fiction, history and myth. The real Crusoes, some of the later ones described by Conrad, were captains of ships and agents of national expansion.

Cook, it has been said, was as definitively the Captain as Johnson was the Doctor. The two men were linked to their titles, and Captain is one of the most potent titles in the literature of adventure. But Johnson may also take a moment of our attention, as a contrast to Cook. We have seen how he dissuaded Boswell from sailing with the Captain, and he had reasons we would all find impressive. In Dr. Johnson's *Letters* we find that he did not "wish well to explorers," because "I am always afraid that they will end in conquest and robbery" (1:308). He spoke for many men of letters in making that reservation.

And yet there is a sense in which the explorer figure captured the imagination of even the writers of his time, and took them with him on his voyages. Thus in *The Task,* Part II, William Cowper says, lines 107–8,

> He travels and expatiates, as the bee
> From flower to flower, so he from land to land . . .

And, lines 114–16,

> He travels, and I too. I tread his deck
> Ascend his topmast, through his peering eyes
> Discover countries . . .

And it was of course Cowper who wrote the most famous line about *Crusoe:* "I am monarch of all I survey." Yet Cowper was not, being an evangelical Christian and an embodiment of moral anxiety, the type most susceptible to Cook and Crusoe and adventure enthusiasm. But along with his contemporaries, he was swept away.

Such then was the intellectual matrix in which the Crusoe story reentered Europe's imaginative life in the late eighteenth century, where it remained powerful for at least a century and a half. The ideas the story seemed naturally linked to were liberal, national, secular, expansive. They were on the side of free thought, democratic politics, and economic development, of course of the capitalist kind. They strengthened the desire for an overthrow of the petty princes (who included bishops and archbishops) and the growth of a united nation-state in Germany, like those in England and France. The Crusoe story was one of the myths attached to that train of thought.

5

Der Schweizerische Robinson (1812)

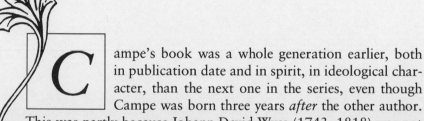ampe's book was a whole generation earlier, both in publication date and in spirit, in ideological character, than the next one in the series, even though Campe was born three years *after* the other author. This was partly because Johann David Wyss (1743–1818) was not a professional author, and his book was not so much written as slowly evolved in the bosom of the Wyss family. It was published on someone else's initiative and at the end of the author's life.

But a more important reason for the sharp difference in character was the occurrence of the French Revolution, and then the general reaction against radical ideas, between the two books' dates of publication. Campe's book was published on the very eve of the Revolution, and his ideas were prerevolutionary, in some sense prorevolutionary. Wyss's book had opposite sympathies and came out long after the Revolution. At least the frame around the story could only have been written then. And perhaps the parts written earlier acquired new power, as a consoling and reviving fantasy, from the anxiety aroused by the French Terror. Wyss's intellectual temperament seems to have been molded by the reaction, and could be described in terms of political sentiments, while one would speak of ideas in describing Campe.

The Author and the Book

Wyss was rector of the Protestant Cathedral in Bern. He was the son of a Johann Anton Wyss (1721–1803), who, though apprenticed to a baker, studied artillery in his spare time, became a soldier, and rose to be the colonel commanding all his city's artillery. He was in charge of the arsenal, the weapons factory, the cannon foundry, and the powder-mill. Johann David therefore grew up in a house of military interests, and, it would appear, of military order.[1]

Having entered the ministry, Wyss served with the Tscharner Regiment abroad, between 1766 and 1775, in the Mediterranean. Switzerland still sent soldiers abroad to earn money as mercenaries. When he settled down in Bern, he devoted most of his energy to educating his four sons, by exercises and hunting in the open air, and by the study of famous voyages, such as George Forster's and Captain Cook's. He also told them a story about a family like their own having adventures in the South Seas. This is the story we know as *The Swiss Family Robinson*. Written down as it was told, it reached the sum of 841 pages, and included sixty illustrations by the third son, Johann Emmanuel Wyss. The book seems to have been begun in 1792 and finished sometime after 1798, because of references in the last chapter to refugees from the French Terror in Switzerland. Between 1797 and 1802 Wyss devoted a lot of his time to such refugees, who were often in his house. They constituted an audience for his story, and he no doubt for theirs.

Wyss apparently called the manuscript, sometimes, *Charakteristik meiner Kinder in einer Robinsonade* (a characterization of my children in the form of a *Robinsonade*). This suggests the way the story changed in his hands from what it had been in Defoe's, to something more domestic. Moreover, Wyss consciously intended the idyll of family life to be the model and myth of state politics. "The family, as the seed-cell

1. Robert L. Wyss, "Der Schweizerische Robinson," *Stultifera Navis,* 12 (1955), 122–35 at 122.

of the civilized state, should be the life-form from which the individual's rights and duties, as well as his idea of happiness, must result."[2]

Changes in the Story

The external changes Wyss made to Defoe's motifs can be summed up under three heads. First of all, he was much more interested in flora and fauna, which he displayed to his reader as the treasures of nature's storehouse. (Campe was interested primarily in Crusoe's skills and in knowledge in the abstract.)

Wyss was not accurate. He made barley and pineapples grow together; penguins and flamingos nest side by side; the onager, said to be male at the beginning, gives birth to a foal; a cow bears a calf without benefit of bull; and the rainy seasons return too fast. Moreover, he was profuse. Every episode introduces some new and exotic bird, beast, or flower, described in the way—by intention at least—a contemporary encyclopedia would use. (The preface, by Wyss's son, Johann Rudolf, cautions parents to have its "facts" checked by their children's teachers.) All this makes Wyss's island very different from Defoe's.

The intellectual style is that of an encyclopedia, or of a contemporary naturalist like William Bartram. Bartram's descriptions of the southern landscapes of the United States, published in 1791, offer several passages like the following, which remind us of Wyss not in their verbal detail but in their vision of nature. "It is very pleasing to observe the banks of the river ornamented with hanging garlands . . . perpendicular green walls with projecting jambs, pilasters, and deep apartments . . . how purple and fiery appeared the tumultuous clouds. . . . The skies appeared streaked with blood or purple flames overhead, the flaming lightning streaming and darting about in every direction around."[3] Here, as in Wyss, exotic nature is presented half as a storehouse, half as a stately conservatory.

Second, this is a profoundly patriarchal story. The family is described

2. Ibid., 125. "Die Familie, als die Grundzelle des gesitteten Staates, soll die Lebensform sein, aus welche die Rechte und Pflichten sowie der Gluecksbegriff des einzelnen ergeben muessen."

3. Downs, *In Search of New Horizons,* 68.

as a patriarchal band, off to the Promised Land, as they set sail from Europe. And the point of most of the episodes is that Father knows best. His wife is a pale and timid figure, referred to (and addressed) as "the little mother," and largely a drag on the adventurous projects. ("What a wise little mother it is!" beams Father.) Johann Rudolf says that she was drawn to show the softer sex the power they have over the happiness of their families.[4] The four sons, however, are being trained to be *men*— like Father—and each one's clearly marked faults are worked on by precept and parable, reward and punishment.

This also is something new and quite unlike Campe or Defoe. In their works the word "man" and its derivatives—manly, manhood, manliness—are sometimes sounded but still lack that hearty resonance that was to become so ominous through the rest of the nineteenth century. The concepts were there, but they did not receive their emotional development before 1800.

Men have a touch of the devil in them (they play with fire, gunpowder, cannon) while women are all angels. The father and the sons sometimes frighten the little mother, who says, plaintively, "You dear, horrible, wonderful people, shall I scold you or praise you? . . . *We* [women] don't frighten people by firing salutes in honour of our performances."[5]

Men are playful, women are nervous. But of course playfulness knows its place, does not go very far, in a real man. Seriousness is dominant. This book makes a cult of authority, for the patriarchal family is the justification of the patriarchal state. The preface says that what the book teaches is above all the value of "the social state, whether in its domestic or its national form, together with the arts and inventions that accompany it for the well-being of every individual."[6]

Third, it is a family book, in which everything happens, not to a solitary shipwrecked sailor but to a group. The members are related to each other by affectional but also hierarchical bonds: husband to wife, father to sons, older brother to younger. There is a lot of play within those bonds. Secrets are kept, surprises sprung, games played. But most of these are forms of play initiated predominantly by the father. The limits of the permissible, the sacredness of the hierarchy, are kept clear.

---

4. Wyss, *The Family Robinson Crusoe*, ix.
5. *The Swiss Family Robinson*, ed., W. H. G. Kingston, 90. All subsequent quotations will be from this version.
6. *The Family Robinson Crusoe*, xi/xii.

There are athletic games for the boys, organized by the father, at which the mother, as a Queen of Beauty, presents the prizes. The triumphs are family ones, celebrated in civic rituals, of a kind familiar in Switzerland; the griefs are family ones, when some member is lost or is in danger. Indeed, the family relations are *the* source of pleasure and emotion, as well as virtue. In the world of this Robinson all pleasures are family pleasures, and the individual's other relations, to God and nature, to landscape and work, are aspects of his family life. All this could hardly be less like Defoe's Robinson.

The story was invented as part of Wyss's education of his sons, which included also his building them toy forts and ships, harbors and regiments, such as he had seen in his military career. He took them hiking and hunting, and they stuffed and studied the animals they shot. In his introduction to volume four in 1826, Johann Rudolf Wyss says the printed version misses the technical zest and skill communicated by the manuscript and the games that went with it. Johann David Wyss was apparently from earliest youth on clever with his hands, and clever at devices and small machines. He had the Robinson gifts.

The book was a family project, but it was an all-male family, though Wyss was married three times. One of the sons painted watercolors for the story; another got the story into print, revising what the father had written. There had been two sisters, but they died young, and we do not hear of them, or the boys' mother, or Wyss's other two wives, making any contribution.

This emphasis on family must recall Campe. He too gave a father-teacher a moral and mythic authority that seems to replace or blend into that of church and state. But the comparison also brings out differences. First of all, Campe's is an educational, not a biological, family. Second, his Crusoe is alone on the island. Above all, Campe's implicit idea of the state is liberal and individualistic. The island is a place in which to escape from oppressive social forces. And insofar as he is at all interested in principles of authority or hierarchy, it is not in any organic or affectional myth of the family. Wyss's is a Romantic version of the Robinson story, though not in any Jean-Paul or *Paul et Virginie* sense of erotic idyll. It is the political philosophy that is Romantic, and the romantics to think of are Burke and Scott, not Blake or Shelley.

Roughly speaking, Wyss's is also an evangelical version of the story. It begins, like most evangelical fiction, in a reaction against Enlightenment rationalism and a recourse to traditional emotional structures. But it is not pietistic; there are no references to Jesus or salvation, or to Luther and his hymns. (This is true of all the versions of Wyss's story I have read, but I should admit that there are others. As I said at the beginning of this argument, *The Swiss Family Robinson* always existed in a number of versions. I have taken most of my quotations from the W. H. G. Kingston translation and edition, partly because of Kingston's immense activity and reputation as a writer for boys in the later nineteenth century.)

In Kingston's version, on their first Sunday on the island, the father preaches a sermon, which expresses the book's theology. There was once a king who ruled over two realms; one was Reality, or Day, the other was Possibility, or Night. (This seems to correspond, very roughly, to Heaven and Earth, or perhaps to Christianity and Paganism.) He gave some people from the second realm the chance to colonize an island in the first. He gave them seeds, lands, and advice, and for a time all went well. But after a while most of them forgot their king or rebelled against him, and so were punished. Admiral Death sailed into their port and seized them for work in the galleys or mines. God's patience does not last forever.

This parable covers some thirteen pages, and morals are deduced from it, appropriate to each son in turn. After which, the little mother reveals that she has saved a Bible from the wreck, and they all read from that. This is a Christianity adapted to the colony-and-empire situation, and shorn of reference to the Gospels or to the schemes of feeling we usually call Christian. If God is like a king who founds colonies, presumably such a king is somewhat like God. One would not call such piety as this evangelical, but one can find something similar in the children's fiction of England in the later nineteenth century, when many evangelical writers were writing adventure. Wyss was their precursor. In the first half of the century, as we shall see, the Crusoe story was sometimes told with a more genuine evangelical stress.

The main feeling in Wyss is quite different. This is the heartiest of all versions of the Crusoe story, if we understand heartiness to be a self-congratulating (and usually male) assertion of pleasure in being who one is and doing what one does. The implication is that the heart is the core or root of the personality, the organic interpenetration of body and soul, thought and feeling, ethics and aspiration. Each action and emotion is so felt as to reinforce the core of the individual and the core of the group. Nothing is allowed to foster separateness or criticism.

In *The Swiss Family Robinson* every joke, every meal, is a sacrament of togetherness. There are lots of jokes; every mistake anyone makes (of course Father does not make any) is funny; and much of nature is funny. There are also lots of meals, which are described with gourmet relish. Everything on the island tastes better than at home, and they manage to procure turtle, oysters, caviar, and wine for themselves. Eating together is a ritual of domestic heartiness. And there is a strongly rising curve of emotional gratification, as in *Robinson Crusoe,* but more appetitive or consumptive here. Things, notably things to be eaten, get bigger and better all the time. When they catch a salmon, it weighs *fifteen pounds!* (p. 70). And the scale of the flora and fauna rises toward the lion, the elephant, the whale.

Then too the father's ingenuity in taming animals is another kind of heartiness, though the appetite this time is for power. He dizzies the eagle with tobacco fumes, and charms the iguana with music, and tames the onager by biting through its ear. The family is, except of course for the little mother, at ease with violence. The father had taught the boys to shoot, back in Switzerland, and powder and shot are the first things they save from the ship. The episode of the slaughter of the apes is an exception, because they feel shock and disgust at what they have done, but the impression it makes does not linger—with the boys or with the readers in sympathy with the book.

Continuity and Innovation

Despite the differences between them, there are points of similarity between Campe and Wyss. Wyss was, like Campe, a military chaplain, briefly, and spent the second half of his life as a member of the clerisy. That combination of the military with the religious, in the service of a bourgeois class and a national cause, seems to be natural in writers about Robinson. Our story, with its stress on work and its discretion about violence, suits a secularized clerisy. It suggests a *political* heartiness, of which patriotism is perhaps the prime example.

Surely it is no accident that one of the Wyss sons—the Ernest of the story—wrote in 1818 what was to become the national anthem of Switzerland. He also collected Swiss folktales and legends, and did other literary-philological work that reinforced Swiss national identity, just like what Campe did for Germany. (The variety and purposefulness of their masculinist enterprises—literary, linguistic, and educational—can remind one of feminist enterprises today.)

Wyss's nationalism was, however, more conservatively colored than Campe's. Switzerland had long been established as a nation-state—and indeed as a bourgeois republic—to the ruling class of which Wyss's family already belonged. That family, and their version of Robinson, was not charged with the innovative excitement of Campe's aspiration to political change—to a new nationalism that would break the power of church and feudal aristocracy. Their nationalism was linked to support for the church and for the existing ruling class. The Wysses used the Robinson story indeed to *renew* the source of their pride and power—seeing their colonial experience rather the way the English aristocracy was to see theirs.

Another innovation in the story, only apparently unrelated, is the appearance of the missionary theme. Father is a Pastor (in some versions, he lost his patrimony in the Revolution, in 1798), and he sets out to become a missionary in Tahiti, going by way of London and the London Missionary Society. This is a point of juncture between the Crusoe story and the evangelical movement, a juncture of only passing importance in Wyss's story but very significant in the history of the Western imagination.

The London Missionary Society was founded in 1795, and the first missionaries arrived in Tahiti two years later. It was a colonizing as well as an evangelizing party, for of the thirty-nine of them (thirty men, six women, and three children), only four were ordained ministers. The others were trained in English technical skills. There was a draper, a butcher, a weaver, a tailor, a hatter, a bricklayer, a carpenter—so many aspects of, or versions of, Crusoe. And there is some evidence that Defoe's book was favorite reading for them, along with Bunyan and the Bible.

They came from a different caste of British society than the empire's military officers or colonial governors. Most were tradesmen, with little schooling but full of religious zeal. They had had little contact with the world of learning or taste, and got little support from that world, except from upper-class evangelicals.[7] There was a good deal of skepticism about missions among the educated, book-reading public. Dickens, for

7. Grattan, *The Southwest Pacific to 1900*.

example, takes that skepticism for granted, and makes many jokes about missions and collections for their benefit. To the congregations of evangelical churches and chapels, on the other hand, the idea of the Protestant missions was very important. Their awareness of these missionaries gave both the empire, and adventure, a new emotional tone of seriousness. Voyages and settlements now involved the nation's religion, and martyrdom was in the air. The already lurid image of cannibalism now included a Christian martyr. (The prototype, soon to become comic, was the missionary in the cooking pot.) This was a category of motif that Defoe had not touched. Wyss does not develop it far in *The Swiss Family Robinson,* but continuers and adapters of his story carry it further.

These martyrs might be of another nationality from the colonizing power. It was quite plausible for Wyss to send his Swiss to Tahiti, and thus to link his family to contemporary history. Many of the Protestant missionaries in the British Empire were German, or Swiss, or Danish. For instance, Olive Schreiner's father was a missionary to the British colonies in Africa; and Hermann Hesse's grandfather was a missionary in India. The history of Christianity in even India (where the Church of England was established) would have been profoundly different without its German and Danish workers. At least the missionary half of that history would have been different.

Another change was the location of Robinson's island. It was now in the South Seas, and neither where Defoe had placed it nor where Selkirk was marooned. (Campe had situated it in the Caribbean, and *Simplicissimus* set the story in Madagascar.) The attention of the civilized world was now turned to the South Seas, perhaps partly because of the popularity of Cook, and partly because of the designation of Australia as a place to be developed as a colony by the labor of deported convicts. In 1786 for the first time a fleet was commissioned to take seven hundred and fifty convicts from Britain to Botany Bay. The hulks at home were full, and North America would take no more convicts.

The frame story around *The Swiss Family Robinson* reflects this international character to the contemporary interest in the South Seas. The father's story is supposed to be told in a manuscript brought back to Switzerland by Hofrat Horner (a real person), who had sailed around the world on a Russian ship, the *Podesta,* under the command of Captain Krusenstern (a real voyage, which began in 1803 and ended in 1806). According to Madame de Montolieu, Horner was an astronomer from

Zurich. Krusenstern did visit Tahiti, and the New Switzerland island is supposed to be somewhere near there and somewhere near New Guinea. He had German naturalists aboard, his ship was British-built, and his lieutenant had sailed in the British navy. The European nations, or at least their nationals, cooperated as well as competed in their voyages.

The Swiss themselves were exploring and emigrating in some numbers, even though they owned no colonies. In the story, the family calls their island New Switzerland, but they are resigned to seeing it absorbed into the British Empire. Shiploads of Swiss, tempted by promoters' pamphlets telling of paradisal conditions of life, sailed to, for instance, America. In 1735 William Byrd sold 33,000 acres of the Carolinas to Sam Jenner, a Swiss, who got two hundred and fifty of his compatriots to buy this land and sail toward it in 1738. They were responding to his pamphlet description, entitled "New Found Eden," *Neugefundenes Eden,* more than two hundred pages long, and published in 1737. (The immigrants were wrecked and drowned off the coast of Virginia.)

Wyss's book could be called another among such pamphlets, though one of a fictional kind. The father says, about emigrants, "None takes a better place in the great national family, none is happier or more beloved than those who go forth from such homes to fulfill new duties" (p. 250). And the end of the story comes when the English Captain Littlestone sails his brig, the *Unicorn,* to the island, looking for another and *English* castaway. She is Jenny Montrose, who has not only survived but met and fallen in love with Fritz, the oldest of the father's sons, thus uniting the Swiss with the English. Moreover, since the name Jenny Montrose identifies her as a Walter Scott heroine, we may say that in literary terms the Crusoe story here unites itself to the historical romance, the other major adventure story of the time.

The Story's History

Another interesting aspect of the book's composite character and its internationalism is seen in its career after 1813, when the second volume was published. The story was immediately translated into other languages, and into French by Madame de Montolieu, who had an established reputation as a writer for children. This lady, of Swiss origins herself, was born in 1751, and was already famous as the author of *Caroline de Lichtfield,* published in 1813.

She translated Wyss quite freely, and appropriated the story. Her version is dedicated to her three grandsons and two grandnephews, and at the end of the first half she remarked that she was offering her translation to boys in particular. The dedication says, "You will see there [in the story] how union between brothers and friends, activity, courage, confidence in God, and obedience to those who know more about things than you, are necessary in all of life's circumstances."[8] She shows a strong sense of the moral values of the enterprise she and Wyss are engaged in.

Because there was such a demand for a sequel, and because Johann Rudolf Wyss could not or would not produce one, Madame de Montolieu got his permission to write one herself. This lengthy continuation, published in 1824, introduced some female characters and enhanced the role of the mother. However, the first thing the mother does with her freedom is to fall down and break her leg; and the second thing is to get abducted by savages. So if the mother (now called Elizabeth) is more the center of attention, she is no more active or adventurous than she was before. The change is rather that the book becomes more a vehicle of sensibility than it had been. It is apt that Madame de Montolieu sets an epigraph from *La nouvelle Héloïse* before her continuation. The father is now full of Rousseauist feelings as well as morality, and a description of a storm covers a hundred pages. She also introduces another missionary, this time English, called Willis, who preaches restraint to a tribe of savages—who practice human sacrifice and have abducted Jack.

Madame de Montolieu's version of the story, especially in her continuation, is generally pious and emotional. Willis is said to be "one of those zealous and courageous Christians who dedicate their life and energies to the instruction and the eternal welfare of men born in another hemisphere" (4:81). The father too is more religious in these volumes and refers to the Divine Savior. The chapter titles are revealing: chapter 37, "Hope Disappointed; Tempest; Misfortune and Consolation"; chapter 38, "The Thunderbolt and the Lightning Conductor"; chapter 39, "Anguish; Perplexity; Frightful Night; Consolation"; and so on. She

---

8. *Le Robinson Suisse,* vi. "Vous y verrez combien l'union entre des frères et des amis, l'activité, le courage, la confiance en Dieu, et l'obéissance pour ceux qui en savent plus que vous, sont nécessaires dans toutes les circonstances de la vie."

introduces a woman and her two daughters, Madame Hirtel (her husband is a Hamburg merchant) and Sophie and Matilde. Her motive, she
declared, was to tranquilize the reader's imagination about the family's
future while avoiding all that might arouse the passions (p. iv). (Johann
Rudolf Wyss, in his introduction, addressing the question of why there
were no girls or women in his father's story, said the motives might
easily be conceived.[9] This was above all family entertainment.)

Later J. R. Wyss wrote his own continuation (mostly out of his
father's manuscripts) published in 1826, and this was the one most
favored by later publishers, even the French. He replaced Madame Hirtel
and her daughters with Jenny Montrose. Madame de Montolieu's volumes got reprinted only once, in 1829. But Wyss had taken over several
of her ideas; for instance, her ostrich, donkey, and boa constrictor, and
the famous scene in which the boa swallows the donkey. But then
Madame de Montolieu had taken ideas from other precursors. The boa
and the tortoise-shell fountain bowl, for instance, came from *Le Robinson français* of 1822. Other translators and adapters took equally freely
from precursors in their treatment of the story, so that what was read by
children in the second half of the nineteenth century and later was very
much a cooperative effort. And any information about the source, in a
preface or publisher's note, was and is quite likely to be false. Henri de
Suchau, in an 1869 *Le Robinson suisse,* published in London, confi-
dently attributes the book to Johann Rudolf Wyss, teacher and librarian,
who is also credited with *Robinson the Younger.* The story was public
property—it was more anonymous than *Robinson Crusoe*—and even
today J. D. Wyss gets no entry in most Swiss books of literary reference.

The Swiss Family Robinson was immensely popular. When J. R. Wyss
published his continuation, he spoke of a fifth edition to the English
translation (and he does not seem to know of the earlier translation by
William Godwin) and the fifth edition of the French, plus an Italian and
a Spanish edition. There were sixty editions in France in fifty years; in
1837, for instance, there were three new editions and a six-act play, *Le
Robinson suisse.* In 1898 Ullrich listed fifty-six reworkings. In France,
where the book was particularly popular, twenty translations were said
to be in print simultaneously. Perhaps this was because of the strong
French emphasis on family loyalty and family sentiment. In an essay
published in London in 1870 the book was compared to its advantage

9. *The Family Robinson Crusoe,* ix.

with Defoe's version by a well-known man of letters, Charles Nodier. He addressed rhetorical reproaches to Defoe's hero: you love nobody, the dearest necessities of the heart are forgotten, the consoling voice of women, the delightful prattle of children. These things are what Wyss offers. "What is lacking [in Defoe] are those tender anxieties, those mutual solicitudes, those alarms, those joys we share with others."[10] Compared with Defoe's cold masterpiece, Wyss's is a book that could replace all others.

The same comparison is made, and the same conclusion drawn, in England and Switzerland for instance, by Walter Jerrold, in an essay introducing a London edition of 1910, and by H. Kurz in a Zurich edition of 1841. But the French seem the most eloquent or insistent on the point. Perhaps it was the Rousseauist tradition of sentiment in nineteenth-century France that led to this direct reversal of Rousseau's own judgment on *Robinson Crusoe*. The hero's solitariness and self-sufficiency is counted against him. In the twentieth century it was of course not Wyss but Defoe (especially his *Journal of the Plague Year*) who caught the attention of writers like Camus, precisely for his "coldness."

It is worth noting that *The Swiss Family Robinson* has also been popular and outshone *Robinson Crusoe* in another time and place—twentieth-century America—where there was great value placed on family feeling. Walt Disney, and Hollywood in general, has offered us many treatments of Wyss's story. It has been propaganda for family feeling more often than for adventure.

Wyss's story was also popular in nineteenth- and twentieth-century England, where there have been three hundred editions in English, according to Bettina Huerlimann (*Three Centuries of Children's Books in Germany*). It is of interest that the first translation (of 1814) was made by or for William Godwin, and perhaps with the help of his son-in-law, Shelley. At that date Godwin was of course in disrepute as one of the radicals who would have liked to see a French Revolution in England. He had to eke out a covert living as the anonymous translator of children's stories, most of which were in themselves conservative. English culture was finding yet another way to restrict the freedom of dissenters, and to make them say the opposite of what they would have wished. (An earlier example was *Gulliver's Travels*, written as a parody

10. In Nodier's introduction to *The Swiss Family Robinson*, trans. W.H.D.A.

of the *Robinson Crusoe* stories but read as another such.) Godwin's philosophy was anarchist, but his most popular book (that is, the most popular book he published) was this translation, which is intensely conservative, religiously, politically, and socially.

6

Masterman Ready (1841)

In this chapter we meet the first English successor to Defoe's story—the first significant *Robinsonade* in England in one hundred and twenty years. To scholars of English literature, it has often seemed that the subject was born and died with Defoe. But our glances at French, German, and Swiss literature have shown us how wrong that is. The story still exerted so strong an appeal, it seemed to bear upon so many interests, that different ways of telling it continued to be devised; and that was true of all the literatures of Europe.

The Story's New Shape

If Pastor Wyss's version could be called reactionary and partially evangelical, Captain Marryat's, a generation later, was Victorian and wholly evangelical. Both are equally domestic. The people to whom the adventure happens in Marryat's book are an upper-class Victorian family, the Seagraves. Their day always begins with a domestic idyll of family prayers, at which the father or mother reads from the Bible. There are also scenes of mutual collision and upset, out of domestic comedy.

The narrator is pedagogical and inculcates a high standard of propriety on the reader, even via the "rough seaman" after whom the book is named. In the opening scene we hear Ready complain to his captain about the first mate's bad language. "I do wish that Mr. Mackintosh would not swear so; I always think that the winds blow harder, as if angry that their Divine Master should be defied by such poor worms as we are" (p. 19). As the last phrase indicates, this propriety has religious roots, and depressive effects. Ready (who is the book's main moralist) tells his life story in volume two; and he accompanies it with such severe self-criticism that Mr. Seagrave protests: "You analyse yourself very minutely, Ready." To which Ready replies, like a seventeenth-century puritan, "The heart is deceitful and desperately wicked, sir" (p. 137). And even mild Mr. Seagrave warns his son, "More people are laughed into error than persuaded into it" (p. 170).

Most important, the blame for nearly destroying the family—which is saved only by self-sacrifice on Ready's part—falls on Tommy, the liveliest and naughtiest of the Seagrave children. He has let their precious supply of water run away while the family is under siege by savages. Ready has to crawl out to the spring with a cask to save them all from dying of thirst, and he gets killed. Tommy has caused alarms and mishaps throughout the book, but because he is so lively, the reader remained sure that he was to be forgiven—indeed, preferred—according to the conventional morality of fiction. But the plot forces us to take even children's naughtiness judgmentally, puritanically.

This evangelical strain of course goes against the grain of the Robinson story itself, with its upward curve of adventure, optimism, and expectation. The story had been everywhere recommended, and received, as amplifying men's energies and directing outward, to achievement and self-confidence. So much was true even of Wyss's conservative version, and more so elsewhere in Europe.

Robinson in Russia

Robinson Crusoe's career in Russia, for instance, shows how closely it was linked there to cultural modernism and psychological expansion. A translation (from the French) was published there between 1762 and 1764 and reprinted in 1775, 1787, 1797, and 1814. Then another translation, direct from the English, was made in 1811. There were also many abridgments and adaptations circulating in the country. Thus Pushkin had in his library, at the time of his death in 1837, both a London edition of 1831 and a French translation by Borel of 1836, and the translation contained some biographical material about Defoe.

There were also native Russian castaway stories to which Defoe's story could attach itself. One of these, of the early eighteenth century, "Vasilii Koriotskii," in part resembles *Robinson Crusoe,* but the writing of it is never really penetrated by the factual imagination. Then we should remember also Campe's story about the Russian sailors marooned on the Arctic ice.

As for what the Robinson story itself meant to Russian readers, we know that in 1844 the great radical literary critic Vissarion Belinsky wrote enthusiastic praise of Defoe and comparative disparagement of Campe, because the latter had subdued the adventure of the story to its moral. (In Spain too, about this time, literary critics began to prefer Defoe to Campe and the others. Alcalo Galiano gave lectures in Madrid on eighteenth-century European literature, in 1845, and praised Defoe above all other writers of *Robinsonaden.*) This preference implies that the story's adventurous element was being prized in all its unregenerate energy and egotism. Belinsky attacked in particular one version of the story in which a great fuss was made about Crusoe's going to sea, because that was a sin of filial disobedience. Now this was just the sort of moral issue that Marryat, in England, was reintroducing into the story. But Belinsky in Russia, at the same moment, brushed it aside. He pointed to great sea travelers like Cook, Bering, and La Perouse, who had been able to do so much for humanity only because of their passion for travel and indifference to domestic duty.[1] One has duties to *oneself,* Belinsky says (like Rousseau). One has a duty to grow and develop; to become an adventure hero, we might say. Caring for one's parents must not impair one's developing as an intelligent and independent being (p. 91). Crusoe is a hero of modern life, and those who condemn him belong to the past.

M. P. Glinka saw Crusoe in the same terms. He inserted an abridgment and reworking of *Robinson Crusoe* into his *New Children's*

1. Alekseev, *Mezhdunarozhnie Svyazi Ruskoi Literaturi,* 89.

Reading, published in 1819–24, and told his readers that his French tutor had recommended the book to him with the words, "See how much an individual can accomplish. Nature is dead. Man brings her to life" (p. 88). Robinson transforming his island is seen as a sort of Prometheus or Pygmalion.

Belinsky and Tolstoy both wanted to write their own versions of the story for Russian readers, and a version *was* published in Tolstoy's education journal, *Yasnaya Polyana,* in 1862. This was in the period of Tolstoy's faith in modern culture, when he wanted Russian schoolchildren to read *Robinson Crusoe,* to liberate and animate their minds. Herzen, too, another of the great Russian radicals of that generation, had high praise for Defoe's book. All of them read it as the Enlightenment text Rousseau had made of it, while England was having doubts or at least making changes.

The Author

The Victorian or evangelical severity is the more striking in Marryat because he had before written several adventure tales of a much prouder and gayer kind. Take, for instance, *Frank Mildmay,* whose autobiographical hero says—and wins us by saying—that even at seven his ruling passion was pride, and self-love. "If I have gained a fair name in the service, if I have led instead of followed, it must be ascribed to this my leading passion" (p. 7). He is a triumphant narcissist. At sixteen, Mildmay's "person assumed an outline of which I had great reason to be proud, since I often heard it the subject of encomium among the fair sex, and their award was confirmed even by my companions" (p. 53). The reader is expected to like him despite, or because of, this dandyism, which could not be further removed from the morality of *Masterman Ready.*

The change of ethos between the two books is to be explained on both biographical and historical grounds. Marryat's first novels were Regency in both date and feeling, while his later ones were Victorian. The Regency was a period when dandyism, or in general young-manly styles of dashing irresponsibility, felt free to express themselves more fully than they did before or after. Marryat began his novel-writing career in

1829, and wrote prolifically and popularly enough to make, it seems, a thousand pounds a year. But by 1839 he felt his popularity as a writer, and that of his genre, the Regency sea adventure, to be waning. Queen Victoria had come to the throne in 1837, and she soon became a symbol for certain forces for change in the national temperament, a change toward that moral style and mood we call Victorian. Marryat therefore designed a new literary product, suited to the new demand, and *Masterman Ready* was as successful as his earlier books, though so steadily edifying. (I do not mean to imply that he was not sincere in employing this later moral style, only that his sincerity is not the point.)

Many details of his biography suggest how well placed Marryat was to receive and respond to the adventurous messages of his culture. His father had been a chairman of Lloyds Marine Insurance and a West Indies merchant who amassed a fortune of £250,000, while his mother was an American. Thus both lines of his parental heritage spoke to him of the empire, commercial and political. Then he went to sea, at the age of fourteen, to serve under Captain Lord Cochrane, a dashing naval commander, a hero of the wars against Napoleon, who became after 1815 a hero of the liberation movements in Chile, Peru, and Brazil—and in 1818 was involved in a plot to rescue Napoleon and make him emperor of South America. Cochrane was Marryat's personal hero and was admired also by Scott, and by the twentieth-century adventure writer C. S. Forrester.

Cochrane is depicted as Captain Savage in Marryat's novel *Peter Simple*. He was one of Nelson's captains, and his inspiring of Marryat's fiction can be compared with the inspiration Alexandre Dumas got from his father, who was one of Napoleon's generals. (Something similar can be seen in the life of the writer who succeeded Marryat as chief English boys' writer, W. H. G. Kingston, as we shall note.) In such writers the excitements of the historical empire passed into fiction, especially fiction for boys, very naturally.

Then Marryat himself had a distinguished career in the Royal Navy. He devised a code of signals, published in 1837, for the merchant navy; and he fought in the war that won much of Burma for England. His early literary projects were factual accounts of adventure heroes; the first was a life of Admiral Collingwood, and the next an *Age of Nelson*. He was the first writer in the Robinson series to have himself lived a life of adventure, and among adventurers.

Continuity and Innovation

If we ask what other changes Marryat introduced into the Robinson story as he inherited it from Wyss, we must say, preliminarily, that he made it more realistic. This is not primarily the kind of realism we call "moral," since the black-and-white moralism of his story is hardly subtle and cannot compete with the great masters of moral realism, like George Eliot. But in the matter of formal realism, the rendering of season and shoreline, food-gathering and hut-building, Marryat is almost on a par with Defoe, or at least he is closer than the intervening writers. He knows the practical problems the Seagraves would meet on their island, and the solutions he devises for them are both plausible and engrossing. Comparatively speaking, neither Wyss nor Campe spoke with authority on the practical problems of survival.

Then the principal new element in the story is Masterman Ready: "a weather-beaten old seaman, whose grizzly locks were streaming in the wind" when we first see him, on the first page. He in some sense replaces Robinson as the center of interest, which makes a great difference to the hero motif. What Defoe embodied in Robinson Crusoe, Marryat split between two characters. He tells us that his idea had been "to show the practical man in Ready, and the theoretical in the father of the family" (p. xii).

However, besides practice and the practical, Ready also represents the people and hardship. He describes himself as "one who has roughed it all his life, and who has neither kith nor kin that he knows of to care about his death" (p. 31). His lack of education and his worn and deeply grooved face are often insisted on. He is sixty-four, and tells us that that is old age for a sailor. "Because sailors live faster than other people, partly from the hardships which they undergo, and partly from their own fault in drinking so much spirits" (p. 93). Yet, in the storm, when the other sailors take to the boats and abandon the Seagraves to their fate, Ready stays behind. He joins the party of the gentlemen rather than that of his economic class or vocational caste. "I tell you, Mr. Seagrave, I think much more of your children than I do for myself" (p. 28).

In many ways Ready reminds us of Cooper's Natty Bumppo (also, of course, descended from Robinson Crusoe). Natty too represents the people, and is uneducated and unpolished, but devotes himself to the service of the gentlemen he meets—and even more to the service of their wives and daughters. The difference is that Natty belongs to—he imaginatively possesses—the wide open spaces of America, a fact that disguises and mitigates his caste servitude. He is able to choose which of the young men in his stories should become his heirs, and so inherit the American idea. He is a more acceptable, less embarrassing representative of the lower classes, and so are his descendants in countless western adventures. For that reason, American adventure has, paradoxically, given more space to class differentiation than has English or French adventure. Ready belongs to the sea, but not in the sense that Natty belongs to America, because the latter is a reciprocal relationship. America belongs to Natty too. Ready and Natty are, respectively, the English and the American representations of the same idea. Ready is, as a sailor, a figure at the bottom of a rigid social hierarchy. The sea does not "belong" to him.

He is, after all, the Seagraves' servant, however superior his position, morally speaking. They also have a black girl servant (originally a slave, but redeemed because she has been to England, where slavery was illegal), whose virtue it is to care more for and about the Seagrave children than about herself. She is often complimented on this, and it is clear that the appropriate virtue of all such people is self-sacrifice. The devotion of a lower class or race to the children of an upper class is a theme that develops as imperialism develops, and perhaps reaches its climax in Kipling's stories about English boys in India.

Natty protects the daughters of gentlemen too, but in him all this has a more poetic air, because he has in his keeping the idea of America, a priceless jewel that the gentlemen must aspire to inherit from him. The only European figure like Ready I recall is Willis the Pilot, another seaman, who appears in a continuation of *The Swiss Family Robinson*. Willis is the (reinterpreted) missionary figure first introduced into the Swiss Family Robinson story by Madame de Montolieu.

The Seagraves are a ruling class and imperial caste family, more directly related to the actual British Empire than Wyss's Swiss pastor could be. The colonies are sketched in, in the background of the Marryat story. The Seagraves' ship calls in at Cape Town, just before it is wrecked; they are on their way to Australia to start a farm; and Mr. Seagrave has been to India and to the Andaman Islands. And in the epilogue to their adventure it is made clear how imperial their social roles are to be in the future. "Mr. Seagrave, like the patriarch Job after his tribulations, found his flocks and herds greatly increased on his arrival at Sydney. . . . William inherited the greater part of the property from his father, after having for many years assisted him in the management of it. Tommy, notwithstanding all his scrapes, grew up a very fine fellow, and entered the Army. He is now a major. . . . Caroline married a young clergyman, and made him an excellent wife; little Albert went into the Navy, and is at present a commander" (p. 338).

Missionaries and Martyrs

Thus both the evangelical theme and the imperial theme were incorporated into the British adventure tale in the mid-nineteenth century. The emergence of the former of course had to do with the contemporary emergence of the Protestant missionary and martyr. For instance, more or less contemporary with *Masterman Ready* was the martyrdom of John Williams, who was a famous figure in England because of his lecture tours there between 1834 and 1838. His autobiography of 1837, *Missionary Enterprizes in the South Pacific,* was a best-seller. And after he was killed by natives on the South Sea island of Erromango in 1839, chromographs of the scene of his death were sold in large numbers.

Williams had been apprenticed to an ironmonger in London, but after a conversion experience in a tabernacle connected with the London Missionary Society, he decided to become a missionary, and in 1816 was accepted as one and sailed for the South Seas. He went first to the island of Moorea, where he learned the language in the course of a year's stay, and helped build a schooner, doing all the ironwork himself. He then moved to Roiatea, where he built a seven-room house, plastered and whitewashed and painted, with carpets and furniture with turned and polished legs, and, outside, lawns, flowerbeds, and gravel paths.

Williams taught his converts that Christians slept one to a bed, in separate rooms, wore clothes, drank tea, and sat on chairs. Above all he taught them, as the London Missionary Society in general did, that the chief bane of savage life was idleness, and the chief virtue of Christians was work. David Livingstone quoted one of the founders of that society (to which he too belonged) as saying that all a missionary needed was to be able to read the Bible and to build a wheelbarrow; missionaries should be "godly men who understood mechanic arts." We might say that they should combine John Bunyan with Robinson Crusoe.

Thus the missionary took with him the gospel of Daniel Defoe, as well as that of Jesus Christ; both gospels, after all, crystallized forms of spiritual feeling in nineteenth-century England. Williams taught the natives to adze and saw and plane, to make boxes and bedsteads and sofas, and to burn their coral to make lime, to boil sugar, and to work at the forge.[2]

Transferring himself to Rarotonga in 1826, he built a seventy-ton missionary schooner in three months, inventing a bellows and pump along the way, and using charcoal made from coconut trees, rope from hibiscus bark, and so on.[3] The natives were by and large fascinated by Williams for a long time, but some of them (especially the young braves) grew to resent his preaching and eventually he was killed. He became a hero in England, his name sometimes ranked with Columbus, or with John Howard, the prison reformer. In retrospect, he seems a striking blend of the solid, practical, commonsense man with the solitary, driven, restless man—psychologically, somewhat an exaggeration of both opposite sides of Robinson Crusoe. (Masterman Ready, though culturally he has the same meaning, woud be psychologically a "sadder but wiser" type.)

As the Crusoe image thus became in some ways sanctified, it was perhaps natural that the image of "native races" grew more grotesque in the public consciousness. The only precursor in this matter is Defoe, and if we compare Friday with Juno, the Seagraves' servant, we find Defoe more interested and responsive to Friday's otherness. And if we compare his cannibals with Marryat's, the latter are more multitudinous, terrifying, and nightmarish. "The savages were all painted, with their war-cloaks and feathers on, and armed with spears and clubs, evidently having come with no peaceable intentions. . . . " " 'What a fierce cruel set of wretches they appear to be; if they overpower us, they will certainly kill us.' "[4] It is an appropriate new feature of the plot that the Seagraves are rescued at the last possible moment, by cannonballs from a British ship crashing into the bushes that conceal these naked murderers. (This potent image recurs in later adventure tales, with various emotional tones.) Despite these differences and innovations, Marryat's story is clearly an adaptation of his precursors'. In his preface he says that his

2. Daws, *A Dream of Islands*, 32.
3. Ibid., 45–46.
4. *Masterman Ready*, 306.

children asked him to write a continuation of *The Swiss Family Robinson*. He refused, he says, because he could not condone Wyss's ignorance of seamanship, or his unscrupulous inventions in geography and natural history. Marryat claimed a high sense of duty toward his readers.

Marryat's is still, however, a tale told to children, as well as about children—like Wyss's and Campe's. In his second paragraph, the writer half turns away from his narrative to make a didactic aside to his readers. "The captain stood before the wheel, watching the men who were steering the ship; for when you are running before a heavy gale, it requires great attention to the helm" (p. 1). Like Wyss, Marryat begins inside the story, though not quite *in medias res;* and somewhat like Campe, he gives us Ready's life story in serial form—evening narrations, with questions from the audience—in volume two. And many of the main features of both form and content are familiar: the lists of tools, the count of possessions, the tasks to be performed, and the delight in nature's storehouse, of flora and fauna designed to enhance and enrich human life.

Above all, this is a story about a family, whose structure is very like that of Wyss's family, notably in the position of the delicate wife and mother, who never gets to do more than to wave her handkerchief as her men appear or disappear on the horizon, or to sink lifeless into someone's arms. One should say that Marryat is a better writer and a smarter man than Wyss. This is a sketch of the Victorian ideal that one can take seriously, despite the didactic primness that obtrudes in quotations. What makes it interesting above all is the way the role of the father, so wholly the master in Wyss's story, is split between Mr. Seagrave, the educated gentleman, and Ready, the "frontiersman" and hero. This split in the image of the masculine reflects a whole idea of a caste-composed society, where some virtues belong to one class and other virtues to another, but the whole is harmoniously combined, a social idea well suited to an empire. Defoe's Robinson had contained all the virtues in one body.

The other difference dividing *Masterman Ready* not only from *The Swiss Family Robinson* but from nearly every other telling of the Robinson story we have already mentioned. Its severely evangelical ethos runs counter to the spirit of adventure. The story's mood is not expansive; many of the texts Ready cites are powerfully depressive. They derive from moral anxiety as directly as, say, William Golding's images in his much later, anti-adventurous telling of the story. When five of the sailors

are swept overboard early on, Ready says, " 'Master William, did any of
these men imagine, when they left the Cape, or indeed the day or hour
before it happened, that their souls were to be required of them? . . . In
the midst of life we are in death.' " (p. 21). Looking at the Seagrave
children at play, he says to their father: " 'Although nothing pains me
more when it does take place, I often think, sir, it is a great blessing for
a child to be called away early' " (p. 33). And in terms of plot, this story
ends with the death of the hero, which is exceptional among Crusoe
narratives.

The Little Savage

Marryat wrote another version of the Robinson story that is even more
evangelical than *Masterman Ready*. This is *The Little Savage*, a work
published posthumously, in 1848–49, and completed by the writer's
son. I cannot claim that *The Little Savage* is as successful a *Robinsonade*
as *Masterman Ready*, but it is as interesting in conception, and even, in
those early parts Marryat himself completed, in execution. It is unmistakably a Robinson story, not only because it begins with a castaway
alone on an island and ends with his rescue, but because it is enthusiastic
for entrepreneurial ingenuity and productivity. We find the familiar lists
of implements and resources, charged with the familiar subdued glee:
". . . two or three old axes, blunted with long use, a tin pannikin, a mess
kid, and some rude vessels to hold water, cut out of wood." There are
the familiar triumphs of *bricolage:* fish lines pieced together from the
sinews of man-of-war birds and hooks made out of fish bones. There is
the same enthusiasm as in *The Crater* (James Fenimore Cooper's novel,
which came out just before) for transplantation and improved agriculture. (Like Cooper's, Marryat's is a guano island.)

But there is a new note sounded here. *The Little Savage* begins in its
first paragraph to place itself in the Crusoe line: "I believe I am the first
instance of a boy being left alone upon an uninhabited island." But in
fact he had the company of an older man, a sailor called Jackson, and
therewith he had the experience of evil. The sailor enslaves the boy,
physically and mentally, until an accident (leaving the sailor blind) makes
him dependent. In the second paragraph the boy says about Jackson's
reproaches during his dependency, "But I cared not, for I was then

getting stronger, whilst he was getting weaker every day, and I had no love for him." And in the next paragraph, "He called me Boy, and I called him, Master." We scarcely need to be told that the little savage grows up understanding "boy" to mean not "young male" but "slave." We think, though perhaps Marryat did not, of Friday calling Crusoe "Master."

Moreover, the boy himself is not innocent. When Jackson is blinded by lightning, the little savage empties the water pool near their hut in order to make the man completely dependent on him, for drink as well as for food. "I felt an inconceivable pleasure at the idea of my being the master, and he the boy" (p. 21). He throws a rock at the blind man, and, when the man attacks him, cuts his right hand half off with a knife. Cooper, as we shall see, was at this time introducing into the energizing myth of capitalism some disturbing doubts about the fruits of economic success. And Marryat was introducing these even more disturbing suspicions of original sin into the Enlightenment myth.

This religious diagnosis is not separated from other, more secular ones; the evangelical mood had several foci of interest. Marryat stresses quite as much the importance of education and environment. The little savage does not love or trust others because he has not been taught to; he has not been taught those concepts, those words. We are often told how many concepts he lacks. He does not know what a year is, or a ship, because Jackson has refused to tell him. When the boy acquires power, his first demand is to be taught to read, which he learns from the Lord's Prayer. The second half of the book is more explicitly religious. Jackson dies when the boy is fourteen, and soon afterward some rough sailors land on the island, bringing their passenger, a missionary's widow. She is the first woman the boy has seen, a Victorian lady, with a pale face like a marble statue, which rarely smiles and yet expresses love and wisdom. She henceforth represents the author in the story and instructs the little savage quite pietistically.

The sailors treacherously leave the island, abandoning the boy and Mrs. Reichardt, and a new act of the drama begins, on about page 180. The scale of "improvement" of the island expands, because of Mrs. Reichardt's practical skills and some new resources. The sailors leave behind an iron kettle, a saw, nails, five oars, a harpoon, a whale-line, and some sheet iron. Mrs. Reichardt, like Wyss's Mother, carries a basket, which contains brushes, scissors, ink, wax, a magnifying glass, and so on. She knows how to sow, how to make fire with a glass, and so on. She can also demonstrate how much more valuable the kettle is than some diamonds that the boy has found. Such teaching is in accord with Defoe's sermons against gold, but Mrs. Reichardt is more sincerely unworldly than Crusoe. It is notable that she is unsympathetic with the boy's schemes for leaving the island. She often tells him they would do well to stay there, to escape the miseries of the life of civilization. When she reads the Bible to him, and teaches him to pray, there is more of resignation in her religion than there is in Crusoe's.

Mrs. Reichardt is the daughter of a parish clerk and married a German-born missionary to the Sandwich Islands who came to preach in her father's church. We hear of his "pale, grave, and serious features . . . thrilling earnestness of delivery . . . fervent blessing" (p. 186). It is hinted that his religious fervor incapacitated him for domestic happiness, but unlike most nineteenth-century novelists—unlike Charlotte Brontë, writing about St. John Rivers, for instance—Marryat does not condemn the man of faith. The way he puts it is that Reichardt's "holy enthusiasm exalted him above ordinary humanity," and he was so devoted to God's work that he overlooked the claims of his marital partner. And she, unlike Jane Eyre, does not rebel against the subordinate role of being a missionary's wife. When he is killed by savages, and his blood spatters her, she accepts it as a consecration to a life of service.

The little savage is sixteen when Mrs. Reichardt arrives, and she is only thirty-six, but there is no hint of sexual relations or sexual feeling between them. In Marryat's Regency novels, such a situation would certainly be sexual, and in *The Crater* Cooper's hero is in love at seventeen and married at nineteen. (Cooper was not an evangelical.) But the little savage calls Mrs. Reichardt mother, and that relationship, exalted to a spiritual intensity, governs the story's meanings.

The plot proceeds in orthodox Crusoe fashion and the island is developed into another little utopia. The boy saves his mother when she is attacked by a giant python. When a ship is wrecked on the island, they acquire animals and more valuable tools. They develop gardens and improve their crops. And they have also their trials and warnings. They drift out to sea in a boat and come close to death. Explaining history to him, she, like Campe, tells him of Columbus's heroism, but also of the Spaniards' cruelty in South America. Finally the sailors return, now as mutineers, having taken their commanders prisoner. But just as in *Robinson Crusoe,* the castaways first release the prisoners and then, with their help, defeat the mutineers. One of the prisoners turns out to be the boy's grandfather, so the little savage is furnished with a family and fortune as well as a rescue from his island. The plot is romantic and traditional, but the religious ethos is new.

Thus we see that by the middle of the nineteenth century the revisions of the Robinson story came to incorporate moral doubts and difficulties, even in the hands of writers enlisted on the side of the imperial and capitalist myth.

The Legacy

As for the future of the story, *Masterman Ready* introduced a number of ideas or motifs that were taken into the Robinson material, or the adventure material as a whole, ideas that other writers inherited. There was, for instance, the idea of the coral island. Coral islands differ from others in being paradisal. They are associated with bright blue water and surf and coconut groves, and above all with the clean pink coral itself, a semiprecious stone. The natural history of how the cells of the zoophyte grow upward through the waters to build this island as a gift for castaways suggests the whole idea of nature as paradise, which is so congenial to these adventure writers. Marryat says, "In a few minutes they arrived at the cove; the water was shallow, and as clear as crystal. Beneath the boat's bottom they could see beautiful shells, and the fish darting about in every direction" (p. 42). The island at moments seems an asylum, and William and Ready, the story's favorite characters, do not really want to leave it.

Another such motif is the stockade the Seagraves build to protect themselves. (In Stevenson's essay on his writing of *Treasure Island,* he says that he took *his* stockade from Marryat.) It is said here to derive from the East Indies, but it goes with a number of techniques, associated with various imperial frontiers. The blazing of trees to make a trail, for instance, and the building of a log cabin come from America, and other techniques come from the South African colonies.

Another category of motifs can be represented by the fierceness of the sharks around the Seagraves' island; they are always lurking in the shallows, ready to seize a bather by the leg. This version gives a new, or more specific, sense of the danger always to be feared, from animals or natives. This we can connect with a certain militarism. Ready tells

William at some length of the advantages that sailing in the Royal Navy has over the merchant navy: advantages of order, discipline, justice. We feel the pressures of imperial anxiety and imperial pride. On the other hand, the philosophy of history that Mr. Seagrave teaches to William insists that England's empire will fade, just as Portugal's did, and that it may be the turn of the black races next time to establish a world empire. This possibility is not very urgently felt—how could it be?—but it is not offered trivially or paradoxically.

Masterman Ready was very popular, especially in Germany, where one version was retitled *Sigismund Ruestig.* No doubt it owed this popularity to its combination of real adventure with real piety. Serious literary critics have, predictably, said little about the book. (J. G. Lockhart's comparison of Marryat to Defoe, for instance, for the "quiet effectiveness of his circumstantial narrative," is as much as one finds.) It is a nonprofessional critic who says, in an enthusiastic introduction to the Everyman edition of 1970, "no-one could put the taste and texture of pea soup into the reader's throat as Marryat does. . . . To write with such precision about so many subjects, Marryat needed the skills and arts of a carpenter, smith, farmer, hunter, fisherman, doctor, nurse, builder, fighting man, and half a dozen other things besides" (p. vii). However unfashionable his critical idiom, Richard Armstrong here puts his finger on the essential virtue of *Masterman Ready* and of all the narratives in the line that began with Defoe.

Marryat's immediate successor as chief writer for English boys was W. H. G. Kingston (1814–80), an enormously productive writer with nearly three hundred and fifty items credited to him in the British Museum Catalogue. He had, like Marryat, aristo-military family connections and an equivalent in his own life to the figure of Cochrane in Marryat's. His great uncle, Admiral Sir Harry Burrard-Neale, broke the naval mutiny at the Nore during the Napoleonic wars and was a striking figure in Kingston's childhood and youthful experience. Kingston's biographer, M. R. Kingsford, says that Neale was to Kingston what Sidney was to Spenser, and T. E. Lawrence to John Buchan. Thus were men of action linked to men of letters in the sixteenth, nineteenth, and twentieth centuries, and via such connections we see personal and political enthusiasm pass into adventure fiction.

Kingston's first novel was *The Circassian Slave* (1843), set in the Russian Caucasus, a more Scott or Dumas kind of adventure. His most (and deservedly) popular story was *Peter the Whaler,* first published in

1851, like *Moby-Dick,* and reprinted almost continuously for just short of a century. His only strictly defined Robinson story was the slight but interesting *Alone on an Island,* of 1874. But most of his works continued and transmitted this or that part of the Crusoe tradition.

Kingston was, like Marryat in his later years, evangelical in his religion. The nineteenth-century career of the Robinson story in England seems to have been linked to that religious movement. His bête noire was the Roman Catholic church, the antithetical and antagonistic form of Christianity, and he worked in three of the great evangelical causes: the Missions to Seamen, the volunteers (a part-time military organization that put the gentry and middle classes at the head of armed forces), and, above all, emigration. He wrote several pamphlets recommending emigration and giving practical advice to emigrants—a natural extension of his fiction.

Kingston's attitude toward art and high culture was also evangelical in its nervousness. At eighteen he visited Paris, and wrote, "In the evening I saw, for the first time, an opera and a ballet. Delightful as was the music, the impression the whole exhibition made on me was such that I should be very sorry to expose any young persons over whom I had any influence to a similar spectacle; and I cannot suppose that a glaring evil can in any way be counterbalanced by any benefit or pleasure to be derived by listening to the syren voice of the singers."[5] Such arts, significantly linked to Paris and Catholicism, stood as a polar opposite to the excitements of adventure, a polarity of the effeminate versus the virile.

Kingston was, says Kingsford, widely read by "the more masculine, virile, and venturesome element in the population . . . [p. 172] [such as, during the world wars] the Canadians at Ypres, and the Australians at Gallipoli, and the South Africans at El Alamein" (p. 179). He claimed for one of his magazines that it would be a friend to its readers, "when you may be battling with the realities of life under the suns of India, in the backwoods of Canada or the United States, or the grassy downs of Australia, over the wide ocean among the isles of the Pacific, or on the distant shores of Columbia" (p. 185). He edited many magazines and annuals: *The Colonial Magazine and East India Review, Kingston's Annual for Boys, Kingston's Magazine for Boys,* and *The Union Jack.* He also published adventures in series: *Adventures in Africa, Adventures in Australia, Adventures in India,* and *Adventures in the Far West.*

5. Kingsford, *The Life of W. H. G. Kingston,* 25.

We are told that the servants of the empire asked themselves, "What would Kingston think about what I am doing now? Am I measuring up to his standards?" (p. 189). A questionnaire of 1884 got answers from 790 boys about their favorite author, and Kingston with 179 votes came next after Dickens—ahead of Scott, who got 128 votes, Jules Verne, who got 114, and Marryat, who got 102 (p. 194). Among individual books, *Robinson Crusoe* got 43 votes, *The Swiss Family Robinson* 24, *Pickwick Papers* 22, and *Ivanhoe* 20. These figures indicate the endurance of *Robinson Crusoe* and its tradition a century and a half after its publication.

7

The Crater (1847)

T he *Crater,* the aristocratic version of the Crusoe story
by James Fenimore Cooper, is the best of the American *Robinsonaden.* But that is not saying very
much, and one of the questions raised by the Crusoe
story is why there were so few notable versions by American
writers. This is a puzzle because America was the land of adventure,
for its own citizens and for foreigners, and Robinson could be called the
patron saint of the American imagination. He *has* been called something
like that often. We saw that in our sampling of twentieth-century
American autobiographies, like Floyd Dell's of 1926, *Intellectual Vagabondage.* Dell had set out to discuss "the significant stages in the history
of what men and women have thought and felt," but focused naturally
on the stages his own countrymen had been conscious of (pp. 24–25).
The first of those stages he represented by Defoe's book. "Let us begin
with *Robinson Crusoe . . .*" which inspired their games as children. "We
as children loved it for the same reasons as our adult forebears did" (p.
26).

American history tells just the same story as Defoe, Dell said. "When
Captain John Smith, in a colony hard-pressed by hunger, gave orders

that he who did not work should not eat, he abrogated the whole sacred medieval tradition of class-duties and class-privileges. A man, in conflict with elemental nature, could not remain noble or commoner, he became simply *a man*" (p. 31). As Rousseau pointed out, this kind of manliness belonged preeminently to Robinson Crusoe, and Cooper, in *The Crater*, repeatedly claims that Americans are the people best suited to "Robinson Crusoeing it." That is why, in Thornton Wilder's *Our Town*, Defoe's novel is said to be the one book Americans know, apart from the Bible; and why Frank Luther Mott, in his study of American best-sellers, found it especially American. "This is a good book for young America; it teaches while it pleases. . . . Did ever reader fail to put himself imaginatively in Crusoe's place?"[1] Yet there was no American writer of *Robinsonaden* to compare with the French and the Germans.

The same is true of the white dominions of the British Empire, notably Canada and Australia, which have much in common with the United States in cultural mythology. Defoe shaped the colonial imagination, yet it is outsiders who have made most speculative use of that fact. Paul Dottin declared in 1924 that *Robinson Crusoe* "helps to maintain the cohesiveness of the great British Empire" and "contributes to the growth of the Anglo-Saxon hegemony in the world."[2] That is not something the dominion writers themselves said, though there is some evidence that they felt it. Thus in one of the important works of early Australian literature, Marcus Clarke's *For the Term of Your Natural Life*, published in 1870, there is a Robinson episode in which a convict and a gentleman are castaways together, and their relative status is reversed by the experience. Australian society as a whole was expected to follow the pattern of that episode of the Robinson experience. The whole idea of "mates," which so long dominated Australian male experience, depended on two or more men being along together under desert-island conditions so that each might discover his own and the other's real self. Only then could the bonding of man to man occur, out of which all value flows.

The early analyst of colonial experience in Australia, Charles Rowson, took Defoe as his explicit master and Robinson as his implicit hero. His *Tales of the Colonies* (1846) offered itself as "useful history of a settler's

---

1. Mott, *Golden Multitudes*, 33.
2. Dottin, *Daniel Defoe et ses romans*, ". . . aide a maintenir la cohesion du grand empire britannique . . . contribue à augmenter dans le monde l'hégémonie anglo-saxonne."

life . . . [showing] how much may be accomplished by prudence, industry, and perseverance." Alexander Harris, in the other important early guide to settling in Australia, *Settlers and Convicts,* also took Defoe as his master in writing and in ideas.[3] But they did not write *Robinsonaden.* Tales of adventure of other kinds, however, first oral and then written, determined the colonies' imaginative life in the early days, when literature seemed to belong to the mother country. "Literature in the pure sense" (or "literature in the traditional sense" or "serious literature") seems to begin in the colonies with a reaction *against* adventure, a rebellion against the pharisee. Henry Handel Richardson says her own career began when she saw that Australian experience often did not correspond to the adventure tale. That was for her (and other women writers) a liberating experience, giving her something to write about.

The same thing occurred in the African colonies, but a writer like Doris Lessing often acknowledges a debt to the adventure experience. In an interview in 1962 she said that her greatest good fortune was that she had grown up outside England, and so took for granted experience that would have been hard to win as an Englishwoman. She has even contrasted "masculine" and "feminine" tendencies in her own writing and preferred the first. She contrasted a story called "The Pig" with one called "The Trinket Box." The titles alone suggest what she means, but it may be worth saying that the first is about Africans, black and white, and involves guns and violence. We should note also that other white women in Africa, like Isak Dinesen and Beryl Markham, included adventure and hunting elements in what they wrote.

In Canada the first important children's book was entitled *The Canadian Crusoes,* written by Catherine Traill Parr and published in 1852. Defoe was thus one of the early sponsors of writing in and about Canada. But when we turn to the history of Canadian literature as written at present we find Margaret Atwood, in her book called *Survival,* saying something like Richardson in Australia about adventure. "Canadian literature itself," she says, "tells a very different story," something sadder and grimmer than the myth of the place (p. 16). Literature begins with the denial of adventure.

In England itself we know there had always been a conflict of a similar kind throughout the history of the empire. One form the conflict takes, which is especially relevant to Cooper, is over the literary dignity of the

3. Dutton, *The Literature of Australia,* 137.

subject: Should adventure be written as epic or as pastime or as children's reading? Pharisees, possessed by a sense of the greatness of what was happening, wanted to see England's poets write a new *Iliad* or *Odyssey*. Bacon used epic language in his essay "Of Plantations." "Plantations are amongst ancient, primitive, and heroical works. When the world was young it begat more children, but now it is old it begets fewer."[4] But the actually energizing myth of empire, *Robinson Crusoe,* was written in much less elevated language.

Carlyle used the grand style and an epic vision in Cooper's time. "The spoken word, the written poem, is said to be an epitome of the man; but much more the done work. . . . thy Empire, unsung in words, is written in huge characters on the face of this planet—sea-moles, cotton trades, railways, fleets and cities, Indian Empires, Americas, New Hollands, legible throughout the Solar System."[5] But neither England nor the colonies nor the United States produced the literary epics Carlyle suggested. Probably this was because "literature" was divided over whether it wanted such books. Critics and scholars maintained Homer in the loftiest niche in their literary scheme, but many of them—and perhaps those most congenial to later critics—did not want a modern *Iliad*.

Even forgetting about literary quality, retellings of *Robinson Crusoe* are hard to find in America. We are reduced to such small items as James F. Bowman's *Their Island Home* of 1853. This is a story not unlike Ballantyne's *Coral Island* a little later; indeed, Ballantyne borrowed from Bowman. In it a group of boys (three from the United States, one from Scotland, and two natives of the South Seas) set up house together on an island and do battle with savages. This is lively, and fairly realistic, and has some superiority over *Coral Island*. But still it is not a major version of our story. Probably the best-known *Robinsonade* in a mainland American setting was Captain Mayne Reid's *The Desert Home* of 1852. But this was not only written by an English, or Anglo-Irish, author, but was subtitled "The English Family Robinson." *The Crater* does not enter into competition here because it did not have a mainland American setting, while the Natty Bumppo stories are of a different adventure type.

Perhaps the reason for the American (and Canadian and Australian) writers turning away from Robinson was that his story is, mythically,

4. *Bacon's Essays,* 237.
5. Carlyle, *Past and Present,* 152–54.

more about leaving home (the old country, the old continent) than about the new country you arrive at, and is not even, realistically, a story about the emigration experience. American readers remained enthusiastic about the Crusoe story, but American writers wanted to write about what happened when you got to the other side, when you arrived. Americans as a whole wanted to tell and hear the story of the frontier, of the Indians. At least that is what American readers rewarded Cooper for telling them over and over. But he did once, in *The Crater,* tell the Robinson story (it was translated into French as *Le Robinson américain*), and he did so with more zest and authority than he ever brought to his Natty Bumppo romances.

Cooper's Story

The Crater was quickly recognized as a brilliant *Robinsonade,* at least outside America. In Ullrich's 1908 supplement to his bibliography, he lists ten English editions, four German translations, ten French translations, and eight reworkings.[6] Cooper is the one great exception to the generalization about American authors and the Robinson story. Not incidentally, he was also the great American pharisee of his generation.

Thus an important theme of the early Natty Bumppo stories is the inadequacy, the mistakenness, of idealistic Christianity. This faith Cooper embodied primarily in the Quakers, though also in the Moravians. In *The Pioneers* (published 1823, the first of those books), the Moravians are blamed for the "Christianizing," and thus emasculating, of the Delaware Indians, formerly a warrior race; and the Quaker origins of Judge Temple are something he has to exchange for Episcopalianism in order to be a true American gentleman. His estates will fall into the right hands when his daughter marries Oliver Effingham, the scion of an aristocratic English family. The same examination of Quaker idealism, with the same severe judgment against it, is dramatized more vividly in Robert Montgomery Bird's *Nick of the Woods* of 1837. There are even echoes of the same idea in Richard Henry Dana's *Two Years Before the Mast* of 1842.

In *The Crater,* the Quaker theme is quite minor, but it is there, and

6. Ullrich, *Zeitschrift fuer Buecherfreunde,* 493–49.

with the same significance. Now that the colonies have become an independent nation, the United States of America, they must have an army and a navy and must be ready to engage in war. In Cooper's hands, thus, the Robinson story becomes a socially and politically conservative myth, indeed reactionary. The familiar island here grows into a colony, at first idyllically happy and reasonable. "In our island community, most of its citizens were accustomed to think that education and practise gave a man certain claims to control, and, as yet, demagoguism had no place with them" (p. 222).

But this was early in its history. Later a conflict developed between the mass of the population and the governor, Mark Woolston, whose temperament is aristocratic. Cooper's sympathies are explicitly and completely with the governor, who indeed represents the author within the story. "The governor, now, seldom ate with his people. He knew enough of human nature to understand that authority was best preserved by avoiding familiarity. Besides, there is, in truth, no association more unpleasant to those whose manners have been cultivated, than that of the table, with the rude and unrefined" (p. 273). It seems clear that this part of the story expressed Cooper's anger at the "demagoguic" tendencies in America in his time. In particular he disliked the "people's constitution" drawn up in his home state of New York in 1846. The novel, moreover, was written during the months (November 1846–May 1847) when Cooper was disgustedly reading Horace Greeley, who just then was expounding Fourierist Socialism in the *Tribune*.

Conservatism had of course been an aspect of the story's meaning when it was told by both Marryat and Wyss. Marryat had been a naval officer as Cooper had, and both men were defenders of military discipline, including flogging, and enemies of various liberal and humanitarian reform movements of the times. Wyss offered his readers his heartwarming picture of the patriarchal family as a model of the authoritarian state. But neither he nor Marryat described a colony, with a complete political history, from birth to death. Neither tackled the political theme directly or expressed his reactionary views point-blank, as Cooper did.

If we look back to Campe and Defoe, their versions' political implications were liberal. To be alone on an island was a means to release the power in oneself that the hierarchical culture of the homeland repressed. One lesson of their books was that each reader should cultivate self-reliance in order to achieve a similar freedom for himself. In Cooper's novel, however, the enemy of liberty is equality. The closest thing to a

Robinson is not Mark Woolston, the hero, but his brother-in-law, Heaton. He is rather condescendingly commended, and certainly he is not Cooper's representative. "Heaton was a man of singular tastes, which led him to as remarkable acquirements. Among other accomplishments, he was a very good general mechanician, having an idea of the manner in which most of the ordinary machinery ought to be, not only used, but fabricated" (p. 230). Seeing how useful a handsaw would be on the island, he sets to work to build a sawmill. But Cooper's attention is focused not on Heaton, the Robinson figure, but on Woolston, the "governor," the man of politics. When Woolston is rejected by the colonists in an election, the author punishes them by having their islands disappear under the waters of the Pacific, destroying them and all their works.

The Crater is remarkably successful as a narrative in its development of the suspense and in sustaining the rising curve of gratification proper to the Crusoe story. It is, for instance, much more successful as narrative than Cooper's more famous Natty Bumppo stories. It is also remarkable for the amount of contemporary science it brings to bear upon the story. As Thomas Philbrick, the editor of the 1962 edition, says, "*The Crater* is above all a 'scientific' narrative" (p. x). Particularly notable is Cooper's knowledge of climate, geology, agriculture, and astronomy. He draws on Laplace, Lyell, and Herschel, among contemporary scientists, and— more predictably—on Anglo-Saxon explorers like Cook, Beechey, and Wilkes. Like many intellectuals of the nineteenth century, Cooper was an inveterate reader of exploration, and unlike, say, Thoreau, he does not turn them into metaphors or allegories.

The story begins in Philadelphia in 1793, when its hero, Woolston, is sixteen. At nineteen he sails for the South Pacific on a ship owned by Quakers, who have stocked it well with tools and seeds for the benefit of the natives the crew may meet. Cooper makes admiring but amused and condescending references to the Quaker combination of philanthropy, pacifism, and profit-seeking. He identifies himself, by contrast with them, and with evangelicals, as a gentleman. By page 60 (out of 469), Mark and one humble companion, the seaman Bob Betts, are wrecked on a volcanic crater where not even a blade of grass grows. They make several comparisons between their own condition and that of Defoe's hero. The upshot of the comparisons is that *they* have much more work to do for their island. (Such comparisons occur in most *Robinsonaden*.) Much of the first half of the book has to do with how they invent soil by skillful mixing of guano, vegetable loam, seaweed, and dead fish with the volcanic ash they find already there. By page 120 Mark is alone on the crater; a hurricane has swept Bob Betts out to sea in a boat they have just built. He now has the experience of illness with no help, like Crusoe, and for various reasons his relation to God grows more intense and serious. Mark is an Episcopalian, the gentleman's religion, but he is as pious as Crusoe himself.

As Cooper says, "It is when men are prosperous that they vainly imagine they are sufficient for their own wants, and are most apt to neglect the hand that alone can give durable support" (p. 94). This warning note is, we shall see, confirmed by the story's climax as its major message. But there is also a more optimistic implication in these early episodes, a sort of doctrine of progress. Cooper says, "He has lived in vain, who has dwelt his half century in the midst of the civilization of this our own age, and does not see around him the thousand proofs of the tendency of things. . . . That which the Richards and St. Louis of the Middle Ages could not effect with their armed hosts, is about to happen as a consequence of causes so obvious and simple that they are actually overlooked by the multitude" (pp. 139–40). And there are many passages which celebrate those modern forms of knowledge that can make the barren places of the earth blossom like the rose.

By page 158 Mark has built and launched another boat, when suddenly a volcanic eruption lifts his crater further out of the sea and provides him with a more extensive domain. Fifty miles away, moreover, now appears a 2,000-foot mountain, which he names Vulcan's Peak. While visiting this, and delighting in the trees and fresh water now available to him, he sees a boat approaching, which turns out to be the one he built, saved from the hurricane, and having meanwhile made a trip home to Philadelphia. It is sailed by Bob Betts, who brings with him their two wives, two of Bridget Woolston's negro servants, some other eager colonists, cows, colts, babies, and so on. Clearly, Cooper now has a colony on his hands, and we see why Mark's domain has been providentially increased in extent and in natural resources. (He acquires another island, Rancocus Island.) The focus now passes from individual to group enterprise, and its "scientific" subject matter is henceforth political theory rather than agriculture. The same transition can be seen in *Robinson Crusoe*, but there the political part is less striking. On page 217 a war party of Kanaka "savages" attacks the colony, and guns and cannon have to be used to defend this valuable property. Vulcan's Peak, we are told, became a second Gibraltar; though by the scientific employment of an echo, they are able to scare off the natives rather than kill them. (Later Mark learns how to use the blasting to win over the Kanakas and induces them to work for him; he allows them to take part in causing the explosions, and so engages their imaginations.) Then the colonists find and befriend a good Kanaka called Ooroony, so that they can then dethrone the bad Kanaka, Waally. Now they are able to hire Kanaka laborers by the hundred. The scale of Mark's operations, and his profits, far exceeds Crusoe's. This amplification of scale was to be taken further by Jules Verne. To amplify was one way to develop the subject. But in the twentieth century there has been some development in the opposite direction, minimizing the scale, as in William Golding's *Pincher Martin* or Arthur Ransome's *Swallows and Amazons*.

From this point on, only halfway through the book, the reader begins to be surfeited with the glut of possessions and productivity. We also begin to find oppressive, though still interesting, Cooper's attacks on democracy and the spirit of commerce. Cooper was the very opposite of Defoe in his aristo-military sympathies and his distaste for tradesmen. So he cuts a paradoxical figure, as the celebrant but more often the denouncer of capitalism and modernization. "Trade, perhaps the most corrupt and corrupting influence of life—or, if second to anything in evil, second only to politics—is proclaimed to be the great means of humanizing, enlightening, liberalizing, and improving on the human race" (p. 355).

We are told that the colony now began to term Mr. and Mrs. Mark Woolston "the governor and his lady" (p. 227). And, as we know, the governor seldom ate with his people. His brothers arrive in the colony and are given jobs like Secretary of State and Attorney General, while Mark himself is awarded a thousand acres of the peak for his private use. Altogether, we are not surprised to hear that anti-Woolston sentiment arises among the less educated and rational of the lower classes. In their prosperity, they began to "wax fat and kick," Cooper tells us (p. 430). A variety of religious sects compete against each other; lawyers foment a craze for litigation; and newspapers demand a democratic constitution—as was happening in Cooper's home country.

When elections are held, the Woolstons are defeated, and Mark sails away in disgust for a change of scene. And his disgust is of course shared by his creator. Thus, when Mark returns, his ship looks in vain for the crater and the peak. Both have disappeared. Another volcanic eruption has occurred, and all those islands and those ungrateful colonists have been swallowed up. God has punished such unbridled democracy. For a nineteenth-century American novelist to conceive such a plot was to fly in the face of public opinion—which Cooper had the habit of doing.

Victorian Conservatism

The Robinson writer of whom *The Crater* most reminds us, among Cooper's contemporaries, is the Englishwoman Jane Porter (1775–1850), for her *Sir Edward Seaward's Narrative of His Shipwreck* (published in 1852). Porter's publications include two novels discussed as American best-sellers by Mott, and this book was widely and deservedly popular. It is also remarkable as a *Robinsonade* written by a woman. However, it seems there is reason to think she only edited this manuscript, which was written by her brother. (Her own fiction was more Gothically romantic.)

Porter's work synthesizes the adventure tradition in a "classical" way. (It consists of two volumes, of which the first is a version of Defoe's story, while the second is a historical novel in Scott's vein. Edward Seaward, a middle-class boy in early eighteenth-century England, marries a vicar's daughter and takes her off to America (to British Honduras, now Belize), but they are shipwrecked on an uninhabited island. There is a lot of detail about how they survive, quite plausible and interesting, and also a good deal about money and possessions. As Edward and Eliza rise from total poverty to riches, every penny is accounted for, as in *Robinson Crusoe*. They soon acquire black servants in flight from slavery (the usual way for an adventure hero to both have slaves and disapprove of slavery) and rise to seigneurial power, and determine to add their island to the empire. At this point the themes of the story are those of *The Crater,* though Porter develops them more in Scott's way than in Cooper's.

Going home to England in volume two, Edward and Eliza have to appear at the court of George II; here they take part in various power intrigues that involve Sir Robert Walpole and Queen Caroline (as Jeanie Deans does in *The Heart of Midlothian*). Edward is financially successful, is made a knight and the proprietor of his island, and they go home in triumph. Porter gives more detail about the politics of adding new countries to the empire—of how politicians felt about flying the flag over new pieces of land—than other Robinson writers.

It is the Victorian domestic idyll, as well as the political interest, that reminds us of Cooper. The husbands are all that is manly and fiery; the wives are consolers, restrainers, and reminders of religion. And then Porter, though less blatantly than Cooper, writes even the Robinson fable from the point of view of the gentry, and gentility, and the status quo. When Eliza gets her black servants, she "was restored to her former gentlewomanly condition, by this providence," and we feel *glad* that the Robinson episode is over for them. In both the American and the English book we see reflected the historical process of the mid-nineteenth century whereby the gentry both acquired private estates where they could play at being royal and took part in the national adventure of empire.

The Crater's ending, however, though so lurid, is briefly presented. The Woolston party is defeated at the polls on page 441, and the book ends on page 469. Much the greater part therefore is written in the Defoe mode, of delight in growth and development and productivity. Apparently all Cooper's spare time in the 1840s, when he was writing this book, was absorbed by his "Chalet," a farm he had carved out of the forest on the shores of the Otsego. Susan Fenimore Cooper, his daughter, tells us that he was "most thoroughly a pioneer in spirit. He delighted in the peculiarly American process of 'clearing' " (p. xiii). Of course he did not delight in the mess and waste that so many pioneers were guilty of and that he had inveighed against in earlier novels. "It was the work of improvement, in all its different stages, in which he took pleasure, from the first opening of the soil. . . . Almost every morning, writing hours over, he drove to the *Chalet,* looking after the stock and the dairy, the pigs and the poultry" (ibid.). We can indeed feel that enthusiasm transferred into *The Crater*—and it is worth pointing out that Cooper's earlier Natty Bumppo stories fail because they lack that enthusiasm, which is because Cooper then lacked that experience.

But of course the story ends in a way that expresses Cooper's quite opposite experience of *social* and *political* improvements in the 1840s. As Philbrick says, "What had begun as an adventure story in the manner of *Robinson Crusoe* has taken on the scope and seriousness of *Faust*" (p. viii). The capitalist utopia has become dystopia; the literary mode has changed from adventure to jeremiad.

The new features that Cooper introduced into the Robinson material can be divided between form and content. This is a "classical" nineteenth-century fiction, which means it has a stately style and such formal ornaments as poetic epigraphs to each chapter, and a plot that includes romance and happy marriage for the hero. And its contents include a large and noble landscape, human as well as natural, with hundreds of characters, a political constitution, diplomacy, and wars. As far as natural landscape goes, Cooper's descriptions remind us of scientists like Bartram or Darwin, so much do they all stress the formal elegance of nature. Thus Darwin saw in Brazil "the elegance of the grasses, the novelty of the parasitical plants, the beauty of the plants, the glossy green of the foliage. . . . This land is one great, wild, untidy, luxuriant hothouse, made by nature for herself."[7] This scope of vision goes beyond ordinary adventure, indeed beyond classical nineteenth-century fiction, toward the sublime.

Both kinds of change derive from Cooper's determination to present Robinson, and adventure material in general, to adult audiences again; indeed, to turn adventure into epic. The treatments by Campe, Wyss, and Marryat had been explicitly meant for children, and Defoe's story had long been handed over to them. Cooper—and this is typical of the pharisaical idea of literature, so alien to our own times—wanted to engage his adult readers' imagination in the Robinson adventure. Among those new motifs, we must mention the volcano, whose eruptions first create the islands on which the colony develops, and later destroy them. "At first he thought the ship had taken fire, a lurid light gleaming in at the open door of the cabin, and he sprang to his feet in recollection of the danger he ran from the magazine. . . . He had just reached this deck, when he felt the whole ship tremble from her truck to her keep, and a running of water was heard on all sides of him, as if a flood were coming. Hissing sounds were heard, and streams of fire, and gleams of lurid light were seen in the air" (pp. 158–59). Cooper describes it all in what one might call the epic-Robinson style, making everything largely symbolic without losing the character of reality. "To the south, it is true, the eye could not penetrate more than two or three leagues. A vast dun-looking cloud, still covered the sea in that direction, veiling its surface far and wide, and mingling with the vapors of the upper atmosphere" (p. 161).

Closely associated with the describing of volcanoes and eruptions comes the expounding of geology, the history of the earth, in which

7. Downs, *In Search of New Horizons*, 139.

Cooper shows himself very knowledgeable. And associated in a different way is the science of artillery and the explosion of shells. Cooper is clearly interested in every form of the dreadful and awe-inspiring; he may be said to have added to the adventure that element of the sublime that men like Carlyle found missing from contemporary literature. (This was an American thing to do: Richard Henry Dana carried that blend to its finest form in his nonfiction classic, *Two Years Before the Mast*.) After the first eruption, Mark sees in astonishment, "some dark, dense body first looming through the rising vapor. When the last was sufficiently removed, a high ragged mountain became distinctly visible. He thought it arose at least a thousand feet above the ocean, and that it could not be less than a league in extent. This exhibition of the power of nature filled the young man's soul with adoration and reverence for the mighty Being that could set such elements at work" (pp. 166–67).

As for literary form, it is of course Scott whom Cooper follows (here, as in his Natty Bumppo stories) in his attempt to give dignity to his story. An important feature of this subgenre are the humor characters. Bob Betts, Mark's companion, being a simple sailor, sees everything in sailing terms, even the lovely Bridget, Mark's intended. " 'A trim-built and light-sailing craft, Mr. Woolston,' " he says, watching her walk away from them, " 'one of these days she'll make a noble vessel to command' " (p. 25). Such language the reader is of course expected to find comically incongruous with its object, though heartwarmingly appropriate to its speaker. In order to be *appropriate* to Mark and Bridget, the description of their feelings and their behavior must be given in the rhetoric and the gestures of romantic theater. When they meet after their long separation, Mark first sees a "solitary female figure" on the shore, who "extended her arms as the boat drew nearer," and then, "as if unable to stand, she sunk on a rock which had served her for a seat. . . . In two more minutes Mark Woolston had his charming young bride encircled in his arms" (pp. 202–3). This kind of language and gesture was rare in earlier treatments of the story and indeed was ill-suited to its practical realism.

Cooper has also a good deal in common with Marryat, in literary style as well as biographically. Because they loved the sea and seamanship, their descriptions of both are very knowledgeable—though also full of romantic feeling. In both, moreover, we feel a conflict (reflected in the main characters) between a love of the island and the hope of leaving it—the desire to rejoin civilization. In *Masterman Ready,* William and Ready, Puer and Senex, are happy on their island; it is Mr. and

Mrs. Seagrave who need the networks of culture to support them. In *The Crater*, on the other hand, Mark and Bridget would be happy to stay in the colony, if only the colonists were better behaved. This conflict is common in adventure, but it is rather pronounced in Cooper and Marryat.

Of Wyss we are reminded by Cooper's stress on manliness and womanliness—though Cooper, unlike Wyss, is too honest to promise those who follow his prescriptions a life without conflict. Mark is adorably manly in his creator's eyes, but the colonists don't like him. All Cooper's values are defiantly and irritably assertive; nothing "goes without saying" in his books. Defoe is alluded to specifically at times, and implicitly by Mark's meditation on the advantages and disadvantages of his situation in the sixth chapter, and by the similar sessions of fever that Mark and Crusoe suffer. Cooper amply acknowledges his own place in the tradition of writers about Crusoe.

The melodramatic and judgmental end to the story was of course new and was to be taken up as a Robinson motif by Jules Verne in *The Mysterious Island*. (It is worth noting that Verne is as interested as Cooper in the agricultural uses of guano and seaweed.) That ending, which in both cases involves the eruption of a volcano, goes together with the greatly extended scope of the material—the aspiration to the sublime and the epic. From this time on, a scope of prophetic meditation on the fate of civilization is available to the adventure writers, and to their heirs, the writers of science fiction. It is one of the paradoxes of literary history that the respectable artistic fiction, the "serious novel," largely denied itself that scope and aspiration. The poetic and prophetic sensibility, insofar as it touched on public and historical themes, found more of a home in the humble form of adventure.

8

The Coral Island (1858)

B y the mid-nineteenth century, the South Sea islands were well established in the Western imagination as *the* setting for Robinson adventures, and indeed for fantasies of various kinds, ranging from heroic thoughts of missionary martyrdom, via Crusoe, to licentious dreams of unlimited sex. This last use of islands can be said to have begun in the eighteenth century with the French explorer Bougainville, though the English writers repressed that dream for more than a century.[1] Bougainville first sighted Tahiti in April 1768, and his description makes that island sound like a continuous festival of erotic play. The canoes brought out such crowds to greet the French ship (all shouting "friend") that the commander could hardly find a place to drop his anchor. The women were beautiful and naked, and offered themselves, or their men-folk offered them, to the French sailors. Bougainville reported all this in a worldly and "classical" tone. For him, a Tahitian girl "appeared to the eyes of all as Venus showed herself to the Phrygian shepherd," and he named the island "Nouvel Cythère," the new Cythe-

---

1. Daws, *A Dream of Islands*.

rea, the home of Venus.[2] But we learn that an audience of fifty watched the sex act being performed, which suggests a sophisticated as well as an Edenic eros.

One of Bougainville's companions, Philibert Commerson, wrote an account of the Tahitians that said they knew "no other god but love; every day is consecrated to it, the whole island is its temple, all the women are its idols, all the men its worshippers." The island was a utopia that showed "the condition of natural man, born essentially good, free of all preconceptions, and following without diffidence or remorse the sweet impulses of an instinct always sound, because it has not degenerated into reason."[3] Whatever the reality of Tahiti (and recent anthropological accounts differ from Bougainville's less than one would expect), that was the myth. The gulf between that and the Robinson myth was obviously enormous in the exaltation of fantasy over reason as well as in the cult of sex. It was a major change in the Robinson story when it made this alliance with very different cultural interests.

This idea of the South Sea islands is reflected, though more discreetly, in Anglo-Saxon writers—in the accounts by Cook's companion, Sir Joseph Banks, and, in the mid-nineteenth century in Melville's *Typee*. Indeed, it entered the general consciousness then in America, if not in England. This set of images squeezed out other, nonerotic dimensions to the cultural confrontation and exchange. To take a Crusoe-like instance, the islanders were apparently as greedy for the metals that the Europeans used so freely and ingeniously as the Europeans were for the natives' free and ingenious sex. Iron nails were as much the object of the islanders' greed as copulation was of the sailors'. However one balances these different accounts, there were several powerful images of these islands, of which the Robinson storytellers exploited the more edifying. But we may suppose that for some readers even R. M. Ballantyne's sexless narrative had a margin of erotic fantasies derived from other sources.

Ballantyne's Version

In Ballantyne's hands, the Robinson material was reshaped to be boy's reading. It may seem that this was no new development, but the readers

2. Ibid., 2.
3. Ibid., 4.

aimed at by earlier writers like Campe, Wyss, and Marryat were children rather than boys, though certainly male rather than female children. The crucial difference is that "children" means not-grown-up, or at least innocent, while "boy," as the word was so eloquently used by mid-Victorians, connoted more positive qualities. These are the qualities suggested by epithets like lionlike, or noble. "Noble boy" is a frequent formula in the works of Samuel Smiles, one of the most popular Victorian moralists. "Boy" in this sense is one of the group of words associated with "manly" and "manliness." Associated qualities were "pluck" and "heart" and (later) "guts."

These last words have biological origins and are significantly different from the moral qualities recommended to children before, like meekness and prudence and patience. The new words allude to the virtues of a warrior caste, and even to the energies of animal life. Leadership came to be a moral term, but it still had some reference to leading a pack—to animal-group behavior. Boys were seen as cubs or whelps, young male creatures, not unlike young male animals; and the favored ones among them, typically Anglo-Saxon boys, were being readied to lead, to keep order, to maintain discipline—to help run an empire. It came to be taken for granted that English boys were and should be fierce rather than meek, bold rather than obedient. The young David Copperfield, for instance, is rescued from complete misery as a child by his fantasy life as Robinson Crusoe and other adventure heroes. Though Copperfield is to be a domestic novel hero, Dickens does not want him to cultivate resignation but spirit. Dickens's heroes all have to be spirited, and that word is quite divorced from the suggestions of "spiritual."

Thus *Coral Island*'s first sentence runs, "Roving has always been, and still is, my ruling passion, the joy of my heart, the very sunshine of my existence." The speaker, Ralph, is supposed to be the quietest and most bookish of the three boys the story is about, but he has no qualms about presenting himself as an adventurer. Ballantyne's tone is strikingly unlike Marryat's and even Defoe's. Crusoe professes to be, and presumably is, ashamed of his unregenerate itch to travel; he pays his dues to the cult of prudence with obvious sincerity. But Ballantyne's readers are not expected to feel any conflict between the hero's love of adventure and his family or social duty. The claims of family and social duty have, for Ballantyne, faded to a mild pathos. Ralph speaks of a trellised and honeysuckled porch as representing all that. He names himself Ralph Rover, emblematically. His father and grandfather had been sea captains in their active years, and then settled down in a West Country village. That career is what we foresee for Ralph, and what we, as his readers, aspire to for ourselves.

Another change in the geography of the Robinson story is this prominence of the West Country within England. The counties of Devon and Cornwall were just beginning to be sentimentally consecrated as the ancestral home of England's "sea-dogs," the defeaters of the Spanish Armada in Elizabethan times. Charles Kingsley's immensely popular *Westward Ho!* had used and spread that legend just before Ballantyne wrote. Stevenson started his story in the same part of the country. Kipling went to school in a new town named Westward Ho!, called into existence by real-estate entrepreneurs cashing in on the popularity of the legend. *Mutiny on the Bounty* begins in an eighteenth-century West Country village.

Ballantyne's tone is humorous and hearty through most of the book, and so can remind us of Wyss; adventures are full of fun for all involved. The great difference from *Swiss Family Robinson* is that in this story there is no father (or mother, or a counselor like Ready, but above all no all-wise, all-explaining father). Ballantyne's three boys are making their own adventures and their own world. That is the zest of the narrative, which made it so popular.

In Louisa May Alcott's *Old Fashioned Girl* the difference between boys' reading and girls' is made in terms that allude to Ballantyne. While the girls cluster around Grandmother to hear her tales of the past, Tom is reading

> One of those delightful books in which boys are cast away on desert islands, where every known fruit, vegetable and flower is in its prime all the year round; or, lost in boundless forests, where the young heroes have thrilling adventures, kill impossible beasts, and, when the author's invention gives out, suddenly find their way home, laden with tiger skins, tame buffaloes, and other pleasing trophies of their prowess. (Boston, 1870, p. 90)

Here the boys' story is glimpsed from an alien perspective, and Ballantyne's is the relevant version of our story.

His boys are so characterized as to divide between them the traits of boyhood. Their names are emblematic. "Jack Martin" reminds us of the Union Jack. He is eighteen, hearty and lionlike, a noble boy, a natural leader. Ralph is fifteen and "old-fashioned," meaning serious, reflective, even humorless; at least he is said to be so, but he writes the book, which is full of gaiety, and to combine the two traits is beyond Ballantyne's skill as an author. Peterkin Gay, the youngest, is mischievous, fanciful, elfin—more a child than a boy. The two boys learn manliness from Jack, as that quality unfolds in him.

Serious moral and religious themes enter the book in its later parts, but the strongest stress falls (perhaps without Ballantyne fully intending this) on the fun. In the preface, Ralph writes, "If there is any boy or man who loves to be melancholy or morose, and who cannot enter with sympathy into the regions of fun, let me seriously advise him to shut my book and put it away." Later his tone is quite different, but Peterkin tends to remain the favorite character, who predominates in the reader's memory, even though by the book's serious standards of boyishness he is the least worthy. That touch of genre decadence is perhaps the most interesting of the book's innovations. Adventure is coming to be thought of above all as fun.

A continuity exists between *Masterman Ready* and this book in the evangelical piety that accompanies the fun and that is rather crudely juxtaposed with it. At first we hear little more than that Ralph's mother gave him a Bible and a blessing when he left home. But when the action turns serious, we begin to hear biblical texts cited, of a definitely evangelical character. In the last third of the book we get to meet evil pirates and are given horrific images of pagan and cannibal rites in the Fiji Islands (a place that missionary accounts were then turning into *the* site of horror.) For instance, Ballantyne describes a pond full of eels, who are fed human babies (p. 227). There are also pathetic pictures of a native missionary ship, like John Williams's but carrying a black preacher who talks black-minstrel language. We are told that only Christianized natives are to be trusted in matters of trade; and a pirate called Bloody Bill says he never cared for Christianity himself, "but anyone can see what it does for these black critters" (p. 219). When Bill himself begins to turn to religion and despairs over his past sins, Ralph consoles him with the evangelical texts, "Though your sins be red like crimson, they shall be white as snow," and "Only believe."

There are several clear continuities from the motifs of earlier *Robinsonaden*. The story begins with a storm and a shipwreck and the casting up of the three central characters, alone, on a desert island. Jack shows his leadership even in the storm by telling the others to cling to an oar rather than piling into one of the overcrowded boats. It is a coral island, with pure white dazzling sands, surf breaking on the reef, bright blue skies, and sunshine and a lagoon. There is no wreck this time for them to get goods from. (Instead there is what we might call a Romantic-poet substitute for that—a Wordsworth-style abandoned cottage, with the skeletons of a man and his faithful dog in it.) But the boys make cloth from their coconut trees and make pitch with which to caulk their boat from their breadfruit trees. And there are the familiar lists of equipment: a needle, some whipcord, a telescope, and so on.

Like Defoe, therefore, Ballantyne still claimed to be realistic in all he wrote. In fact he made a factual mistake in *Coral Island,* about coconuts, which he had to repent publicly for the rest of his life. It mattered to his audience that he should seem to be dealing in facts. But the sophisticated reader feels no real pressure of reality in reading *Coral Island.* Implicitly, this story is fantasy. One sign of that is that by this time the adventure genre, and the pleasures it offered, was so well established that the boys *welcome* their shipwrecked situation as being attractive and in some sense familiar from the start. The author from time to time makes some gestures toward the doubt and terror the boys are supposed to feel, but they sound conventional. (The later cannibalism, on the other hand, *is* taken seriously.) The reader visualizes this island as one among hundreds in the South Seas, each waiting for a propitious wreck to supply it with a solitary castaway. It becomes easy to imagine (as Jules Verne *did* imagine, and describe) deliberate imitations or installations of such adventures. By the mid-nineteenth century they were part, in some ideal sense, of a well-advertized best-education-for-boys. We stand on the verge of a global adventure ground, a tourist industry, of Fantasy Islands.

Scottish Adventure Writing

Ballantyne had his roots in severely pious early nineteenth-century Scotland. His father had been the youngest of three brothers whose publishing firm was deeply involved in Sir Walter Scott's triumphant career, and his subsequent bankruptcy. The brothers helped preserve the secret of who "the author of *Waverley*" really was by copying out Scott's manuscripts so that outsiders should never see and recognize his handwriting. Thus their households were all involved in the Scott legend. And of the three brothers, our Ballantyne's father, Alexander, was said to be Scott's personal favorite. So the author of *Coral Island* grew up in the cult of the adventure tale.

In 1841, at the age of sixteen, Ballantyne went to Canada to join the Hudson's Bay Fur Company, and his first writings were about Canada. (Scotsmen were emigrating to Canada in great numbers, and the colonies were a logical subject for Scott to write about, but it was left for a later generation of Scots writers to situate their adventures in the empire.) Ballantyne's later works included many set in wild lands that were or might become imperial property. They made him a very popular writer for boys on imperial and religious topics.

Ballantyne lectured and posed for photographs, dressed as a frontiersman, wearing buckskins and mocassins, a beard and long hair, with sometimes a bow and arrows, or snowshoes, or a headdress. He usually brought a rifle and powder horn on the stage and sometimes fired it at the lecture's end with such marksmanship that a stuffed eagle crashed to the floor in front of him. He was a star lecturer for the Lifeboat movement, which set up shore-based boats to rescue sailors from wrecked ships (very popular in nineteenth-century Britain) and other comparable causes. He taught a Bible-reading class and was an elder of the Free Church of Scotland. Many members of the clergy endorsed his books. The Reverend Andrew Thompson of Edinburgh wrote, "The dashing and manly spirit of adventure, the fine manly moral tone of the narrative, seem to me to render these little volumes eminently adapted for circulation among working men."[4] His books were felt to be carriers of moral health.

As we shall see, two of the writers to whom Ballantyne handed on the Robinson material were Robert Louis Stevenson and James Barrie, both also Scottish; and it is worth reflecting on the role played by the writers of Scotland in the tradition of adventure in English. It is roughly parallel with the role played by Scotsmen within the empire. Scotland produced more than its share of missionaries, engineers, and soldiers for the empire. Scotland had especially close links with Canada and India, and when the African Association was founded in London in 1788, six of the twelve founders were Scots, as were half of the British explorers of Africa.[5] And Scotland's writers, from Scott to John Buchan, produced

4. Quayle, *Ballantyne the Brave*, 163.
5. Van Orman, *The Explorers*, 80.

books that reinforced the empire's values, masculine and feminine, adventurous and domestic, with a special charm and fluency.

The statistics of emigration are alone enough to suggest why the Scottish imagination turned toward England and the empire in the nineteenth century. Between 1700 and 1800, the population of Scotland increased by births at the same rate as that of England and Wales, but because of their emigration, the final proportion of Scotsmen to the others dropped; in 1700 it was one to five, in 1800 it was one to nine. By 1853 Karl Marx calculated that four-fifths of the United Kingdom's emigration was from Scotland or Ireland.[6] Moreover, it is calculated that about 52 percent of the emigrating Scots were young, between twenty and thirty-five—the most vigorous. It was said that the most desperate migrants from the Highlands went to the industrialized Lowlands, while the rich, in money or spirit, went to North America.[7] Adventure stories are of course closely tied to propaganda for emigration, as we saw in discussing W. H. G. Kingston.

Under these circumstances, it is not surprising that the quality of the native Scots literary tradition—of writing about Scotland—suffered between 1825 and 1880. It is usually said (by David Craig, for instance, in the work cited) that this was because nineteenth-century Scots writers had nothing to offer but nostalgia for their past. But to say that is to ignore the adventure writers. The image of Scotland itself may have been sad, but there were many proud legends of Scotsmen abroad. In 1893, on the occasion of Stevenson's death, Lionel Johnson said, "The wandering Scotsman, patriotic and energetic, pushing his fortunes at the ends of the earth, canny and practical, yet moved forward always by the memory of his old home, is a familiar figure in the real life of experience and in the imaginary life of literature."[8] Stevenson took his themes from Ballantyne, though also directly from Scott.

The Scott adventure was of course quite unlike the Defoe adventure. It was, for one thing, aristo-military in its ethos. That is why *The Coral Island* is not easy to place in direct relationship to *Waverley*. But the moment we think of Scott's greatest heir, Alexandre Dumas, we see an important connection. Jack, Ralph, and Peterkin are younger and pre-sexual brothers to Athos, Porthos, and Aramis, the Three Musketeers,

6. Craig, *Scottish Literature and the Scottish People*, 273.
7. Ibid., 274.
8. "Robert Louis Stevenson," *The Academy*, 3 June 1893.

the archetypes of laughing male comradeship. (The same pattern was borrowed by W. H. G. Kingston, who wrote many volumes with titles like *The Three Midshipmen, The Three Lieutenants,* and *The Three Admirals,* the three being English, Scots, and Irish, respectively.)

Ballantyne thus married the Robinson story to the Scott–Dumas line of heroes. The action in *The Coral Island* includes many simple escapes, from sharks, from storms, from cannibals, but its ethos is also quite aggressive and militarist in places, more like Dumas than Defoe. When Jack is fighting the cannibals, he reverts atavistically to being a Viking, a Berserker. When necessary, we see, the decent young Englishman can revert to the primeval savagery of his forebears and beat the modern savage at his own game. This was an adventure motif that was to become popular with Rider Haggard and the other adventure writers at the end of the nineteenth century, but it was new in Ballantyne's day. "Jack uttered a yell that rang like a death-shriek among the rocks. With one bound, he leaped over a precipice full fifteen-feet high . . . with one blow of his staff, Jack felled the man with the club" (p. 171). Later he duels with a gigantic chief and kills him to save a young girl.

Such savagery is not to be found in Scott's novels, and yet Scott included enough fighting to disturb Scottish literary critics. Edwin Muir found that Scott's fatal flaw was that he crammed his novels "full of quarrels described in a romantic vein which was quite foreign, for instance, to Fielding."[9] Muir used the English writer as the criterion of the normal and put Scott's flaw down to Scotland's having been conquered, and so having lost its "organic culture." This, he thought, impaired the moral realism of its writers. Scott saw himself as a Borderer, who belonged not to any civil society but to a clan country, where disputes were settled by the sword. Border countries are, like islands, the locus of adventures, because the rule of law is feeble there. Thus, though Scott was "a man to whom the established order was sacred," that order did not originate in his own country, and did not seem *natural* to him (p. 137). It was something imported from England.

In other words, it was because Scotland was a conquered country, not an "organic community," that Scott wrote adventure novels. (I myself would want to qualify that by saying that Scotland was also a conquering part of the British Empire, and that its *dual* character, conquered and conquering, fostered its adventure sensibility. The empire promised

9. *Scott and Scotland,* 124.

Scotsmen a romantic destiny very unlike that they would have at home.)
Muir asks, "What happens in the story of adventure? The characters, or
at least those that engage our sympathies, break the laws of civilized life
and yet as by magic escape the consequences of their actions" (p. 170).
But the same is true of non-Scottish novelists of adventure, for instance,
Dumas in France.

It is the laws of adventure Muir quarrels with, as most literary critics
do. "For a while, that is to say, the hero enjoys all the pleasures of
lawlessness, since he exists in a sort of dateless Border country, outside
the law; then society, firmly but benevolently, gathers him into its arms,
none the worse of his holiday, and quite certain henceforth to be a
decent and orderly citizen . . . this arrangement of experience, so
convenient and so unconvincing . . . " (p. 169). This criticism of
adventure probably finds a sympathetic echo in the minds of most
literary readers, whose experience and values accord so much better
with the domestic novel and the organic society. Nor is Muir unpersua-
sive when he suggests that being a Scotsman inclined Scott to write
adventures. But the Scottish fate was not merely to be conquered; it was
also to go forth to conquer, as imperialists.

Innovations

Let us return to Ballantyne and his links to his precursors. The boys are
not, like Defoe's hero, future traders by ethos or anything else. Their
affiliation is, like that of Scott's heroes, rather to other castes, to the
military (Jack) or the ministerial (Ralph). The story's stress falls on skills
useful to an officer in managing his men: skills like swimming and
"scientific" boxing; and on the importance of always being alert and
observant (p. 121).

These values relate to the ethos of the public school as it developed
during the nineteenth century. We note that Ralph would rather go
without his breakfast than without his morning cold bath. (The public
schools made the cold bath a morning ritual, to give a good moral and
muscular tone.) Then the habit of being observant (being in control of
one's experience) was apotheosized at the end of the century in Kipling's
Kim and the Sherlock Holmes stories. The reading of adventure was an
extension of that ethos (and indeed adventure tales were read, semi-

officially, at those schools) because it prepared one for authority. Thus Jack knew all he needed to know, and could take command when they landed on the island because he had been a great reader of travels and adventures (p. 25).

Ballantyne insisted on toughness in his boys, though this is more blatant in other stories—for instance, the very popular *Gorilla Hunters*—more than in this one. (Kipling took up the theme of *Gorilla Hunters* in *Puck of Pook's Hill*.) He wrote autobiographically, "I was deeply impressed with the importance of boys being inured from childhood to trifling risks and slight dangers of every possible description, such as tumbling into ponds, and off trees, etc., in order to strengthen their nervous systems."[10] This is a premonition of the later G. A. Henty, usually taken to be the ne plus ultra of exaggerated manliness. (Henty succeeded Kingston as chief British boys' writer, producing a steady flow of books that were still coming out in 1905, three years after his death. He also edited Kingston's *Union Jack* magazine for a number of years.)

Ballantyne continues, "The muff of a boy who from natural disposition, or early training, or both, is mild, diffident, and gentle . . . [if he is also afraid of rain and dogs and indifferent about swimming] will, when he becomes a man, find himself unable to act in the common emergencies of life; to protect a lady from insolence; to guard his home from robbery; or to save his own child should it chance to fall into the water."[11] We might set beside that a passage from Henty's *Through the Sikh War* (1894). It comes from a letter the hero gets from his uncle in India. "Can you thrash most fellows your own age? Can you run as far and as fast as most of them? Can you take a caning without whimpering over it? . . . Are you good at planning a piece of mischief, and ready to take the lead in carrying it out? For though such gifts as these do not recommend a boy to the favor of his schoolmaster, they are worth more out here than a knowledge of all the dead languages."[12] In Henty's biography we read that his books were "essentially manly, and he used to say that he wanted his boys to be bold, straightforward, and ready to play a young man's part, not to be milksops. He had a horror of a lad who displayed any weak emotion and shrank from shedding blood, or

10. Quayle, *Ballantyne the Brave,* 148.
11. Ibid., 149.
12. Quoted in Jenni Calder's *Heroes.*

winced at any encounter."[13] According to modern criteria, of course, both Henty and Ballantyne were ludicrous posturers. But in their day they were powerful lawgivers of manliness, and Ballantyne added that strain of meaning to the Robinson story.

Another modification of the tradition, affecting the skills adventure heroes acquire, is that some in Ballantyne are associated with the natives, instead of being insistently English, as in Defoe. The boys make moccasins for their feet, giving up shoes, for instance, and Jack makes fire the way the natives do, and surfboarding is presented as attractive, though a native sport. But the natives continue to be presented as moral lightweights compared with the Englishmen. We see a group of them playing on the beach so light-mindedly that they do not grieve, or even pause in their play, when one of them is accidentally drowned (p. 256). Their kings obey no moral laws; a chief may kill and eat a dozen of his subjects any day and no one would object. The boys themselves, though capable of seriousness, are full of fun.

Peterkin supplies most of the comedy, being a small boy wielding a giant club, or pretending to be a fierce pig hunter. And, as in *The Swiss Family Robinson,* Nature supplies a good deal of comedy herself, in the form of squealing pigs or spouting cliffs. (These are motifs that William Golding was to take up, giving them an opposite significance.)

And if the Robinson story here blends on one side with the Scott–Dumas romance, on the other it blends with pirate stories, a genre of adventure that began in English literature with Defoe, like so much else. But it has always been a much less edifying genre, morally, historically, and practically, than the Robinson story. Pirates, it is notorious, take no interest in work. Their identity is largely composed of gaudy costume, lurid cursing, and evil exploits. Thus when pirates arrive on Coral Island, it is in the form of a man of "immense stature and fierce aspect." He is deeply bronzed and wears a Greek skullcap and a broad shawl of violet silk around his waist. This does not promise much in the way of hard work or prudent morals.

The pirate gang abducts Ralph, who bravely conceals from them the whereabouts of Jack and Peterkin. They take him on their expedition to Fiji, where they trade in sandalwood, but treat the natives brutally, firing cannon in their midst. Ralph and a disaffected pirate called Bill steal the schooner and sail back toward Coral Island. When Bill dies, Ralph has

13.   Fenn, *G. A. Henty: The Story of an Active Life,* 334.

to learn to manage the whole ship by himself. (All this part leads directly to Stevenson's *Treasure Island*.) Ralph draws strength from reading the Bible and *The Voyages of Captain Cook*. Cook was still the greatest hero of all those who sailed the South Seas, and throughout Ballantyne's book the reader feels the writer relying on the general public interest in the islands. But his other books are set in widely separate parts of the world. He mapped out the whole globe in terms of adventure areas.

The Scott kind of romance-adventure enters the story mainly in relation to the native populations. Jack tells the other boys that they must sail to Chief Tararo's island to make him allow Aratea, an interesting black maiden, to marry the man she loves (p. 276). This is a chivalric romance. The boys become Aratea's "true knights," like the heroes of Scott, Dumas, and Kingsley, and not like Robinson Crusoe. Aratea has been converted to Christianity by a missionary from the London Missionary Society. Her lover is also a Christian. On one side of their island is a native Christian teacher, sent there by the Wesleyan Methodists. He does not drink, and the cottages built by his flock are, like John Williams's, described in glowing terms of neatness and taste (p. 292). The unconverted, pagan natives, on the other hand, are horrifying and disgusting in both large and small matters. When a chief dies, his wives are strangled and buried with him (p. 293).

The story ends with a hectic series of rescues, recaptures, and re-rescues, which betray Ballantyne's uncertain hand as a shaper of plots. But his work nevertheless advanced the career of adventure in several ways. If we restrict ourself to *Coral Island* alone, it did lead directly to *Treasure Island*. But Ballantyne's work as a whole, less directly but importantly, led on to Barrie's story and play *Peter Pan*. Insofar as Peterkin Gay becomes the story's central character, he makes Jack and Ralph seem comparatively dull, and the adventure seems an occasion for fun. It then requires only a step or two for Peterkin Gay to become Peter Pan, the boy who will not grow up, and for the island to become Never-Never Land. Sometime between Ballantyne and Barrie, it became necessary to envelop the adventure in conscious fantasy in order to take adult pleasure in it.

Finally, it was from *Coral Island* (together with Verne's *Deux Ans de Vacances*) that William Golding started when he took up the Robinson theme. *Lord of the Flies*, the most famous version of Crusoe in the twentieth century, is of course an inversion. Here both Barrie's conscious fantasy and Ballantyne's unconscious kind are stripped away, and dark meanings begin to emerge from the edifying myth. The hearty laughter of the pig hunt turns to hysteria and horror. Ralph and Jack keep their names in the later book (though Golding's Jack is a sinister parody of Ballantyne's), and Peterkin becomes—it is the most unkindest cut of all—Piggy.

9

L'Ile mystérieuse (1874)

The contrast between *The Crater* or this book, on the one hand, and the British *Coral Island,* on the other, brings out a general truth: that after the mid-nineteenth century the more serious and ambitious versions of the Robinson story were told by non-British authors. The British seem to have given the subject over to juvenile readers and minor writers. Was this because Britain was then in a new historical phase, interested in running an empire, not in starting a colony? Or was it because in the English system of literature the novel was dominated by women, who had never been such great readers of adventure? Was the long prose narrative in England irresistibly affiliated to feminine concerns? American writers like Cooper (but also Twain and Melville) and French writers like Verne (but also Balzac and Dumas) belonged to systems of literature in which serious novels were built around male protagonists, and so the adventure form was not so clearly marked off as alien.

Not that Verne himself was "taken seriously" by the representatives of French literature; he was never, for instance, admitted to the Académie française. but he was read so widely that he became and remained an important force in French reading culture. In 1956 a group of ambitious young writers, including Michel Butor and J. G. Le Clezio, wrote tributes to him under the general title, "Nous devons tout à Jules Verne." Pierre Macherey devoted a chapter of his book on literary theory to *L'Ile mystérieuse,* and Roland Barthes chose that book to be the topic of his deconstructionist seminar, after Balzac's *Sarrasine* (the discussion of which led him to write *S/Z,* a major text of modern criticism).

Verne's several versions of the Robinson story show the connections between that story and the world hegemony of the Anglo-Saxon nations. His stories preach the gospel of progress and modernization, and he often outlines for his readers the Anglo-Saxon virtues. Thus in *The Long Vacation (Deux ans de vacances),* he lists the three rules on which he says Anglo-Saxon education is based: "1, If you are afraid to do something, do it. 2, Make the greatest effort you are capable of on every occasion. 3, Don't give up when you're tired. Fatigue is a part of any kind of useful work" (p. 98). Clearly these are universal, if highly ascetic, moral virtues to which every reader is expected to aspire. The Anglo-Saxons are simply ahead of the other nations. Not that Verne lacked patriotic pride, or resentment toward France's rivals. But he saw France's greatness as lying in the part she played in the great international enterprise that the Anglo-Saxons led.

Verne saw and dramatized the story of the English the way they themselves saw it. In *Dick Sands (Le capitaine de quinze ans)* of 1878, his hero is the English boy Dick Sands, and the villain is a Portuguese who practices slavery. The Portuguese were then widely treated as the villains of the slave-trade story, of which the English were the heroes. The book includes a sketch of the career of the famous missionary David Livingstone, one of the heroes of England and Scotland. (His *Missionary Travels and Researches in East Africa* had sold 30,000 copies at 31 shillings each, plus another 10,000 at 6 shillings each.) Verne helped spread the cult of Livingstone, which brought together the antislavery crusade and the missionary legend in the service of England's moral prestige. The cult of exploration was one of the cultural forces that kept the Robinson story alive.

Within the idea of the explorer there was a certain dialectic, between the morally orthodox and the morally heretical. Livingstone was an official hero. His admirers described him as being "as pure and tender-hearted as a child, full of humanity, simple-hearted," while at the same time a man of tremendous achievement and wisdom.[1] But there was an opposite to him among the English explorers of Africa in the worldly immoralist and open atheist, Richard Burton, who founded the Anthropological Society in 1863 explicitly to counteract missionary influence. To Burton and his friends Livingstone seemed a poor naked mind, "dressed in the daubings of Scotch theology." They mocked him and his colleagues with talk of Nigger Worshippers, missionary exporters, and so on. Livingstone, on the other hand, said the true story of Burton's life "could not be told without disgust—systematically wicked, impure, and untruthful."[2] Burton was the hero for moral heretics. But it was Livingstone Verne celebrated as explorer.

Verne's idea of the adventurer—perhaps we might say the French idea—was more Napoleonic, more theatrical, than the English. In *The Mysterious Island,* Cyrus Smith is very Anglo-Saxon: a version of Crusoe or Cook, as we shall see. but he is counterparted by the much more romantic figure of Captain Nemo. In the earlier *Adventures of Captain Hatteras (Les voyages et aventures du Capitaine Hatteras),* the hero is again presented as very English. He is lean and wiry, "with a calm, rigid face, and thin compressed lips, and cold though fine eyes" (p. 277). Again a version of Cook or Crusoe. But Hatteras turns out to be a monomaniac, who drives himself and his men too hard. At the book's climax he goes mad and leaps into a live volcano at the North Pole—not a Crusoe gesture.

Generally speaking, Verne's literary imagination is rhetorical and theoretical, less practical and empirical than that of the English adventure writers. This is true of his style and structure, and of his plots, as well as his characterization. In many ways this makes him less authentic as a Robinson writer, but it does make available to him certain dramatic motifs that belong to the theme of technological progress but which the English writers denied themselves. Thus, in *A Trip from the Earth to the Moon (De la Terre a la Lune)* of 1865, we find a passage that sounds quite modern, much more so than most things in the English Robinson tradition. "An appalling, unearthly report followed immediately, such as can be compared to nothing whatever known, not to the roar of thunder, or the blast of volcanic explosions. No words can convey the slightest idea of the terrific sound! An immense spout of fire shot up

1. Mallery, *Masterworks of Travel and Exploration,* 473.
2. Van Orman, *The Explorers,* 30.

from the bowels of the earth as from a crater. The earth heaved up and with great difficulty some few spectators obtained a momentary glimpse of the projectile victoriously cleaving the air in the midst of the fiery vapors" (p. 238). It is no accident that it is not an English author but again Cooper who provides the closest comparison, in his description of Mark Woolston's volcano erupting in *The Crater*. In the same book, it will be remembered, the hero wins the loyal cooperation of his Kanaka workmen by including them in the privileged circle of those who are allowed to cause explosions.

Verne's literary affiliations are generally rather different from Defoe's. (Among science-fiction writers, H. G. Wells is closer to Defoe.) Verne did of course read explorers, but he also liked nonrealist writers like Edgar Allan Poe. In 1864 he wrote an enthusiastic essay on Poe, in whom, he said, "the spirit of analysis and deduction reaches the outside limit of intelligence."[3] This enthusiasm is at first glance surprising, because Poe has, in both America and France, been claimed by serious (i.e., highbrow) literature. For instance, Verne was in this essay reviewing Baudelaire's famous translation of Poe—and he clearly found Baudelaire's preface perverse in its account of Poe, just because that account was so esoteric, so highbrow-literary. And Baudelaire's attitude was fairly typical. Hippolyte Taine also drew a contrast between literary types in the persons of Poe, "the damned poet," and Defoe, "the sensible bourgeois."

But Verne has in fact something in common with both opposites. He is like Poe in his fondness for huge caverns and polar-surrealist landscapes, and for codes and cryptograms and puzzles and solutions. Such tastes are, after all, often middlebrow, though we now associate them with highbrow art. Contemporary French critics are now interpreting Verne to make him read like Poe, so as to claim him too for "literature." But this is perverse ingenuity. More naturally, Roland Barthes, in his early *Mythologies,* took Verne as a representative of bourgeois realism, and drew a sharp contrast between the Nautilus, the submarine in *Twenty Thousand Leagues Under the Sea (Vingt mille lieues sous la mer),* and Rimbaud's "bâteau ivre," the symbol of the modernist, antibourgeois imagination.

3. *Textes oubliés,* 115.

Verne's Imaginative World

Verne told the Robinson story several times; sometimes with the word Robinson in the title, as in *The School for Robinsons (L'Ecole des Robinsons)*. He said his childhood reading had been dominated by *Robinson Crusoe, The Swiss Family Robinson,* Mayne Reid's *Desert Home* (translated as *Le Robinson du désert*), Cooper's *Crater* (translated as *Le Robinson américain*), and the French *Le Robinson de douze ans* by S. Malles de Beaulieu, published in 1825. Of them all he liked best Wyss's book, which had "the family, the father, the mother, the children and their different aptitudes. How many years I passed on their island! With what ardor I involved myself in their discoveries!"[4] This comes from an interview of 1899, intended for American readers. Verne wrote two continuations of Wyss's book.

L'Ile mystérieuse Verne called his Robinson while he was working on it. Long before, in a letter of 1865, he wrote, "I dream of a magnificent Robinson. I absolutely have to do one. It's stronger than I am. I'm getting some magnificent ideas."[5] And because of the huge body of work he produced, and its enormous international readership, Verne can be called the story's most important heir and transmitter, at least in the second half of the nineteenth century. Ullrich's Supplement of 1908 lists translations of *L'Ile mystérieuse* into Swedish, Dutch, English, Danish, Italian, and German.

In an English-language translation of Verne's works in 1911, the Introduction called him "the expander of horizons" and "a universal teacher," and tried to claim him as being more Anglo-Saxon than French. Though he is suspiciously popular, "the conscience of the moralist can here approve the eager pleasure of the reader, and bid youth continue in this glorious light of wonder and adventure. There is not an evil or uncleanly line in all the volumes."[6] (Evil and uncleanness are, as usual, associated with sex and cynicism, as offenses against manliness.) Verne, it continues, has been attacked by "those who could only make a mock of what was too open and too honest for them to comprehend" (p. ix).

4. Costello, *Jules Verne,* 29.
5. Vierne, *L'Ile mystérieuse de Jules Verne,* 21. "Je rêve à un Robinson magnifique. Il faut absolument que j'en fasse un, c'est plus fort que moi. Il me vient des ideés magnifiques."
6. Charles Horne, Introduction to the Prince of Wales Edition of *The Works of Jules Verne,* viii.

(These mockers would of course be people of advanced literary taste; perhaps readers of Henry James.)

The stress of this praise falls on the moral character of Verne's work, a moral character appropriate to specifically masculine modes of action. "He spoke for the great mass of men, giving them such tales as they could follow, upholding always such a standard of courage and virtue, simple and high, as each of us can honour for himself, and be glad to set before his children. It is not only 'boys' literature' that began with Verne. One might almost say that man's literature, the story that appeals to the businessman, the practical man, began then also" (p. ix). One need not endorse all the presuppositions of this critic, Charles Horne, to agree nevertheless that Verne's fiction was, and was intended to be, in harmony with the ethical, political, and "scientific" interests of the average nineteenth-century male reader.

Verne linked the Robinson story to both international power politics and scientific-technological developments in specifically modern ways. One of the books about his work divides his writing career into three phases. The first phase (from 1863 to 1878) is called "The Mission of the Great Powers, or the Voyage's Direction."[7] This phrase, the Voyage's Direction refers to Verne's use of "voyage" to title his series of novels. His characters, this scholar says, were not individuals but representatives of the great powers. The nations he was interested in were the expanding ones—England, the United States, France and Russia—those that "had charge of humanity." He saw it as the function of these *nations* to help each other, and thus humanity, to conquer the earth. (He thought they deserved the title "nation" more than other countries—we might prefer to say that they were empires or incipient empires.) The group of friends to which he belonged, all influenced by the ideas of Saint-Simon, saw it as the work of progress, performed by the colonizing powers, to "make fruitful a territory rich but underdeveloped."[8]

Verne's imagination was geographical and geopolitical. He held the whole world in his hand and felt its roundness. He imagined piercing it to the center, or leaving it behind. He continually played with the idea of traveling all around the globe, in several novels besides *Around the World in Eighty Days (Le tour du monde en vingt-quatres jours)*. And in *The Children of Captain Grant (Les enfants du Capitaine Grant)*, he

7. Huet, *L'Histoire des voyages extraordinaires*.
8. Ibid., 29.

sets his protagonists traveling across sea and land along a line of latitude. In both these last two books his serious protagonists were British, and Frenchmen figured only in comic roles. In his work as a whole he had eighty English heroes, thirty Russians, and ninety Americans. (Twenty-three of his sixty-four novels take place inside the United States.) *The Adventures of Three Russians and Three Englishmen in South Africa (Les aventures de trois Russes et de trois Anglais dans l'Afrique Australe)* is set in 1854 and is about rival teams of astronomer-surveyors who are in South Africa to measure the angle of the meridian in order to derive from it the precise length of a meter. Their work is interrupted by the outbreak of the Crimean War, but the two teams part still united by the bonds of brotherhood in science, which will ultimately prove stronger than those of war.

It was the cause of disgruntlement in France that Verne so flattered the English in these early stories. He defended himself by saying, "I consider the English excellent protagonists when it is a question of extraordinary or scientific voyages."[9] But in later years his sympathies ran almost the opposite way. "If the world had any idea of the injustice which these English, so proud of their guineas and their naval power, have perpetrated throughout the world, there would not be enough insults in the human language to throw in their faces."[10]

Verne suffered the same reversal of feelings about scientific and technological progress. He began as an enthusiast for the new modes of transport, in the air and under the sea as well as along the surface, and for giant bridges and dams, new fuels, new minerals, new elements. It was the main social function and message of his *Voyages extraordinaires* to keep up with, and to keep a wide-spreading public up with, all the new developments. But in the last phase of his career, after 1897, he wrote dystopias, like *The Astounding Story of the Barsac Mission (L'Etonnante histoire de la Mission Barsac)*, in which science and technology are the means by which a black population is enslaved.

The Extraordinary Voyages

The Jules Verne who wrote *L'Ile mystérieuse* was still an enthusiastic partisan of science and progress, and the hero of this story is an

---

9. *Textes oubliés*, 358.
10. Chesneaux, *The Political and Social Ideas of Jules Verne*, 141.

American engineer. Verne called him Cyrus Smith, though the standard English translation changed Smith to Harding. His vocation is his identity, and he is most alluded to as "the engineer," *l'ingénieur*. He is a man perfectly adapted to surviving on a desert island, and he solves at a glance problems (for instance, how to make fire) that baffled his companions and the reader. (He takes the glass cover off his watch and uses it as a burning glass.)

The story is unmistakably a revised and up-to-date version of *Robinson Crusoe*. It begins, in accordance with tradition, with men cast away on an island during a storm; but these men were traveling by balloon and fall onto the beach out of the sky. Though almost entirely unequipped, they set to work, not only to build themselves shelters, but to subdue the whole island to their purposes. They build mines, kilns, and factories and alter the landscape by means of explosives. The familiar Robinson story is immensely expanded and its pace speeded up, so that the story passes before the reader's eye like a film running too fast.

The Mysterious Island is of course a group story, like Wyss's, not a solitary's, like Defoe's. As we have seen, Verne said he preferred the former. But there is no family in Verne's stories. The most vividly presented human relationships are that of father to son, and that of master to servant, and then that of comradeship: all of them male relationships. Verne's forte as a writer is not to describe or analyze relationships of any kind, but the master-to-servant kind he does depict often and with some vividness. His first novel, *Five Weeks in a Balloon (Cinq semaines en ballon)*, has Joe, *Around the World in Eighty Days* has Passepartout, and this novel has Nab the negro and Jup the ape. Verne seems to take an interest in the idea of the perfect servant, which corresponds to the interest in the perfect woman in love novels; in his first voyage, he apostrophizes Joe: "Rare and honest Joe! A servant who orders your dinner exactly to your taste, who packs your portmanteau and never forgets the shirts and socks, who keeps your keys and your secrets, and never gives up either."[11]

In the second half of the book, Verne reminds us of neither Defoe nor Wyss but of Cooper: by his interest in volcanoes, by his large-scale and broad perspective, and by his apocalyptic conclusion. Between Cooper and Verne, Ballantyne is a mere parenthesis—although in others of his Robinson stories, like *The Two Years Holiday*, Verne is close to Ballan-

11. *Five Weeks in a Balloon*, 204.

tyne. He is like Cooper also in his stress on manliness. 'One must say, also, that these colonists were 'men,' in the beautiful and powerful meaning of the word. Engineer Smith could not have been seconded by more intelligent companions, nor with more devotion and zeal."[12] The word recurs all the time, and with a spiritual, almost religious stress. The caste-hierarchy of the colonists is also a hierarchy in manliness, with Smith at the top. He is always being commended by the others as "Quel homme!" or "Voilà un homme!" It was often remarked by readers and admitted by Verne, that his heroes had no relations with women, in which they were being loyal to the first Robinson story.

Verne's writing career began with an enthusiasm for Alexandre Dumas, whose friend he became and whose example he imitated. (His Captain Nemo clearly owes something to Dumas's Count of Monte Cristo.) But when he met the publisher Jules Hetzel (born P. J. Stahl), one of the great literary entrepreneurs of nineteenth-century France (Victor Hugo and George Sand were also among his authors), Verne's career took a different turn. Hetzel gave him the idea of writing a series of adventures that would dramatize the advances of contemporary science. In a preface to Verne's *Geographie illustrée de la France,* Hetzel wrote, "Our civilization is endowed with a force growing so rapidly that no country, however remote, could escape from its investigations, elude its domination. The day is no longer far off when it will have searched out, even in their last depths, the mysteries of still inaccessible countries. That is not an empty hypothesis, it is a certainty."[13]

One of the most interesting of the Extraordinary Voyages is the first, *Five Weeks in a Balloon,* of 1864. It puts together, without disguise, a patchwork of recent travelers' accounts of Africa. Livingstone, Burton, Barth, Speke, are all often cited. It begins at a Royal Geographical Society meeting in London in 1862. All the members, we are told, are explorers. "All of them either physically or morally, had escaped shipwreck, fire, the tomahawk of the Indian, the club of the savage, the stake, or Polynesian cannibals." (p. 181). His hero, Fergusson, is a "member

12. Verne, *L'Ile mystérieuse,* 107. "Il faut dire, d'ailleurs, que ces colons étaient des 'hommes', dans la belle et puissante acception du mot. L'ingénieur Smith ne puvait être secondé par de plus intelligents compagnons ni avec plus de dévotion et de zèle."

13. Huet, 12. "Notre civilisation est douée d'une force si rapidement croissante, qu'aucun pays, si reculé qu'il soit, ne saurait échapper à sa domination. Le jour n'est plus bien éloigné où elle aura fouillé jusque dans leurs dernières profondeurs, les mystères des pays encore inaccessible. Ce n'est pas un vaine hypothèse, c'est une certitude".

of the Church Militant of science." He "longed for the glories of Mungo
Park, of Bruce, Caillé, and Levaillant, and even of Selkirk and Robinson
Crusoe, who were to him in no way inferior. How many happy hours
had he passed on the Island of Juan Fernandez? He sometimes approved
of the ideas of the shipwrecked sailor, sometimes he denied the propriety
of his plans and projects . . ." (ibid.). But always Robinson was a living
presence to him, and had Fergusson been on that island, he would never
have left it. He would have been as happy there as a king without
subjects.

Fergusson crosses Africa by balloon, and all across the continent
natives attack both him and it, on religious grounds; science is hated by
superstition, though the natives also worship the balloonists as divine
beings. Fergusson is taken to be the son of the moon goddess, and he
performs "miracles," with the aid of ordinary Western science. The
native culture, or lack of it, is a matter of casting spells, sacrificing
animals, getting drunk, and chanting. The balloonists rescue a dying
French missionary; and thus the story pays tribute to all the current
images of Western piety and progress.

Hetzel and Verne were liberals. Hetzel acted as private secretary to the
poet Lamartine in the revolutionary government of 1848, when the poet
was briefly minister for foreign affairs. He was arrested in 1851, when
Louis-Napoléon took power, and lived in exile in Brussels until 1859.
He and other of Verne's friends, like Ferdinand de Lesseps (the engineer
of the Suez Canal) and "Nadar" (a balloonist and photographer) and
Jacques Arago (a traveler and travelwriter), were under the influence of
Saint-Simon's social theories.

L'Ile mystérieuse has been described as a Saint-Simon parable, or a
hymn to the glory of labor, or (by Chesneaux) as a hymn to a culture
ruled by scientists. Saint-Simon wanted "steam and electricity for all
tasks; in place of the exploitation of man by man, the exploitation of
the globe by mankind."[14] In 1832 The Producer, the first Saint-Simon
newspaper, published articles to promote "a careful, regulated, fraternal
cooperation in the exploitation of the globe in the light of scientific
knowledge."[15] Engineering and colonizing projects were dear to idealistic socialists then. Enfantin, the leader of the Saint-Simonians, gave his
blessing to the French colonization of Algeria; and Fourier was interested

14. Chesneaux, 69.
15. Ibid.

in such schemes as discovering the Northwest Passage, or stabilizing the Northern Crown (the aurora borealis, which would, it was hoped, be brought under control by the spread of agriculture into the Arctic Circle.) This sense of progress is of course the nineteenth-century expanded equivalent of Defoe's sense of progress, expressed explicitly and realistically in his *Essay upon Projects* and implicitly or mythically in *Robinson Crusoe*.

Verne's *Robinsonade*

L'Ile mystérieuse reminds us of Defoe in many ways. One part, the story of Ayrton, who led a mutiny on a ship and was marooned, reminds us of Defoe's constant interest in mutinies at sea. Several of Defoe's stories begin with such a situation. The idea of a mutiny is the obverse of the cult of captaincy, which is so central to the adventure tale. Just so, "Jules Verne, who felt so strongly about everything to do with navigation, seems to have been obsessed with the problem of authority on ships, and naval mutinies are given considerable space in his writing," says Chesneaux (p. 93). The same concern was felt, of course, by Cooper and Dana, and others in the Defoe line.

The words "engine" and "engineer," so important to Verne, are used significantly in *Robinson Crusoe*. The full modern sense of "engineer" was not available in the early eighteenth century, but one of Defoe's principal English heirs in the nineteenth century, Samuel Smiles, wrote a popular compilation called *The Lives of the Engineers*. (Talking of Cyrus Smith, Michel Tournier calls *ingénieur* a superb word, "où se mêlé le génie et l'ingéniosité.")[16]

Then Verne emphasizes the advantages of Protestantism. On the mysterious island (Lincoln Island, as the castaways name it), Easter Sunday is celebrated in Protestant style. "All agreed to sanctify this day by rest. These Americans were religious men, scrupulous observers of the Bible's precepts."[17] Engineer Smith is compared with William of Orange, the Protestant hero (and friend or patron of Defoe). In the

---

16. *Le vent paraclet*, 214.
17. Verne, *L'Ile mystérieuse*, 112. "Tous convinrent de sanctifier ce jour par le repos. Ces Américains étaient des hommes religieux, scrupuleux observateurs des préceptes de la Bible."

earlier story, *The Adventures of Captain Hatteras,* the crew of a ship
that sets sail for the North Pole has been chosen as Protestants, because
"it has always been found in long voyages that assembling the men for
reading the Scriptures and common prayer is a powerful means of
promoting harmony and of cheering them in hours of despondency" (p.
224). Many of the traditional Defoe motifs recur in Verne, such as the
superiority of iron over gold, or the slogan that necessity is the best
teacher.

Like Defoe, Verne had a passion for geography. He told Marie Belloc
in 1895, "I have always loved geography, as others specialized in historical studies. [That is the difference between him and Dumas.] It is certain
that my taste for maps and the great global explorations is what has led
me to compose this long series of geographical novels."[18] He wrote a
two-volume *Illustrated Geography of France* and a three-part *History of
Great Journeys and Great Travellers.* The climax to the latter is the
career of Alexander von Humboldt, Campe's pupil, whom Verne calls
"the very ideal of the traveller." Von Humboldt saw "the connection
between geography and the other physical sciences."[19]

As the world was explored, it was also subdued, leveled, smoothed
out. Tunnels, causeways, railways were built. Railways were a favorite
project among Saint-Simonians, and in fact some of those who began as
idealistic dreamers of social change in France ended as directors of a
railway system. It was thus no accident that we are told that Cyrus Smith
had been in charge of railways in America before the action of this story
begins. Smith is one of the more vividly characterized of the Robinson
figures. We are told that he is a true North American, meaning that he is
thin, bony, lean; forty-five or so; wears mustaches, but not a beard; and
has a head fit to be engraved on a medal. "Very well-informed, very
practical, very 'débrouillard', to use a French military term, he had a
superb temperament, for, while staying master of himself, whatever the
circumstances, he fulfilled in the highest degree the three conditions
which together determine human energy: activity of mind, and body,
impetuosity of desire, power of will."[20] He was of course the sort of

18. *Textes oubliés,* 357.
19. Verne, *The Exploration of the World,* 371.
20. Verne, *L'Ile mystérieuse,* 16. "Très instruit, très pratique, très 'débrouillard', pour
employer un mot de langue militaire française, c'était un tempérament superbe, car, tout en
restant maître de lui, quelles que fussent les circonstances, il remplissait au plus haut degré les
trois conditions dont l'ensemble détermine l'énergie humaine: activité d'esprit, et de corps,
l'impetuosité des desirs, puissance de la volonté."

engineer who had done all the manual work he asked his men to do. (In this way, he is like Defoe's historical hero, Peter the Great.) His muscles, literal and metaphorical, have superb tone.

Smith's companions represent other types of contemporary adventure. One is a journalist who writes his dispatches under fire, and is compared with Henry Stanley, ". . . having roamed over the whole world, soldier and artist . . . true hero of curiosity, of information" (p. 18). But others are rather followers of heroes, for Verne has the modern sense of caste. Thus Pencroff is a sailor who, when Smith makes fire, stares at him awestruck. "If, for him, Cyrus Smith was not a god, he was assuredly more than a man" (p. 82). Then there is Nab, "sometimes naive, always smiling, obliging, and good" (p. 18). He is a liberated slave who loves Smith to the point of wanting to die for him—a Friday figure. There is a dog also eager to die for Smith, and later the ape, who is quickly trained to love and serve his human masters.

The story thus depicts an elaborate hierarchy of caste and species dominance, with, at the top, in apparent paradox, the emblem of democracy, the engineer. This is a paradoxical caste system, because at the top is neither priest nor king, and neither pomp nor ceremony. The rulers change their trades all the time, as Robinson did, and work harder each day than the last. "Now, from the brickmakers and potters they had been up to then, the engineer's companions were going to be metallurgists" (p. 125). They make tools—hammers, hatchets, saws; they bake bricks to build an oven in which to smelt iron; they make electricity; they make sulfuric acid—"a nation's industrial importance can be measured by its consumption of this"—and then they make niter and glycerine, and so the most powerful of all explosives.

"There is nitro-glycerine. . . ."[21] It was indeed that terrible compound whose power is perhaps tenfold that of ordinary gunpowder, and which has already caused so many accidents. . . ."[22] It seemed the whole island trembled on its base. A series of stones hurled itself into the air, as if by a volcano. . . ."[23] A triple Hurrah escaped their breasts![24] Pencroff murmured 'Say, he's going good, our engineer. . . . But do you know,

21. Ibid., 147. "Voilà de la nitro-glycérine . . ."
22. Ibid., 148. "C'était en effet, ce terrible produit dont la puissance est peut-être decuple de celle de la poudre ordinaire, et qui a déjà causé tant d'accidents . . ."
23. Ibid., 149. "Il sembla que toute l'île trembla sur sa base. Une séries de pierres se projeta dans les airs comme si elle eût été par un volcan . . ."
24. Ibid., 151. "Un triple hurrah s'échappa de leurs poitrines . . ."

Mr. Cyrus, that with that charming liquid you have created, one could blow up our entire island?' . . . 'No doubt at all, the island, the continents, and the world itself.' "[25]

All this is an international engineering triumph, but it also belongs to one nation primarily, to the United States. In *The Adventures of Captain Hatteras,* we read that "the Yankees, the first mechanicians in the world, are engineers by right of birth" (p. 133). And the story of Lincoln Island is in some ways a parable of America's rise to world dominance. Pencroff says, "If you like, Mr. Smith, we will make a little America out of this island. We'll build towns here, we'll set up railways, we'll install a telegraph" (p. 73). He asks that the castaways call themselves colonists; and all agree to add the island to the United States as the thirty-seventh state. (It is no longer the British Empire that is the residuary heir of all these adventures.)

Innovations

The principal innovation Verne introduced into the Robinson story was his largeness of scale. We have already spoken of what he shared with Cooper in that regard, and of his multiplication of the Crusoe figure by six, but we must note also his alliance of this story with other adventure stories, most notably his own. *L'Ile mystérieuse* is in effect an anthology of sequels, since it introduces, in its second half, characters and themes familiar to Verne's readers from two of his most popular earlier novels, *Twenty Thousand Leagues Under the Sea* and *The Children of Captain Grant.*

The themes of these earlier stories were, in some ways, alien to the Robinson material. The different kinds of adventure mesh together, but the hegemony no longer belongs to Robinson. Captain Nemo, in the submarine story, is one of the great avenger figures, Byronic or Napoleonic. His mysterious monogram, *N,* reminded nineteenth-century readers of Napoleon. The fact that he, in this story, takes Cyrus Smith under his protection from the moment the castaways arrive on the island

---

25. Ibid. "Pencroff murmura 'Allons, il va bien, notre ingénieur.'" . . . 'Mais, savez-vous, M. Cyrus, qu'au moyen de cette charmante liqueur que vous avez fabriqué, on ferait sauter notre île entier?' 'Sans aucun doute, l'île, les continents, et la terre elle-même.' "

means that the Defoe idea of self-help is undermined. He sends them all they need packed up in a box. The ultimate power turns out to be Romantic-Gothic—in some sense supernatural.

As for the Captain Grant story, that contributed the character of Ayrton, who, when found marooned on an island, had atavistically degenerated from manhood to animalism. This anthropological melodrama is also at odds with the Robinson ethos. The effect of solitude on Ayrton is so much the reverse of its effect on Crusoe that one feels one of the two must be exaggerated. Thus Verne's expansion of the material changes its character, and leads to the dystopic apocalypse at the end. This work comes comparatively late in Verne's career, when his stories had blacker meanings. (But we should remember that he described melodramatic scenes involving volcanoes early in his work.)

From as early as page 440, out of well over five hundred, Smith begins to suspect that the colonists' luck—that luck so important to all Robinsons—has turned against them. And when, on page 531, the survivors see the volcano destroy their colony, "the colonists' first feeling was a profound sadness. They scarcely thought of the danger which directly threatened them, but of the destruction of the soil which had given them shelter, of this island which they had made fertile. What good would it have done henceforth to harvest, to gather, to hunt, to increase the reserves in the Granite House. . . . [T]he crater, then widely open, projecting towards the sky such an intense light that, simply by the effect of reflection the atmosphere seemed to be incandescent. At the same time a torrent of lava, swelling from the new peak, spread out in long cascades . . ."[26]

This vision cannot but act as a prediction, to warn the reader against any exalted confidence in progress. However, Verne in effect offers an alternative ending, embodying a different and upbeat vision of the human fate: the colonists are rescued, and settle in the United States, and become extremely prosperous again. The result of superimposing the later upon the earlier ending is to make the story completely ambiguous, as Barthes points out.

26. "Le premier sentiment des colons fut d'une profonde douleur. Ils ne songèrent guère pas au péril qui les menaçait directement, mais à la destruction de ce sol qui leur avait donné asile, de cette île qu'ils avaient fécondé. . . . a quoi eût servi désormais de moissonner, de récolter, de chasser, d'accroître les réserves de Granite House. . . . le cratère, largement ouvert alors, projetant vers le ciel une si intense lumière, que, par le simple effet de la réverberation l'atmosphère semblait être incandescente. En même temps, un torrent de laves, se gonflant de la nouvelle cime, s'épanchait en longues cascades."

The second of the two, the one consonant with Defoe's Robinson
story, is the one most widely circulated, for instance, in Russia. In 1933
the Soviet Writers Circle put Verne at the head of the list of authors
deserving translation, along with Defoe and Swift; and in his *Pour une
théorie de la production littéraire* of 1971, Pierre Macherey has said that
there have been two great audiences for Verne: one nineteenth-century
bourgeois France, the other twentieth-century communist Russia. The
two roughly concur in liking the optimistic ending to *L'Ile mystérieuse*.
Macherey quotes from Cyrill Andreev's preface to the 1955 edition,
which admits the flaws in Verne's science but acclaims his philosophy.

These sound to literary readers like voices out of the past, but as late
as 1978 Verne was the fourth best-selling author worldwide, with
twenty-six million copies sold and translations into forty languages. The
figures for Shakespeare were about one-third of that. The Robinson
story is still a myth men live by.

10

Treasure Island (1883)

As a boy, Robert Louis Stevenson met R. M. Ballantyne, and it was an encounter, he said later, that influenced him to become an author himself. However decisive that meeting really was, Stevenson, as a Scottish adventure writer, stands historically between Ballantyne and Buchan, or perhaps it is better to say, he stands ideologically between Scott and Barrie, between the Whig historian and the master of whimsy. Different as these five are from each other, they have in common an allegiance to the idea of the British Empire, which they served as writers, via the idea of adventure. British literary adventure would have been seriously impoverished if the Scottish men of letters had refused their cooperation.

One could apply to Stevenson and his love of adventure a personal/national analysis like that which Muir applied to Scott. Stevenson was, as Jenni Calder says, a son of the established middle class in Scotland.[1] His family had worked for three generations, ringing the coast of Scotland with lighthouses and creating the ship service of the Northern

1. *Stevenson and Victorian Scotland,* 4.

Lights. Thomas, our Stevenson's father, built more than thirty light-houses. But Robert Louis Stevenson could not and would not carry on the family tradition, even in the literary form of realistic tales about engineers. He was an only son who rebelled against his father. He hated his father's moralism, so suspicious as it was of art. He hated pharisees, as we saw in his remark about Benjamin Franklin in his opposition to Jesus Christ. As a student, Louis saw himself as a Bohemian Christ figure; for instance, he put compassion above the "moral" law, and cried, "Give me the publican and the harlot."[2] If we use the term "Galilean" as an opposite to pharisee, we can apply it to Stevenson, although it must mean "spiritual" in a highly aesthetic or literary sense, and, by a further paradox, we find that it led Stevenson to the writing of what had seemed like a pharisaic form—adventure. He was Scotland's apostle of art and defier of Puritanism. He hated missionaries, wanted to live with a prostitute, and exulted in the debaucheries of earlier Scots poets, like Burns. But he associated that bohemianism with the literary form that had served the pharisees.

In all this he was in step with, or only a little ahead of, the avant-garde of his time. In the 1870s the giant novelists and moralists of the Victorian era were coming to the end of their lives, and of their influence. Stevenson never refers to George Eliot, Matthew Arnold, or John Ruskin. In his *Lay Morals* he says that the Bible itself has become too familiar and has lost its message. His father, who had treated him so severely, asserted the infallibility of the Bible with the conviction of personal infallibility. But he (Thomas Stevenson) died broken in will and even in mind. The story of the personal relations between him and his son seems to parallel the history of ideas in Scotland.

Naturally, Robert Louis Stevenson always bore the imprint of the moralism he first accepted and then rejected. His nurse, Alison Cunning-ham, had told him tales of the martyrdom of the Covenanters, the grimmest of Scottish religious zealots. His own first book, printed when he was sixteen, at his father's expense, was a historical account of an abortive rising by Covenanters in 1666. He told Barrie that he consis-tently read Covenanting books (some of which were adventures, but with the most tragic endings) until he was nearly a man. It was Dumas, after Scott, who suggested to him the kind of gay adventure writing he himself developed. He also remained fascinated by his family's history

2. Ibid., 23.

of lighthouse engineering, feeling that he should have been able to write his stories while also doing their kind of work.

Adventure therefore was to him a way of defying an inherited masculinism and moralism, without entirely breaking with it—making a mitigated defiance. And he connected that defiance with being Scottish. In *The Silverado Squatters* he said that if you are born Scottish, "you generally take to drink; your youth, as far as I can find out, is a time of louder war against society, or more outcry and tears and travail, than if you had been born, for instance, in England."[3] Muir might say that Stevenson felt able to defy Scottish moralism beause he could rely on the larger and more worldly morality of England, the imperial nation. (That was true also of Buchan and Scott and the other Scots writers.)

Because of this hectic romanticism in Stevenson, and because of the book's plot, some may object that *Treasure Island* does not belong in this discussion. There is nothing about work in Stevenson's book; and the elements of the Robinson story that it does contain are blended with material from other kinds of adventure—notably, the kind deriving from Scott and Dumas. The writing of this story marks another stage in fact in the process by which the Robinson story had become nonviable or unwritable in Great Britain by 1900. That nonviability shows itself in, for instance, Kipling's writing no version of the story. The age of imperialism for which he and Stevenson wrote was not interested in *edifying* adventures. It needed other stories, grimmer or more splendid. The empire was now a matter of world power, of guilt and grandeur; it needed a Kipling, not another Defoe.

Just for that reason, however, all the different strands of adventure had become so interwoven in boys' literature in England by 1881 that *Treasure Island* comments on the Robinson story even by its omissions and perversions. We are always being reminded of Defoe's *Robinsonade* and its revisions as we read Stevenson. *Treasure Island* is after all about an island, and a castaway, and a survival. The author himself admits, in his Introduction of 1894, that he took the parrot from *Robinson Crusoe* and the stockade from *Masterman Ready,* while the figure of Ben Gunn, the marooned sailor, seems to be, like Verne's Ayrton, developed out of Alexander Selkirk. It would be absurd to omit such a book from our discussion.

3. Ibid., 21.

Aestheticism

What is new in this story is the aesthetic charm Stevenson confers on his version. This is a carefully calculated charm, of a kind usually associated with a different kind of writing—that aimed at "connoisseurs of literature." That phrase fits several of Stevenson's earliest admirers, like Edmund Gosse, Andrew Lang, Walter Raleigh, and Sir Arthur Quiller-Couch. We see this most obviously in the story's bright visual and sensual images, which are not to be found in Defoe or his direct heirs.

In the second paragraph of the story we read, "I remember him as if it were yesterday, as he came plodding to the inn door, his sea-chest following behind him in a wheel-barrow—a tall, strong, heavy, nut-brown man, his tarry pigtail falling over the shoulders of his soiled blue coat, his hands ragged and scarred, with black, broken nails, and the sabre cut across one cheek, a dirty livid white" (p. 11). And in the very next sentence this visuality is supplemented from the musical sense in the song, "Fifteen men on the dead men's chest," which is to be a motif of the whole book. This is followed by an appeal to the sense of drinking and taste, when he calls for rum, which, "when it was brought to him, he drank slowly, like a connoisseur" (p. 12). Much of this material, to do with the inn, Stevenson took from Washington Irving's "Wolfert Webber" in his 1824 *Tales of a Traveller. Treasure Island* is a patchwork of such borrowings.

Nearly every image is sharp and bright, no matter what the object. "The rest of the arms and powder we dropped overboard in two fathoms and a half of water, so that we could see the bright steel shining far below us in the sun, on the clean, sandy bottom" (p. 104). Or the black spot: "The printed side had been blackened with wood ash, which already began to come off and soil my fingers; on the blank side had been written with the same material the one word, 'Depposed' " (p. 181).

To link these effects with others Stevenson offers, we might suggest the aesthetic category, "the picturesque." He himself says that he and his father each found in *Treasure Island* "his kind of picturesque." This reminds us that Thomas Stevenson, despite his Puritanism, was sensitive to the adventurous—that that severe Scottish culture had its adventurous element. Nearly every Scot, after all, read Scott. "Picturesque" covered a whole taste. It included, besides the strictly pictorial and the music of the language and so on, picturesque ideas and topics: for instance, eighteenth-century England, with its ports, ships, and sailors, but also the moral idea of evil. This last is surely what most profoundly sets *Treasure Island* apart from other versions of the Robinson story, which have no figures of individual evil. There are tribes of cannibals, painted and feathered and frantic, but to transform that blurred image of savagery into a vivid, plausible individual like Long John Silver was to make a significant change.

We have of course already seen Marryat's evangelical portrait of a bad man, Jackson, in *The Little Savage*. But Jackson is not picturesque; he is simply sinister, and his story is sordid. Silver, on the other hand, is confessedly his creator's favorite character. He and Blind Pew, and Israel Hands, and Black Dog, all are creatures around whom the writer's and the reader's mind lingers, thrilled and fascinated. This book takes into itself and aestheticizes the topic of evil, which the Robinson writers had avoided. It associated evil with amputation and mutilation (Pew's blindness, Silver's leg) and good with bodily grace and vigor. But it thereby turned evil into one of the colors in the palette of the picturesque, an embodiment of the moral elasticity of adventure. (Stevenson, like John Buchan later, began his literary career with more conventionally "aesthetic" writing, remote from any kind of action. The continuity between that and adventure of course lies in the aversion of both from moral realism of the Victorian kind.)

Blind Pew was "plainly blind, for he tapped before him with a stick and wore a great green shade over his eyes and nose; and he was hunched, as if with age or weakness, and wore a huge old tattered sea-cloak with a hood which made him appear positively deformed" (p. 27). And indeed this idea of deformity is luridly developed in Stevenson. As a kind of verbal and auditory equivalent, we have the ravings of Bones and Gunn; and as a "supernatural" equivalent, the shudders of the treasure hunt. A sort of climax is given by the sophisticated murders: Silver throwing his crutch and felling the fleeing Tom, and Jim shooting Hands involuntarily, under the impact of the knife with which Hands pinned him to the mast.

The reader is invited to admire the writer's skill, but also his moral license. Stevenson defined the artist as a *fils de joie,* by analogy with the sophisticates' phrase for a prostitute or a courtesan, *fille de joie.* He thereby put his stress on the pleasure the artist can give and denied him or her the moral respectability the Victorian writers had claimed for themselves. In "Letter to a Young Poet," in *Scribner's Magazine* in 1888, he wrote that the son of joy "gains his livelihood by pleasing others, and has parted with some of the sterner dignity of man."[4]

The change in Stevenson paralleled a change in all English literature in the 1880s and 1890s. Aesthetic categories supervened upon moral ones. You can see this change happen in the different ways Barrie presented Stevenson to the world. In an early essay, he declared Stevenson not to be a novelist at all, but a wanderer of the byways of literature.[5] That was because, Barrie said, Stevenson was indifferent to the affairs of life and death that concern most of us; he was uninterested in the immortal soul and in life after death.

"The cry is to arms; spears glitter in the sun; see the brave bark riding joyously on the waves. . . . His [Stevenson's] brain will only follow a coloured clue, and so he is chiefly picturesque, and, to those who want more than art for art's sake, never satisfying" (p. 254). It is specifically in the treatment of religion, subsuming other kinds of moral seriousness, and in the characterization of women and personal relations, that Stevenson fails, according to Barrie. "Scottish religion, I think, Mr. Stevenson has never understood, except as the outsider understands it. . . . Adventures suit him best, the ladies being left behind" (p. 256).

But he changed that judgment. In Barrie's later memoir of his mother, he says that only her claims upon him held him back from following the older writer to Samoa. (She asked him to wait until after her death before he set off for Vailima, Stevenson's famous house there.) So, since Stevenson died before she did, "I shall never go up the Road of Loving Hearts now, 'on a wonderful clear night of stars', to meet the man coming towards me on a horse . . . the dear king of us all" (p. 96). Stevenson was by then the king of all Scottish writers. (Perhaps just as important, in this later essay, Barrie makes much of his mother's reluctant delight in Stevenson's writing.)

Similar changes were occurring outside Britain. French critics developed an interest in the adventure novel—seen as an English form of fiction—which took Stevenson's stories and essays as a starting point. Stevenson had contrasted the adventure novel with the novel of character in essays in 1882 and 1884, which were reprinted in *Memories and Portraits* in 1887. Marcel Schwob was impressed by these ideas, and by

4. Maixner, *Robert Louis Stevenson: The Critical Heritage*, 313.
5. Barrie, *Margaret Ogilvie and Others*, 250.

Treasure Island, which he read in 1888. In the 1890s he and Camille Mauclair espoused this "English" kind of fiction in preference to the "narcissistic novel" written by, among others, André Gide. By the turn of the century, however, Gide himself was working on *Les caves du Vatican,* which he then saw as an adventure novel, and his literary allies had taken up these ideas. What they meant by the phrase was not very close to *Robinson Crusoe* as we have understood it, but Defoe was in fact the novelist they most often cited and discussed.[6] Above all, they were the counterparts in France of those people in England—the Stevenson enthusiasts—who were trying to change the status of the adventure novel and the structure of literature as a field.

This literary change happened at the same time as, and in connection with, a political change. In "The Politics of Stevenson," Christopher Harvie points out that the men of letters who showed early enthusiasm for Stevenson (for instance, Edmund Gosse and Walter Raleigh, Leslie Stephen and Sidney Colvin) had been liberals in the 1860s, but in the 1870s and 1880s turned away from politics toward literature, and insofar as they remained political became Conservative (Unionist was the current term) and imperialist.[7] An election book of 1885, entitled *Why I Am a Liberal,* claimed Stephen, Huxley, Tennyson, Browning, and Arnold as Liberals, but by 1886 they were all Unionists because of Gladstone's Irish policy. (He wanted to give Ireland Home Rule.)[8] Stevenson himself in 1887 proposed to move his family to Tipperary, to the frontier, as it were, in order to defy the Home Rulers. This was the period of conscious imperialism in politics, and of bluff masculinism in literature and journalism. Both were summed up in the person of Stevenson's chief promoter, W. E. Henley.

The boys' story, already less profoundly moralized than adult fiction, was the place where Stevenson (previously the author of small and precious essays and anecdotes) performed this transformation, the aestheticization of literature. (The other great figure in this process, besides Stevenson, was Kipling, the scandal of English literature.) One source of Stevenson's innovations was no doubt French writers of the exotic and picturesque. Another was Dickens, whose characters, long before Stevenson's, performed themselves on a kind of stage, with artificial lighting

6. See O'Neill, *André Gide and the roman d'aventure.*
7. Calder, 109.
8. Ibid., 112.

and trapdoors and movable scenery. His heir was Barrie, whose Captain Hook certainly derives from, degenerates from, Long John Silver.

The idea and form of adventure offered such writers an escape from the moral constraints, the seriousness, of nineteenth-century fiction. Just so, inside the novel, the idea of the search for the island, as it inspires Squire Trelawney and Doctor Livesey, is the idea of a holiday from work and duty and serious reality. These characters are right for Stevenson's purposes because they are glad to "become boys again." Indeed, Stevenson is to be distinguished from Scott (and Kipling) just for his lack of historical seriousness. He is not interested in the forces behind, for instance, piracy, or in any other kind of social causation, or any historical depth. His story is all a bright and decorative mural. "The Man Who Would Be King," for instance, is more *about* nineteenth-century India than *Treasure Island* is about eighteenth-century England. (*Kidnapped* is not so strikingly cut off from Scottish history, but still it is hardly to be compared with Scott or Kipling for historical insight.)

Another way in which the moral potentiality of the story is voided is by the stress on clues (the map and its mysterious markings) and the suspense (the Hawkins' clock strikes just as Jim reads out the message, "You have till ten tonight.") and the general invitation to guess what the writer is going to do next (p. 32). This is not part of the reading contract offered by Defoe and his direct heirs. Stevenson is more artificial; the chapters begin and end with tableaux, and within them theatrical scenes are set up with clear delineations. Jim is led into a great library, where "the squire and Doctor Livesey sat, pipe in hand, on either side of a bright fire" (p. 42).

It should be noted that though Stevenson gives us lists of objects, as Defoe does, they are of a different kind, because these are not objects of use, but randomly quaint. When the Hawkins finally open Bones's great sea chest, "A strong smell of tobacco and tar rose from the interior, but nothing was to be seen on the top except a suit of very good clothes, carefully brushed and folded. They had never been worn, my mother said. Under that, the miscellany began—a quadrant, a tin cannikin, several sticks of tobacco, two brace of very handsome pistols, a piece of bar silver, an old Spanish watch and some other trinkets of little value and mostly of foreign make, a pair of compasses mounted with brass, and five or six curious West Indian shells" (p. 33). All this stimulates the imagination, but differently from *Robinson Crusoe*. We might put that phrase, "stimulates the imagination," in quotes here because the stimulus Stevenson gives is not to practical action but to conscious play. Work has no place in this world. (Thomas Stevenson drew up this list for his son, which reminds us how much adventure-imagination went with Puritan moralism.)

Continuity and Connections

We see the book's continuity with Stevenson's precursors, Ballantyne and Kingsley, in the use of the West Country setting, and in the dedicatory poem. "To the Hesitating Purchaser" names

> Kingston, or Ballantyne the brave,
> Or Cooper of the wood and wave.

It asks if we respond to sailor tales and tunes:

> Storm and adventure, heat and cold,
> If schooners, islands, and maroons,
> And buccaneers, and buried gold . . .

Stevenson declared imagination to be especially the property of children. Therewith he silently subverted the structure of literary culture, insofar as that is built on a theory of trainable imagination.

In "My First Book" Stevenson described how he first drew and painted the map of the island as a way to entertain his schoolboy stepson, and then found himself writing—but still playfully, of course. "It was to be a story for boys; no need of psychology or fine writing; and I had a boy at hand to be a touchstone. Women were excluded" (p. xxiv). "Psychology" is probably an allusion to Henry James's fiction (perhaps "women" is too). James was in those days always cited as the representative of serious literature; Stevenson himself distinguished James's novel of character from his own novel of action.

In his account of the writing, Stevenson made the story seem to evolve, like Wyss's, in a group of his friends. He said that he drew silver from a friend (the patriotic poet and editor W. E. Henley) and that he found an enthusiastic audience in his own father. "I had counted on one boy; I found I had two in my audience. My father caught fire at once with all

the romance of his original nature. . . . it was *his* kind of picturesque"
(p. xxvi). (Mr. Stevenson's original nature probably means his character
as it would have been, but for spoiling by Puritanism.) The adventure
tale henceforth claims to form a link between generations, by returning
men to their true (i.e., boyish) nature.

Fanny Stevenson tells us in her preface to the 1905 edition of the
book, "My father-in-law would sit entranced during our daily chapter,
his noble head bent forward, his great glowing eyes fixed on his son's
face. Every incident of the story could be read in his changing counte-
nance. At any slip in style, or taste, or judgment, he would perceptibly
wince." The fierce moralist had been transformed into an aesthete;
Puritanism was vanquished. Mrs. Stevenson felt free to condescend to
his religious fervor. "I shall always believe that something unusual and
great was lost to the world in Thomas Stevenson. One could almost see
the struggle between the creature of cramped conventions and environment, and the man nature had intended him to be" (p. vii). She asserts
literature's mission to liberate the imagination from moralism, literature
being the servant of adventure and empire.

This is the more interesting because of the bitterness of Stevenson's
early fight for imaginative freedom. Scenes in which a young man is
cruelly scolded and insulted by a father figure are frequent in his fiction.
The Stevensons had done great work, modernizing the coastline of Great
Britain, and their imaginations were prosaically powerful, like Defoe's.
But within the family, as in society as a whole, in the 1870s the factual
imagination yielded to the fanciful, to art and the aesthetic; the serious
adult imagination of literature yielded to the boyish.

Among his predecessors, it is above all Scott from whom Stevenson
derived. But this is the Scott of historical costumes and colorful "theatrical" fiction, not Scott the serious historian and moralist. When we read
about Jim Hawkins preparing to set off on his adventures, the tone is
simply romantic and excited. "I lived on at the Hall under the charge of
old Redruth, the gamekeeper, almost a prisoner, but full of sea-dreams
and the most charming anticipations of strange islands and
adventures. . . . Sometimes the isle was thick with savages, with whom
we fought, sometimes full of dangerous animals that hunted us, but in
all my fancies nothing occurred to me so strange and tragic as our actual
adventures" (pp. 48–49). This thoughtless glee and greed for suspense
is far from Defoe's analysis of Crusoe's itch to travel, or even from Scott.

Jim's romanticism is in fact a variant on Edward Waverley's dreaminess, which, however, Scott *mocked*.

There were other literary sources for *Treasure Island*. Washington Irving has already been mentioned, but Stevenson also acknowledged his debt to Charles Kingsley's *At Last*. It was in that book he read about an island off Puerto Rico, called Deadman's Chest. He also made use of three books by W. H. G. Kingston: *Peter the Whaler, The Early Life of Old Jack,* and *Mark Seaworth,* which is partly about a desert island. And there were literary derivations from his own book. According to Harold F. Watson, whose *Coasts of Treasure Island* is an authoritative scholarly work, the best of these is W. D. Howden Smith's *Porto Bello Gold* of 1924. This narrates events that took place before those in Stevenson's book, which show how the treasure was acquired from the Spaniards.[9]

For obvious reasons, Stevenson (and Kipling) demands to be compared with great literary artists whom we would not think to align with Ballantyne or Verne. Conrad, for instance, makes an important use of islands and castaways, whose experience is like that of Stevenson's castaways, and the reverse of that described by Defoe or Marryat. *On the Beach at Falesa* is a short novel by Stevenson that has quite a lot in common with Conrad. Even Treasure Island is as sinister, in its juvenile way, as Conrad's islands. The difference is that in Stevenson's writing the balance between glamour and horror inclines more definitely to the former.

Another writer close to Conrad and Stevenson, both socially and artistically, was Stephen Crane. He came to live in England, while Stevenson and Kipling went to live in America. Such crossings were typical of these decades, especially for adventure writers. (These were, after all, the years of Anglo-American imperialism, and writers like Kipling and Stevenson were very popular in America.) Both the Englishmen married American women, and Stevenson went on from America to the South Sea islands. He in some sense fulfilled the adventure dream, living in Samoa.

Stevenson built himself there a kind of baronial manor, directing the clearing of the site himself in 1891. He called it "Vailima," and built it of Californian redwood, and furnished it with seventy tons of the Stevenson family furniture, sent out from Scotland. He said it was *his*

9. Harold F. Watson, *The Coasts of Treasure Island* (San Antonio, Tex., 1969).

Abbotsford, his version of the famous Borderland baronial mansion Scott built from his earnings. He filled it with family members and dependents. His mother and his cousin came from Scotland, and his wife's children and grandchildren. Stevenson even treated his servants as a Highland clan. He was their chief, and they gave him absolute obedience.[10]

Stevenson tried to play a part in the politics of the island: both the politics of the great powers, which were appropriating spheres of influence there, and the politics of which local chiefs should have suzerainty. He talked of these feuds in the terms of the Jacobite Rebellion of 1745 in Scotland, and drank toasts to his favorite chief, Mataafa, with the traditional Jacobite words, "To the king over the water." This was imperial adventurism.

Thus Stevenson lived out empire-and-adventure on the proceeds of his literary fantasies about them, which were lavish proceeds. There were six editions of his complete works within the twenty years after his death. And then came a literary reaction against him, datable from 1914. That is the year in which Frank Swinnerton attacked him on literary grounds, but it is also the year of the Great War. The reaction against Kipling dates from the same time. In terms of the world of letters, both men's reputations were prolonged henceforth only in disgrace. But *Treasure Island* remained immensely popular with readers. The British Museum Catalogue lists ninety-five editions, plus six plays, and it has been turned into films and even comic books.

10. Daws, 180.

11

Peter Pan (1904)

D espite the growing unease of gifted writers with the Robinson story—the growing tendency for them to treat it humorously or nostalgically, not to tell it straight—*Robinson Crusoe* itself remained a potent cultural factor in England. It was even perhaps at the height of its influence over children in the last part of the nineteenth century. In 1882 an official instruction to school inspectors, disapproving of some school readers, made up of extracts, said, "Such works as *Robinson Crusoe,* Voyages and Travels, or Biographies of eminent men (if of suitable length) are to be preferred. In Standards VI and VII a single play of Shakespeare, or a single book of one of Milton's longer poems . . ."[1] It suggests *Robinson Crusoe's* preeminence that that was the only title specified.

As for testimony to its influence on individual readers, there is a mass of it. George Borrow learned to read on Defoe's book. For months, he said, "the wondrous volume was my only and principal source of amusement. For hours together I would sit poring over every page till I

1. Gregg, *Modern Britain,* 530.

had become acquainted with the import of every line . . ."[2] Hitherto
Borrow had refused to learn to read, but, having heard some of this story
read aloud, he taught himself reading to find out what happened next.
The power of the story was irresistible.

In *Among the Idol-Makers,* L. P. Jacks tells us how his father bought
him a copy, in 1868, and how the purchase changed his life. "Had the
eyes of my father chanced upon some other book, all would have been
different. Had he bought me *The Fairchild Family,* or *Sandford and
Merton,* or Miss Edgeworth's *Tales,* or *Tom Brown,* then the lady who
is now my wife would have belonged to another; my present children
would not have been born, my strange life would not have been lived;
and these lines would not have been written."[3] If we translate his remarks
from the individual into the general mode, from the personal to the
cultural, the statement becomes even more suggestive.

No other reading so captured Jacks's faith and set his mind on fire.
During his impressionable years, he was dying to get cast away on a
desert island himself. "Not for all the kingdoms of the world would I
have exchanged my keg of powder, my cap of goatskin, my fortification
and my raft."[4] (We should note how he, like Fergusson in *Five Weeks in
a Balloon,* sets the allure of Robinson adventure in opposition to worldly
ambitions. It is a form of spirituality.) *His* haunting passion—he contrasts it with what the Cumberland landscape meant to Wordsworth—
was for an island; for this he ransacked libraries, and read voyages, and
pored over maps, like Stevenson and his heroes.

But though so influential, after 1900 the Robinson story was decadent
in England. One sign of that decadence was that it lost its clear
individuality and became continuous with other adventures; another
was that it became the object of condescension. That is why these
chapters on Stevenson and Barrie are rather different from those before
and after, and why *Treasure Island* and *Peter Pan* both are and are not
versions of the Robinson story. Barrie's play both is and is not an
adventure story.

Everyone talked about the genre adventure, but indulgently, or self-
indulgently. It was the culture's major reservoir of cliché images, and

---

2. Borrow, *Lavengro,* 24.
3. De la Mare, *Desert Islands and Robinson Crusoe,* 245.
4. Ibid.

cliché feelings. The Stevenson admirer Leslie Stephen used to invigorate himself by chanting adventure ballads aloud. It is a habit reported to us in distaste by his daughter, so influential or representative in her circle; and the post-1918 phase of British literature was to begin in a general reaction against adventure motifs. Stephen, Virginia Woolf implies, was acquiring a *false* vigor, boosting his virility quotient, by his chanting.

In *The History of Mr. Polly* (published in 1910), H. G. Wells presented to us, as did many other authors then, a Cockney clerk whose brain had been addled by the reading of adventures. "He would read tales about hunters and explorers, and imagine himself riding mustangs as fleet as the wind across the prairies of Western America, or coming as a conquering and adored white man into the swarming villages of Central Africa. . . . He was beloved by queens in barbaric lands, and reconciled whole nations to the Christian faith. . . . He explored the Amazon, and found, newly exposed by the fall of a great tree, a rock of gold . . ." (p. 13). This was Polly as a boy. Later he read the traveler La Pérouse and delighted in "the frankest revelations of the ways of the 18th century sailorman, homely, adventurous, drunken, incontinent, and delightful . . ." (p. 128). *Treasure Island* shows its influence there.

Indeed, adventure, plus a few licentious authors like Boccaccio and Rabelais, constitutes literature for Mr. Polly, even English literature. "Mr. Polly had been drinking at the poisoned fountains of English literature, fountains so unsuited to the needs of a decent clerk or shopman, fountains charged with the dangerous suggestion that it becomes a man of gaiety and spirit to make love gallantly and rather carelessly" (p. 80).

We see that the hegemony over adventure has passed to other types, to the Three Musketeers story primarily, and Robinson and Defoe have been forgotten. This is all the more remarkable in that Wells, like Defoe, belonged to the "decent clerk or shopman" caste himself; indeed, if Defoe was ever reborn in English literature, it was as H. G. Wells. We also see that the hegemony over literature has passed to adventure, and we marvel at how strong the influence of Kipling and Stevenson then was to sweep away the memory of Victorian humanism.

It is not, however, in Wells and *Mr. Polly* but in Barrie and *Peter Pan* that we find the most remarkable example of this delight in the decadence of adventure, combined with a sustained faith in real-life adventurers and the empire they were still building.

Barrie's Version

The subtitle to Barrie's play is "The Boy Who Wouldn't Grow Up," and that shows the way in which his story reversed the tendency of earlier versions of Robinson, for the boys in the latter were always ahead of their young readers in adulthood in both skills and responsibilities. Indeed, incipient manliness is an essential part of the idea "boy" even for Barrie, but it was more an erotic than a practical manliness, and he wanted to freeze that growth and preserve the bud in perpetuity. Max Beerbohm, in a perceptive review of the play, said it expressed the essentially immature genius of the playwright. He said, "Some fairy once waved a wand over him, and changed him from a dear little boy to a dear little girl."[5] It is surely more exact to say that the fairy fixed him *as* a dear little boy, preserving the outgrown childishness as well as the incipient manliness.

In his dedication, Barrie talks of how the real-life boys about whom he wrote the play gradually ceased to believe in the fantasies (of flying, and fairies, and so on) that he had spun for and around them. He next tried to involve them in the world of adventure. "In these circumstances, I suppose, was begun the writing of the play of Peter. . . . [I]t was a last desperate throw to retain the five of you for a little longer . . ." (p. 4). The imagining, the telling, the appeal to their judgment, and the writing itself were all attempts to preserve a fantasy. "The rebuffs I have got from all of you! They were especially crushing in those early days when one by one you came out of your belief in fairies and lowered on me as the deceiver" (p. 15).

Barrie describes his triumph when he won one of them back to be a child again, to believe again—for a moment—in fairies. But he also followed an opposite strategy, and involved them in the adventure tale, the next stage on in fantasy, the boy's stage that follows the child's. The difference Barrie made was to link adventure to the fairy tale so closely. Adventure, even in the Robinson story form, was now the next stage in fantasy.

Within the play the center of this sustaining and protective fantasy is the Darling children's bedroom, which Mrs. Darling has made into "the hub of creation, by her certainty that such it was, and adorned it to match with a loving heart and all the scrapings of her purse. The door

5. Birkin, *J. M. Barrie and the Lost Boys*, 118.

on the right leads into the day nursery, which she had no right to have, but made it herself with nails in her mouth and a paste-pot in her hand" (pages 17–18). It is the mother, not the father, who is the source of power—of course, playful power—in Barrie's family (which is therefore the opposite of Wyss's).

The family origin and orientation of Barrie's story nevertheless wins *Peter Pan* a place in the series begun by Campe and continued by Wyss and Marryat (and Stevenson, who brought a grandfather in as second boy). But what a strange, perverse family! In the telling of the Peter Pan story, as in the Darling family on the stage, the father counts for nothing, at least in the way of authority. The mother is a radiant absence, adored by the storyteller (who is not her husband) but ineffectual in the action. The imagination is ascribed to the children themselves, but in fact belongs to the unnamed cuckoo in the nest, Barrie.

Barrie was the cuckoo in the domestic nest, displacing the Davies boys' father and finally becoming their literal guardian. And he was the cuckoo in the cultural nest, displacing Defoe and Ballantyne, while seeming only to supplement them. Adventure was being reduced back to fairy tale; England's morality was being seduced back to fantasy and charm by her most faithful servant.

Of the three "family writers" of the Robinson story, the closest to Barrie was Stevenson, in several ways. Captain Hook, with his mutilated arm, clearly derives from Long John Silver and his mutilated leg. And the authors' feelings about these characters are similar. If Hook *is* Peter, as the stage directions suggest, he is surely Barrie's favorite; just as Stevenson loved Silver better than any other of his characters. Stevenson and Barrie were both geniuses of ambivalence and play.

Above all, they take a similar view of women and children. Henry James, in an essay on Stevenson of 1883, defines that view in a way that amounts to a prediction of *Peter Pan*. "To [Stevenson's] view," he says, "the normal child is the child who absents himself from the family circle, in fact when he can, in imagination when he cannot, in the disguise of a buccanneer. Girls don't do this, and women are only grown-up girls."[6] Thus James sees the cult of the boy in Stevenson, to be repeated in Barrie; and, being not an adventurer but a writer of adult fiction himself, sees the strangeness of that cult. "What he [Stevenson] is most conscious of in life is heroism—personal gallantry, if need be, with a manner, or a

6. Smith, *Henry James and Robert Louis Stevenson*, 135.

banner. . . .[7] [E]verything he has written is an apology for boyhood."[8] This is the source of Barrie's feeling for adventure, too, which he makes one degree more self-conscious than Stevenson did. Women, and the mode of moral realism associated with them, are the enemy of adventure.

To begin at the humblest level and mode of ambivalence, the adventure elements in *Peter Pan* playfully mix up different kinds of story. Captain Hook is a variation on the Byronic and dandy elements to be found in the avenger type—the Count of Monte Cristo, for instance, or the Master of Ballantrae. "The elegance of his diction, the distinction of his demeanour, show him one of a different class from his crew, a solitary among uncultured companions. . . . In dress he apes the dandiacal . . ."[9]

Then the native race is said to be Redskin, but their tribal name is the Piccaninnies, and their heroine, Tiger Lily, speaks pidgin English. Pirates and mermaids and fairies mix together, and many of the stage directions are written in an ironical pastiche of adventure prose. "The brushwood has closed behind their scouts as silently as the sand on the mole; for hours they have imitated the lowly wail of the coyote; no strategem has been overlooked, but alas, they have trusted to the paleface's honour to await an attack at dawn, when his courage is known to be at its lowest ebb" (p. 71).

There is a similar ambivalence about the play's themes; for instance, women and their relation to men. In the dedication Barrie says, "Wendy has not yet appeared, but she has been trying to come ever since that loyal nurse cast the humorous shadow of woman upon the scene and made us feel it might be fun to let in a disturbing influence" (p. 13). This surely suggests, in its playful way, a desire to keep the two sexes apart as long as possible in order to save boyhood from the reality principle. On the other hand, Mrs. Darling is a radiant presence as well as absence, because she is surely the implicit audience; the whole fantasy is surely being offered up to her—a tribute to the Virgin Mother—for her to display to rival parents in proof of her triumph. She is "the loveliest lady in Bloomsbury, with a sweet mocking mouth, and as she is going out to dinner tonight she is already wearing her evening gown, because she knows her children like to see her in it. It is a delicious confection made by herself out of nothing and other people's mistakes (p. 19).

7. Ibid., 133.
8. Ibid., 131.
9. Barrie, *Peter Pan*, 42.

Wendy's motherliness, on the other hand, is surely felt to be an inferior fate. One of the Lost Boys tells her, "What we need is just a nice motherly person," and she replies, "Oh dear, I feel that is just exactly what I am" (p. 51). What she had hoped to be was Peter's beloved. But that was not to be. By the end of the play she is flying so badly that she has to use a witch's broomstick (p. 93). Like everyone else in the play, but especially the women, she wants to lay her hands on Peter, but he is not to be touched, not to be caught. He is infinitely desirable boyhood, which infinitely desirous womanhood can never possess.

Barrie's revision of the story clearly corresponded—by the testimony of its popular success—to an important change in English imaginative life. In the dedication Barrie speaks of beginning to play with its theme a quarter of a century before, which would be around 1890. This was when England began willfully to cherish its Pans (in E. M. Forster's stories) and its Pucks (in Kipling's *Puck of Pook's Hill*) and its Kims and its Mowglis, and to address its more soberly named Georges and Williams as "Boy!" Maurice Hewlett, a friend of Barrie, wrote a play, *Pan and the Young Shepherd* at the same time Barrie was writing his. Hewlett's first line was, "Boy, boy, wilt thou be a boy for ever?"[10] Kipling's Brushwood Boy is addressed as "Boy." And this was not only England, as we shall see. America, for instance, had its Bad Boys, like Huck Finn and Tom Sawyer. They were not conceived so categorically as darlings, but they too were seen inside the toy theater of adventure.

Peter is the object of desire, for Tinkerbell, and Wendy, and Mrs. Darling. And this desire has its element, its trace, of sexuality; it is rooted in his identity as a boy, incipiently a man. He is, we are told, cocky and conceited. He defines himself as "Wonderful boy!" and he is eager to fight and give orders.[11] His ego is the force behind and within the whole island. On the other hand, he is a child. He is scared at the thought that he might really become a father, might be trapped into manhood (p. 66). He ran away the day he was born because he heard his parents talking of what he was to be when he became a man. But he is manly—with all the ambivalence of manliness. He is brave enough to die ("To die will be an awfully big adventure"), but not, Barrie tells us, brave enough to live (p. 61).

10. Birkin, 63.
11. Barrie, *Peter Pan*, 58.

Cultural Changes

This diagnosis of English manhood was current at that time. We find it in Conrad's *Lord Jim,* in A. E. Housman's poems, in Pater's "Emerald Uthwart," and above all in Kipling. Besides Kim and Mowgli, one need only think of "The Brushwood Boy" or "A Conference of the Powers," or the boy in "Cold Iron." Everywhere manhood appears as a crushing burden, which everyone hates to see imposed on the beautiful boys who have up to adolescence been cherished as the living icons, the totems of their race and class. But the will of writers like Barrie and Kipling does not falter. Manhood is all the more glorious a destiny by reason of its severity. Boys must become men, and boyhood must be conceived in the terms invented by the adventure writers. Barrie tells us in the dedication that he and the Davies boys imagined themselves as rivaling Captain Scott in his attempt to reach the Pole (p. 11). (After Scott's heroic death, his son became another of Barrie's adoptive children. Barrie laughed at the clichés of heroism, but he cherished its truths.) The boys were taught how to make fire without matches by the Canadian adventure writer Ernest Seton-Thompson on his visit to London (p. 10). And the play of course assumes familiarity with Dumas and Cooper and Ballantyne.

Another of Barrie's plays, *The Admirable Crichton,* is a reprise (as well as a send-up) of the island story. Its point is the incompatibility of the adventure ethos, from Defoe to Kipling, with actual life in England. Of course the play is ambivalent, being by Barrie, but to some degree it presents that incompatibility as England's shame.

An English aristocratic family is shipwrecked and the butler rises to the challenges of adventure. So does the daughter of the house, Lady Mary, who becomes a bow-and-arrow hunter, swimming a river in pursuit of her prey. But she is slavishly enamored of her former servant. When he, now so powerful, alludes to his shameful servant past, she tells him he speaks of it like a king. He replies, "In some past existence I may have been a king—who knows? It has all come to me so naturally, not as if I had had to work it out, but as if I remembered." And he quotes some lines by Stevenson's friend Henley—

> I was a king in Babylon
> And you were a Christian slave.[12]

12. Barrie, *Plays and Stories,* 75.

This is, like Kipling's "The Man Who Would Be King," a climax to that vein of suppressed excitement that runs through adventure from *Robinson Crusoe* on, however mockingly expressed; the idea that an Englishman can become a king just by leaving his island home and taking English skills and English character to less fortunate parts of the world. England was a nation of kings, as long as Englishmen remained adventurers.

Barrie as much as Kingston wanted his *Peter Pan* boys to be adventurers and not aesthetes. (When, later in life, he was their guardian, he discouraged any enthusiasm for ballet and opera, recommending cricket and football instead, just like Kingston.) Indeed that pressure can be felt within the play itself. Peter of course sees grown-ups like Barrie adoring him for his boyishness, but he must continue to make himself as tough as possible—make himself another Jim Hawkins or Jack Martin. (Something similar can be seen in Barrie's great contemporary, Marcel Proust, who wanted his Saint-Loups to remain fiery duelists, even while they sank under the influence of "Marcel.")

George Bernard Shaw said *Peter Pan* betrayed the boys involved because it appealed over their heads to adult consciousness: what they took seriously, it took fancifully. But contemporary accounts show the actual audiences as containing a mixture of generations, all of whom were equally pleased. It was Barrie's triumph to devise a fantasy in which boys could enjoy both pretending adventure and mocking the pretense. This is not unique; something similar no doubt occurs in most societies that make a privileged domain out of childhood. Children's imaginative playing together often combines fantasy and mockery, and television cartoons for children often include parody and pastiche. Thus Barrie's triumph was to recognize the time and place in which that phenomenon could be made into adult art. For the character, and the popularity, of Barrie's play, shows the perfect control of his art—far finer than Twain achieves in his stories about boys. The exquisite play of ambivalence in Barrie suggests that this conscious fantasy had in England become so central a cultural topic that even a brilliant artist need not transcend it.

Barrie came from a poor and nonconformist family in Scotland, so he had a considerable distance to traverse to end up as principal entertainer, or minor-key celebrant, of the Edwardian empire. His father had been a Chartist, a political radical, but he evidently counted for little in the family. His mother, though devout, was delighted to see her son become a writer; and his relation to the adventure form and theme was, by his own account, typical.

In the dedication he depicts himself at the age of eleven as feverishly consuming "sanguinary" tales about desert islands, but as at that age learning (from a high-class magazine) that such reading was shameful (p. 7). Allegedly he thereupon carried his copies secretly out of the house and buried them. At twenty-one, he says, he craved to be a real explorer, "one of those who do things instead of prating of them"; and if later he gave up that ambition, "because noone would have" him, he began writing plays that had islands in them (ibid.). This suggests plausibly enough the history of adventure as reading matter and inspiration in the minds of the early audiences for *Peter Pan*. However, this account of his career omits significantly the phase that first made Barrie famous—when he wrote domestic comedies in what was called the Kailyard style. (That phrase suggested humble domesticity.) Writers of this school wrote about Scotland's poor, provincial, and morally narrow dissenters. These were comedies of manners, aiming at moral realism, and with women as major characters—the opposite of adventure.

Barrie went to London as a journalist in 1885 but wrote about Scotland—about his home town of Killiemuir, and the sect of the "Auld Lichts." His attitude to the people he describes is "tenderly mocking." He and his reader, being men of letters, are of course unlike those they read about, but he makes his characters quaint, touching, lovable. These stories and novels were published in religious weeklies, like *Good Words* and W. Robertson Nicoll's *British Weekly*. In this phase Barrie wrote his reproof of Stevenson. It was not until 1891, after his mother's death, that he began to write for the theater; and by 1900 he was writing about and for Englishmen. Stevenson (ten years his senior) had shown him the way from a Scottish to an English audience.

As we have seen, Barrie always associated the claims of adventure with Stevenson, assuming, in the first half of his career, that any such enthusiasm was immature—maturity having to do with his mother, his home town, Scotland, and religion. That is why his mother's secret preference for Stevenson's tales (later revealed or alleged) is so important. In *Margaret Ogilvy* he describes how he and she read books together. *Robinson Crusoe* was the first book they shared—and the second; and she prodigiously admired an African explorer whom Barrie had as a friend. She loved to picture him at the head of his caravan, now attacked by savages, now by wild beasts. But she was very afraid that he wanted to take Barrie with him on explorations, and that she would never allow. Indeed, she wanted her son to be a minister, or a professor, rather than even a writer.

Barrie's devotion to his mother is as ambivalent as everything else in his life and is undermined by a strong wish to have broken away and engaged in adventure himself. In the second half of his career the strongest emotion he expresses is a love for boys (boy-men), which focuses on their fierceness, their egotism, their will-to-power, their appetitiveness. But that loyalty to boyhood and manhood was accompanied in *Peter Pan* (and elsewhere) by subversive feelings, mirrored in the defeat of the father. Mr. Darling (played by the same actor who played Captain Hook, the villain) is said to be "really a good man as bread-winners go . . . at home the way to gratify him is to say that he has a distinct personality" (p. 21). In fact, he is a blustering bully and coward who ends up in the doghouse.

The paradoxical breadth of Barrie's subject's appeal is shown both by the popularity of the play (actresses have made careers out of playing the name part) and by the many forms it took in Barrie's own oeuvre during the quarter century he refers to—roughly speaking, up to 1914. He treated it in *The Boy Castaways* (a book with titles and photographs but no letterpress), in *The Little White Bird* (Peter here is a baby, who thinks he is a bird, and flies about, and lives on an island in the Serpentine Pond in Kensington Gardens), and in *Peter and Wendy*, a novel, and so on.

It is also worth noting that a large part in bringing *Peter Pan* to the stage was played by the American impresario Charles Frohman, who loved it and believed in it from the moment he saw the script, and supported Barrie in all his extravagances of money and fancy. (At the moment of Frohman's death, he quoted Peter's line, "To die will be an awfully big adventure.") So it appealed to the American (and European-Jewish) imagination of that moment in history, as much as to the British. In America, however, the subsequent career of adventure was to differ from its course in England, because of other cultural factors and historical forces.

For instance, while Barrie was writing *Peter Pan*, an American was living out a Robinson adventure. Joshua Slocum (born 1844; died 1909) built himself a boat and sailed around the world in it between 1895 and 1898. He was conscious of his adventurer's heritage, and visited Juan

Fernández, the Robinson island: "The blue hills of Juan Fernandez, high among the clouds, could be seen about thirty miles off. A thousand emotions thrilled me when I saw the island, and I bowed my head to the deck. We may mock the Oriental salaam, but for my part I could find no other way of expressing myself."[13] He visited Selkirk's cave and his lookout and left feeling "feasted" with the experience (p. 158). Richard Henry Dana paid a similar tribute to that island and its Robinson memories in his *Two Years Before the Mast*. It was a genuflection in the cathedral of adventure.

Though uneducated, Slocum was highly self-conscious about his public role. He exhibited himself (alongside Buffalo Bill) at the Pan-American Exposition of 1901, visited Theodore Roosevelt at the White House, wrote his book, which was first published serially in a magazine, and was hailed as being in the line of Thoreau. Adventure was still a living tradition in America.

The success of *Peter Pan* is essentially a matter of theater history, and not to be measured in numbers of books printed; but it is nevertheless striking that the National Union Catalogue lists some ninety-nine editions, if one includes *Peter and Wendy,* plus many translations. Perhaps most important is the number of picture-book versions, and cartoons, static and animated. This is the version of our story that still first impresses young minds.

13. Slocum, *Sailing Alone Around the World*, 152.

12

Le solitaire du Pacifique
(1922)

T he Great War broke out just after Barrie wrote his dedication to *Peter Pan*. The horrors and futilities of that experience undermined the image of manhood, and therewith the Robinson story, for the continent of Europe. In America that effect was by no means so strong, and edifying adventures could still be written even by serious artists; Kipling found an heir in Hemingway. But in England and France adventure for some time lost its power to convince; the Robinson story could attract men and women of letters only as an occasion for satire.

These are rough generalizations, to which there are many exceptions. On readers who were not men and women of letters, the literary effect of the war was less clear-cut; my attempts at history here are all biased in the "literary" direction. Even within the field of literature, 1930 in England saw the publication of both Walter de la Mare's *Desert Islands and Robinson Crusoe* and Arthur Ransome's *Swallows and Amazons,* a work of adventure fiction and a work of nonfiction about adventure, both written with great care and taste. Nevertheless, both those writers were conscious of being outside the mainstream of modern sensibility. Ransome was writing for children, while de la Mare contrasted Defoe with Henry James, the representative modern writer for serious readers, and admitted the lack of subtlety in *Robinson Crusoe*. Among contemporaries who, like himself, did love island stories, de la Mare cited John Masefield, another poet popular in schools. (The potent young poets, like T. S. Eliot, had no truck with adventure—and for that reason it took them some time to get admitted to schools.) Ransome's story is a Barrie-like version of pirate wars, played out by upper-class children on a lake with an island in it. The tone is not Barrie's; the adventure is not *mocked;* but it is set within a heavy frame.

In America, on the other hand, 1932 saw the publication of *Mutiny on the Bounty*, by Charles Nordhoff and James Norman Hall, which became a best-seller and was made into movies more than once. The topic came out of the tradition of English adventure and had been used by foreign authors before. Jules Verne had written about the historical event on which it was based, and it belonged to the family of Robinson stories.

The two authors, both American, had served during the war in the Lafayette Escadrille and were heroes of combat. They and their book were commended by Ellery Sedgwick, the editor of the *Atlantic Monthly*, as antidotes to modern 1920s cynicism. "Both had lived with intensity lives high above the conflict, and to both the stridency and (as they felt) the vulgarity of post-war civilization was past endurance . . . reticent and illusive, there was something in each of them that in its pure essence I have not known elsewhere. Conrad called it romance."[1] Sedgwick, himself one of the old guard of letters, helped the two young men find a subject to write about that would satisfy their sense of romance and its attendant moral purity. That blending was something that modernism in the arts rejected. We might cite Hemingway and Fitzgerald as examples of the "cynical" new treatment of romance and morality that *did* seem convincing, though shocking, then—and that was to become the mainstream of serious literature.

The Mutiny on the Bounty story is about a South Sea island and has many elements of the traditional adventure. It is told by a West Country gentleman, like Stevenson's, or Kingsley's, or Ballantyne's. And within American culture their success was paralleled by that of Richard Halliburton and Martin and Osa Johnson: popular adventurers and writers about adventure, for the middlebrow American public. This seems to

1. Foreword to Nordhoff and Hall, *Mutiny on the Bounty*.

mark the difference between America's cultural situation and England's. And yet one could find equivalents for de la Mare's bookishness in America and for Halliburton's boyishness in England. We let de la Mare represent England and Halliburton America because of what feels like a different balance in literature's conflict of interests in both countries. This tilted toward adventure in America and away from it in England.

The same is true of France. Perhaps that country had its equivalents for Nordhoff and Hall (indeed, it *had*), but those who continue a movement always claim less attention that those who diverge from or oppose it. And so the important thing for literary history is that France published two outright mockeries of the Robinson story in the years 1921 and 1922, just after the war ended. One is Jean Giraudoux's *Suzanne et le Pacifique* and the other, Jean Psichari's *Le solitaire du Pacifique*. Of these the first is the more interesting because it is so typically a twenties book. It shows how naturally a send-up of the Robinson story went with those other exercises in cynicism and frivolity that we find in England, France, America, and everywhere in the 1920s. I use the Psichari title for this chapter mainly because it is a somewhat more evocative phrase, but the book is interesting in its own right.

Jean Psichari was Greek by birth, though he became a professor in France and married the daughter of one of the most famous of French professors, Ernest Renan. (His own son, Ernest Psichari, was one of that adventure-seeking group of young Frenchmen who are sometimes called the generation of 1914.) His first published books were written in Greek and date from 1888. He was a Greek nationalist and ready to be aggressive against great powers who overlooked the newer or smaller countries. Psichari wanted to help found a literature written in modern Greek, which would help his country acquire self-consciousness and self-confidence.

Le solitaire du Pacifique, was begun in 1904, as part of that enterprise, and finished in 1919. Psichari said he was following Dumas's example in giving some social and psychological foundations to the excitements of adventure. As far as this *Robinsonade* goes, however, Conrad would have been a better choice as sponsor. Part of the story's attraction for Psichari, for instance, was that it let him mock those overweening adventurers, the English. (The similarity is not that Conrad meant to mock, but that he too identified the English with adventure, and we feel in both authors the perspective that the smaller and peripheral nations,

Greece and Poland, took on the great enterprise of white empire.)
Psichari's earlier novel of 1892, *Jalousie,* had been a challenge to *Othello,*
a defiance of Shakespeare. This was a sardonic protest against the
prestige given to *Robinson Crusoe*—"one of the masterpieces, we are
told, of our neighbors, friends, and even allies: the English."[2] We should
recall the enthusiasm of certain French writers in the 1890s for Stevenson
and the English adventure tale.

Psichari's story follows Defoe's quite closely, in order to quarrel with
it more sharply. His hero, Yanni Petroyanni, is a Greek sailor of silent,
difficult temperament who is marooned on Juan Fernández in 1739 and
remains there for twenty-one years, like Robinson. The captain who
leaves him behind has been reading Defoe's book. He finds Defoe "a
disastrously bad writer" and throws the book into the sea in disgust.[3]
"It is not a sailor but a carpenter who has written that. . . . Him a
solitary? Pardon my laughter! Solitude! He hasn't even an idea of it."[4]
Thus the burden of the captain's (and the author's) contempt is both
psychological and aesthetic. By the standards of late nineteenth-century
high culture—deeply interested in the dialectic of solitude and society
(as we see in Conrad)—*Robinson Crusoe* was a trivial and superficial
book. "It isn't about solitude. It's the manual of the perfect English
colonizer."[5] Defoe's Crusoe is, in fantasy form, a political figure, a
projection of philistine entrepreneurs or administrators, with neither
artistic nor spiritual authority. Now Psichari's Robinson story will show
forth the truth.

Of the three Juan Fernández islands, Yanni lives first on Santa Clara,
which is a silent paradise, with no life on it. The theme of survival, so
important to all sympathetic treatments of the Robinson story, is slighted
here. Yanni has plenty of food and no dangerous animals to threaten
him. He also has plenty of tools and scorns to use them. What does
threaten him are his own fears and hallucinations. (Here is where we
think of Conrad.) But the tone in which even these are described is witty
and sprightly. Chapter 5 is entitled "The habits we love can sometimes
cost us dear," Chapter 6 is "The solitude which flees itself," and Chapter
7, "The voices of Bald Mountain." (This mountain, with its voices—

2. Psichari, *Le solitaire du Pacifique,* 8. "Un des chefs d'oeuvre, affirme-t-on, de nos
voisins, amis, et même alliés; les Anglais."
3. Ibid., 19. "Un écrivain désastreux . . ."
4. Ibid., 20. "Ce n'est pas un marin, c'est un charpentier qui à écrit cela. . . . Ça un
solitaire? Laissez-moi rire! La solitude! Il ne l'a pas seulement réalisée par la pensée."
5. Ibid., 21.

Psichari's anthropomorphic animation of the island—was to be taken further by Golding and Tournier.)

The main idea Psichari develops is what he calls "synanthropie": the perception that man can be man only inside a network of cultural situations involving other men. Solitude therefore contradicts humanity even in principle. Here again we meet a premonition of Tournier and a parallel with Conrad, though Psichari's handling of the theme is less portentous. Chapter 22, for instance, is entitled "The alternation of loves and hates." In solitude, where these opposite feelings do not alternate, but fuse or confuse, there can be no "humanity." Psichari deplores this—Tournier will welcome it.

Yanni disobeys the Robinson ethic flagrantly. For instance, he deliberately sets fire to the forest on Santa Clara. And Psichari disobeys the ethic of realism. Yanni finds on his beach a plank that has floated in, with his name carved on it; and to get from Santa Clara to Masatière, he simply entrusts himself to the trunk of an orange tree and floats there. On this second island he turns imperialist. There are goats and dogs there, and he makes the dogs his servants and the goats his subjects. We see him through their eyes, as Zeus the fire-bringer. He also becomes a hunter and loses the power of speech. He is compared with Selkirk in his degeneration. But Psichari lived in the era of Nietzscheanism. Unlike Selkirk, Yanni is naturally compensated in animal vitality for his loss of human verbality. He becomes a magnificent animal, a Tarzan. (Edgar Rice Burroughs created his ape-man hero just a little earlier.) He has escaped civilization and its discontents.

Yanni spends fourteen and a half years on Masatière. He makes love, romantically as well as physically, with a young goat. But then appears a beautiful Venetian blonde, called Myrielle, who makes herself costumes out of the island's flowers and feathers, which are like the works of Paul Poiret, the famous couturier of Psichari's time. Finally they are rescued, but settle down on the third island, Masafuere, to enjoy their children and receive visitors.

Giraudoux's Version

One might guess that the frivolous touches in the later part of this tale belong to the postwar period of its writing. Certainly they are what it has in common with Giraudoux's version. Here Robinson is a woman, called Suzanne, who writes her own story. She is a young girl when the story opens, shortly before 1914, and is living in Bellac, Limousin. Provincial life is described with a 1920s mixture of condescension and revulsion. Suzanne and her friends yearn to escape, to Paris and beyond, to exotic lands. But they affect by day to feel contempt for the secret life they lead by night, in dreams—"that strange life to which we were secretly pledged."[6] This other and exotic life is represented by the names of modern and immoral authors, like Verlaine and Loti.

Having won a competition (for composing the best epigram on the subject of boredom) held by an Australian newspaper, Suzanne gets a free journey around the world, and sets out with her governess-companion. The companion takes the teachings of adventure seriously. Aboard ship she studies the stars and prepares for shipwreck, making her plans to take command of the survivors if the captain and the other officers are disabled. Suzanne, on the other hand, scorns all this, and Giraudoux is on her side. Before they sail, she has met a Firbankian group of young people, and they mean more to her than any white heroes or black cannibals on any island. (Firbank in England, Fitzgerald in America, the dandy writers generally, are those whose voices we seem to hear echo in Giraudoux.)

When the wreck does occur, it announces itself only as a slight shock to the vessel. The headlights turned on on the bridge remind Suzanne of a car breakdown on a country road (p. 76). Various people sacrifice themselves so that Suzanne may survive, and she floats away on a raft well stocked with bottles, an umbrella, and a fur robe. (As we saw in Psichari's book, floating is an anti-Robinson mode of motion.) Thus all the conventions of the Robinson story, moral and practical, are flouted.

As her island first emerges from the mist, we see a rococo Paradise, two miles by three. "A thousand rainbows, upright or aslant, joined the stream to the hills. . . . Every tree liberated a red or golden bird that it had held through the night as a hostage for the dawn . . . everything that was needful to appease my hunger and my thirst, lying almost within reach of my hand. . . . Banana trees offering me a thousand bananas (p. 83) . . . holes from which bees flew out; holes from which honey itself was running; and even birds' eggs in their nests, within easy reach of that human being who had never yet passed by" (p. 84).

6. Giraudoux, *Suzanne and the Pacific*, 24.

Suzanne sweeps her beach with a broom made of marabou-feathers, and (like Psichari's Myrielle) makes herself a dress out of string and bird-of-paradise feathers. She decides to make a career out of being an idler and a millionaire. She spends a week deciding which feathers to use for her beds. She tattoos herself, eats at whatever hour she pleases, and displaces reality with her fantasies. (In all this, Tournier is to follow Giraudoux closely.) She names things arbitrarily, with words whose sounds appeal—mangroves, mandrakes, manchineels. Thus the action, as well as the decor, is rococo, and will remind us of early Wallace Stevens poems—a profusion of mahogany trees and cockatoos.

Suzanne is disappointed by nature's lack of malice: the poisons of poisonous plants seem to have no effect on her. She defies our sense of reality and realism, which she associated with the Robinson story. She scorns that story's heroes: "To speak like the Protestants in their tales of shipwreck . . ." (p. 132). She finds the remains of someone who died on her island, who must have been male because he had busied himself with all kinds of useless *work* (p. 144). He has carved the measure of a meter on the rock, and subdivided it laboriously into centimeters (like a Verne hero) and has carved the Puritan motto, in Latin, "Distrust yourself" (pp. 144–45). When she discovers that he had been an Italian, Suzanne is disconcerted; she had felt so sure that such a Puritan must be a Northerner. Her own values are of course opposite—southern and youthful. "Youth alighted on the corals, the parrots, and the baobabs. In my thought the word *young* was added to every word as an open car is added in springtime to every tram in Europe" (p. 125).

When Suzanne finds a copy of *Robinson Crusoe* and reads it, she of course hates the main character:

> This Puritan weighed down with rationality, certain that he was Providence's only toy, did not even entrust himself to God. . . . [I have departed from Redman's translation here.] Every minute for eighteen years—as though he were always on his raft—he was fastening cords, sawing stakes, and nailing planks. This bold man was constantly trembling with fear, and it was thirteen years before he dared to reconnoitre all his island . . . (p. 225). He required a table to eat, a chair to write, wheelbarrows, ten kinds of baskets. . . . Already encumbering his poor island, as his nation would encumber the world, with tin-plate and rubbish. . . . He was perhaps the only man—so superstitious and such a busy-

body did I find him—that I would not have liked to meet on an
island. Never burning his fortress in an enthusiasm for God,
never dreaming of a woman, devoid of divination, and without
instinct. . . . [Far from learning from or imitating him, like earlier
castaways, Suzanne had some instructions for Robinson.] "Don't
lose six months in making yourself a prie-Dieu; kneel down
there!" (p. 226).

Here we see the implicit polemic of the book become explicit. A program
is drawn up for future protesters against the Crusoe cult. Friday, for
instance, becomes the hero of Defoe's story, for Giraudoux as later for
Tournier. Suzanne says, "Friday plunged into me, to my very heart, by a
shorter road than that of a pearl diver. Everything that Friday thought
seemed natural to me: what he did, useful . . ." (pp. 227–28). She has
no reproof or advice to give *him*. He knew how to live.

The wittiest pages of the book are of frivolous satire against high
culture and its prescriptions. Suzanne reflects on the seven cardinal sins,
the nine muses, the canon of classics; because she has heard of three new
authors—Mallarmé, Claudel, and Rimbaud—but knows nothing about
them, she complacently invents for them all sorts of modish literary
virtues. These ideas, then, extend the attack on Crusoe to other standard-
ized icons of establishment culture.

The Great War breaks out and runs its course while Suzanne is on her
island. The roar of its battles reaches her ears in appropriately muffled
and accidental forms—as the corpses of dead sailors that float up on to
her beach. Then in 1918 three young English millionaire astronomers
come to her island to observe an eclipse (as if this were a Verne story,
again). They provide her rescue, and she falls in love with all three of
them. One of them carves on the rock there what could be called the
book's motto, "This is Suzanne Island. Where Polynesian demons,
terrors, egotism, were conquered by a young girl" (p. 264).

On her way home to France, Suzanne hears in New York that the
Armistice has been signed; and she sees pictures of the statesmen who
sign the historic document, all of whom seem to her to have sadly canine
features. And when she finally lands in France, and for the first time a
Frenchman approaches her, she feels a deep emotion, which is rudely
dashed when he announces himself as a Controller of Weights and
Measures. He is another Crusoe. She bursts into tears. Crusoe has
conquered after all.

A certain ambivalence toward the idea of the Controller is suggested by the fact that, in Giraudoux's later *Intermezzo* (1933), the heroine, Isabelle, *chooses* another such in order to bring stability into her life, and by the biographical fact that Giraudoux's own father was a civil servant.

Giraudoux often introduces figures from one of his works into another, and Suzanne writes letters from her island to "Simon," who is the more or less autobiographical hero of Giraudoux's earlier novel, *Simon le Pathétique*. This is one of the many ways in which Giraudoux stresses the playfulness and ambivalence of what he is saying. He was a writer very like Barrie in that way; Georges Lemaître has noted his "elusive, evasive, detached attitude to life."[7]

Connections

Like Psichari (and Tournier later), Giraudoux often used parody in retelling traditional stories. In his play *Amphitryon 38* (1929), the number 38 referred to the number of versions of the Alcmene myth that preceded his own, and his *The Trojan War Will Not Take Place* (1935) was a parody of the *Iliad*. But a closer comparison, as I have suggested, is with Barrie and *Peter Pan*. Both writers began with whimsical journalism, both liked to put children or adolescents at the center of their works, and both achieved a career as their homeland's leading middlebrow dramatist. Looked at personally, both also show an unhappy relationship to masculine maturity. Giraudoux's *Simon le Pathétique* corresponds to Barrie's equally autobiographical or confessional *Sentimental Tommie*. Both were devoted to their mothers and seem to have been locked into a long, perhaps a permanent, immaturity in consequence. And both were fascinated, but with ambivalent feelings, by stories of adventure and exploration like *Robinson Crusoe*. (Giraudoux wrote a play, *Supplément au voyage de Cook,* which is based on Diderot's *Supplément au voyage de Bougainville.*)

Barrie was significantly the older of the two, and already a successful writer in 1914, which perhaps explains why he remained nevertheless loyal to the national myth he so impudently mocked. (In the matter of

7. See Reilly, *Jean Giraudoux,* 19.

dates, and some traits of temperament, Giraudoux was closer to postwar British dandies, like, for instance, Osbert Sitwell.) But both he and Barrie were servants of the middle-class audience and yet antipathetic to the pharisees. Giraudoux's novel *Bella* (1926), for instance, describes two families of opposite moral styles. The preferred one is all feckless charm, the other "all upright, all intransigent, with their health and their work, and always dressed in black."[8] The latter operate only by rules, have unmitigated respect for the law, and see themselves as being totally honest. This antagonism toward "respectability" discharges itself in Giraudoux's work, as it does in Barrie's, in humor, whimsy, and the playful cult of adventure. And in *Suzanne et le Pacifique* he shows how clearly he recognizes *Robinson Crusoe* as a source of such pharisaical rectitude.

Michel Tournier's attraction to the Robinson story has similar sources, and there is an additional parallel between the two writers in that both were attracted to France's national enemy, Germany, and at times of severe national antagonism. It was of course German culture that attracted them, not Prussian or Nazi militarism. But it comes as a shock to read Tournier saying that in 1944 he turned away from the war to study Plato, "clothed, comforted, warmed, by the absolute conviction that Germany rightfully belonged to me, and would be given me at the desired moment, liberated from her Wehrmacht and her Nazis."[9] Both writers played with the subject of a captured French soldier who finds happiness as a prisoner in Germany and assumes a German identity. Giraudoux turned that idea into a very successful novel and play *(Siegfried)*. This undermining of nationalist politics runs parallel to the undermining of racial and gender superiority in the Suzanne novel.

Giraudoux had powerful allies among his contemporaries in his anti-Robinson work, allies who also made use of the island story reinterpreted. One of the most powerful images of freedom in the world of art and ideas was the life story of the painter Paul Gauguin, who left France to live on an island in the South Seas. He had felt from childhood on the desire to be an Indian or a "savage." This was part of his revolt against bourgeois culture. Like Giraudoux's Suzanne, he had read about the islands in the exotic novels of Pierre Loti. Quite the reverse of Robinson,

8. Ibid., 55.
9. Tournier, *Le vent paraclet*, 85.

he did not mean to teach the islanders anything, but to learn from them. When he finally set out for Tahiti, after years of planning the move and talking about it, he was forty-three. It was 1891, and the Symbolists of Paris gave him a farewell banquet, with speeches. Mallarmé spoke of Gauguin as an exemplary figure, a man superbly dedicated to art, who was seeking a new strength in this self-imposed exile. No one seems to have alluded there to Robinson Crusoe, but it is nonetheless clear that Gauguin's was designed to be a diametrically opposite enterprise.

On Tahiti Gauguin built a lifestyle that reversed nineteenth-century bourgeois values. He lived with a promiscuous girl, Tehaama, and accepted her infidelities. He learned to think of himself as *arioi,* one of the erotic priesthood of the islands, who had horrified Cook's contemporaries. Later he moved on, to the Marquesas, to rejuvenate himself in a setting of "savagery." His death there gave him a glamour comparable with that which John Williams gained from his island martyrdom, granted the opposite values of the two men's audiences.

Gauguin's story was retold for England by Somerset Maugham in his best-selling novel, *The Moon and Sixpence.* Indeed, many of Maugham's stories about the islands, especially those about white men who went native and found happiness, carried the same message as Gaugin's life story. This contradiction of so many eighteenth- and nineteenth-century messages became one of the truisms of 1920s art.

In Germany, on the other hand, a book was published just after the war that kept faith with the Robinson story even while it shared the French skepticism about society. This was the three-volume *Die Hoehlenkinder* (published 1918 to 1921) by "A.Th. Sonnleitner" (Alois Tluchor, 1869–1939). It is about a small boy and girl whose grandmother takes them, in order to save their lives from village enemies, to a secluded and uninhabited valley, where, after her death, they must learn to survive by themselves. Their technical expertise is at the level of the Stone Age, but they learn to make fire and to tame animals, and the boy (who takes on the dangerous and difficult tasks) begins to discover metallurgy. This story was very popular with German children of ten to sixteen, and reached a fifty-third edition in 1963. There was of course more poverty and disorder in Germany than in England or France in the years after 1918, and a strong movement to leave the cities and found communes. This story may perhaps be seen as a precursor of our contemporary adaptations of the Robinson story, to the theme of survival in a postnuclear wasteland. Giraudoux's book and Psichari's, however, must take up more space here because of the frankness of their dialectic. They show how the reaction against patriarchy after World War I could dramatize itself as a satire on the Robinson story.

13

Lord of the Flies (1954)

I n 1954 and 1958, soon after World War II, England produced two versions of the Robinson story that were as sardonic in their reversal of the original story's values as the two French versions produced after World War I. These were William Golding's *Lord of the Flies* and Muriel Spark's *Robinson*. Golding's, the more famous, was also much closer to the original. But they were alike in various ways; for instance, both mounted their attacks on Defoe's Protestant myth from a recognizably Catholic point of view. This had not been true of Giraudoux or Psichari, although, or because, they were writing in a Catholic country.

Perhaps one should call Spark and Golding's point of view not so much "Catholic" as that of the Catholic writer. This was a concept that had established itself in various European countries during the 1930s and 1940s—though it was much older than that in France—and had been strengthened by the experience of the war. In England it had been associated with the names of Graham Greene and Evelyn Waugh. In Spark's case we find the terms Protestant and Catholic used fairly openly, if somewhat paradoxically. Spark's literary career began under the protection—critical and financial—of Waugh and Greene. In Golding's case there was no such personal connection, and the "Catholic" ideology is recognizable mainly in his stress on original sin and his attacks on natural grace. Such attacks had been associated in earlier ages with Protestantism, but by the 1950s in England everyone understood them to be the mark of the "Catholic writer."

Such writing was a powerful strategy in the ongoing war between culture and civilization, between the artist and the pharisee, between Suzanne and Robinson. The Catholic writer felt himself besieged by post-Protestant civilization, with all his natural allies lost causes, as Catholicism itself was. He therefore represented culture, in the sense of a critical resistance to modern civilization. Thus the Robinson story, a myth of Protestant and progressive triumph, was his natural enemy.

It seems likely, however, that the loss of the empire was as potent a source of the anticivilization and antihumanist mood of English writers then as any revival of Catholicism. The acquisition of colonies and the practice of ruling them had been a powerful stimulus to English pride and vitality for more than 250 years. For much of that time England had been the greatest world power. The effects of the possession of an empire were to be felt throughout British civilization, in the political and educational systems, as well as in public buildings, music, paintings, and literature. Now it was gone, and it was felt to have been an intoxicant, a toxin. England had to go through a (still continuing) period of withdrawal.

As far as writers went, the embodiment of the empire in literature must have been one of the most potent ways in which it was felt; and of all literary forms, the adventure tale was the one most linked to empire. It was thus natural that many antiadventures should be written after 1945, and among them two anti-Robinsons. However, the surface ideology was religious or sectarian.

The concept of the Catholic writer developed in late nineteenth-century France (Léon Bloy was one of the originators). Such a writer, in fiction, described "out of date" Catholic practices like special devotions, the cult of the saints, the belief in miracles, obedience to priest and church, denial of divorce and birth control, and so on, plus "up to date" practices of secular, post-Protestant culture. He or she described both in such a way as to disturb any complacent assumption that the latter were superior. This was a development from black or Gothic romanticism, which had often been used against Enlightenment common sense and decent virtue. But the Catholic writers practiced a romanticism as much gray as black. Catholic ideas and practices were made to look, at the beginning of a story, dowdy and foolish next to their modern rivals. But by the end of the story it was the modern rivals that looked foolish. The apparently dowdy was revealed to be deeply true and powerful. (G. K. Chesterton's detective, Father Brown, is a neat example.) This scheme of effects appealed to a deep distrust of "progress," a moral anxiety about natural happiness and natural virtue, a deep distrust of everything that *Robinson Crusoe* promised.

In Catholic writers such as Graham Greene, François Mauriac, Evelyn Waugh, and T. S. Eliot, we soon recognize as Catholic a gray accumulation of defeat and decay, an atmosphere of hope and energy being buried in the humanly meager and meaningless. The defeat of virtue and talent and the successful malignancy of the environment—understood as townscape and climate, but also as culture and even psyche—all this, rendered as suffocation, dullness, and pathos. The writers are on the side of those characters who hate the world, even when they are the worst sinners.

This attitude affected their treatment of "innocent" adventurers, who in some sense love the world. There is, however, a paradox to note here: Greene and Waugh wrote sympathetically about men who, during World War II, reverted to the adventure attitudes they had learned as boys, and even to the adventure tales they then read. In *The Heart of the Matter* and *Men at Arms* we see such men renouncing their adult sophistication—the liberalism and libertinism of post-1918 England—and turning back to pre-1914 adventure. But this was a mockery of liberalism rather than an endorsement of adventure, at least of any Robinson kind. (Other adventure types had always been more compatible with Catholic angst because of their alienation from civilization; for instance, Greene said the war had taught us to take seriously John Buchan's warning that only a thin partition separates civilized life from barbarism.) The truth for these writers lay not in any revived Robinsonism, but in this paradoxical Catholicism, which could not have been more hostile to all edifying or optimistic adventure. The Crusoe story was always a potential Aunt Sally for Catholic ideologists, though Greene and Waugh never took aim directly at it themselves.

Golding proved himself their most successful heir. His oeuvre in fact includes two anti-Robinsons, for *Pincher Martin* takes on and subverts another aspect of Defoe's story. If *Lord of the Flies* is about a group of boys on a coral island, *Pincher Martin* is in some ways closer to Defoe, for it is about a solitary shipwrecked sailor, surviving, against odds, on a shelterless sea-bound rock. The sailor's experience, however, is in every way opposite to Robinson's, being physically and morally hideous, and it ends in death. Formally, moreover, this novel undermines the myth in another way, by revealing at the end that the whole sequence of days of survival was this sailor's hallucination, for he had died almost immediately. Thus formal realism itself is mocked. Golding seems driven by a vindictive hostility to the whole Robinson genre.

In Muriel Spark's story we have a literal Robinson living on a literal island. This Robinson is a Catholic (his full name is Miles Mary Robinson), but he is identified with Protestant rationalism, moral integrity, and barrenness of spirit. (He eats out of tins and makes nothing grow on his island.) A key symptom is that he, like the other male characters in the book (who are otherwise very unlike him), is hostile to the cult of the Virgin Mary and to the popular trust in her grace. He is also associated with the empire, for he was born in Gibraltar, and into a wealthy military family. He is thus a Protestant Crusoe figure, despite being nominally Catholic.

He lives alone on an island in the Azores, which he has bought from the Portuguese government, to be a retreat from the world and its corruptions. Its only visitors are the seasonal laborers who come to harvest the pomegranates that grow there. The narrator and protagonist of the story is a woman, as in Giraudoux's story. But Spark's representative is a born Protestant, newly choosing traditional Catholic values. Spark's story is, however, not so unlike Giraudoux's as that might suggest, for it has a strong strain of dandified frivolity. Like Giraudoux's and Golding's, moreover, it seems likely to have suggested some points to Tournier. Like *Vendredi,* for instance, this Robinson's island has a swampy place, called the Furnace, which gives access to caves underground, and which is so described as to seem one of the island's secret places, in a sexual or somatic sense.

The plot of Spark's book is too unlike Defoe's to reward our retelling it here. We will just note that her Robinson, disturbed in his retreat by the survivors of a plane crash, and distressed by the muddle and mess of "humanness" that they bring with them, disappears in circumstances that he contrives in order to make them suspect each other of murdering him, so that they set to murdering each other. This is a case of that typically Protestant or post-Protestant dislike of humanness, as the Catholic writer saw things.

Golding's Version

Spark's story is said to take place in 1954, the year of Golding's novel, and there are some hints in *Robinson* that Spark was inspired by some features of his story. For instance, the action in both begins with a plane crash. Golding's story is, however, a true rewriting of the Robinson material: of Ballantyne's *Coral Island* and Verne's *Deux ans de vacances* in particular. Golding shows us yet another group of British schoolboys marooned on a desert island, without supervision, and challenged, therefore, to show themselves true adventurers. But in his version the boys revert to savagery and murder. We gather that only civilization, corrupt though it is, saves human beings from always living like that. Both civilization and nature are corrupt; but civilization is merely feeble, while nature is evil.

Golding does not make anything of the story's themes of technical ingenuity or those of survival techniques. The boys build a fire, but the reader's attention is directed to the symbolic meaning of this activity, not to its practical achievement. The island supplies them with fruits, but the interest of that is in the diarrhea they cause, because that undercuts the romance of the boys' situation. This book's attention is all focused on the nightmarish moral possibilities of the castaway life— the hideous forces, political and moral, that would creep out of the darkness of the soul if civilization, that drab but necessary daylight, were removed.

Golding's Jack Mayhew is, like Ballantyne's Jack Martin, a natural leader; but (or so) Jack Mayhew is also a psychopath. Soon after meeting him we see that his eyes are restless, and we soon guess that he is morally mad. (Wartime propaganda about Hitler had taught the British to associate charismatic leadership with psychosis.) Ralph, the well-meaning but ineffectual representative of decent values, is no competition as a leader. He is the son of a naval officer, and the British officer class is Golding's symbol for the old-fashioned values that used to defend us against chaos but that, in a postimperial world, no longer do. While Ballantyne's charmer, Peterkin, renamed Piggy, is transformed into a fat, clumsy Cockney swot, like a degenerated Jeremy Bentham or one of H. G. Wells's satiric self-depictions; the embodiment of graceless and pathetic rationality, admirable inside the walls of a city, but useless in a landscape of savagery.

It is the familiar island, and the boys have the familiar survival and rescue problems. Like Verne's castaways, Golding's solve the problem of fire with a piece of curved glass. But this time the glass comes from Piggy's glasses, fragile emblem of the civilized life, without which he is blind and defenseless. Ralph institutes a perpetually burning fire to act as signal to any ships that may be passing, and this is the boys' only hope of rescue and return to civilization. (The book works largely by means of symbols, and fire is perhaps the major one, with its manifold anthropological meanings.) But the boys assigned by Ralph to keep the fire burning are inspired by Jack to want to be hunters instead, a concept associated with tribalism and paint and meat orgies and killing rituals— associated ultimately with the worship of the Beast, the bestial principle divinized. They are reluctant and inefficient guardians of the fire, linked as it is to domestic and settlement values.

It is that bestial principle which has authority over men; that divinization is their doing. When Simon thought about the Beast, "there rose before his inward sight the picture of a human at once heroic and sick" (p. 121). Simon is the most spiritually gifted of the boys, and it is to him that the Lord of the Flies speaks his meaning. The Lord of the Flies, a dead pig's head, seething with insect life, is one of the forms the Beast takes. The boys, though heirs to the empire and the Enlightenment, fall down and worship the evil principle. In Golding's world the mad and evil are naturally stronger. (If the good is to triumph, or even to maintain equilibrium, it will have to be by means outside nature.) Thus at various moments Jack seems to have been defeated. His childishness and craziness have been exposed to the general view, as Hitler's were. But each time the majority finally follow him. They *prefer* evil. The criteria of common sense and common decency cannot command any fervent loyalty. (They used to, or we thought they did, when the sun never set on the British Empire.) First Simon and then Ralph are made into scapegoats and hunted like pigs by the whole tribe. Piggy is crushed to death by a giant rock, which one of his playmates deliberately sends rolling down upon him.

Finally, the adult world returns in the form of an officer in naval whites. He speaks to them in the accents of Ballantyne or Marryat, accents that sound hollow to those who have just read Golding. " 'I should have thought', said the officer, looking at the boys uncomprehendingly, 'I should have thought that a pack of British boys—you're all British, aren't you?—would have been able to put up a better show than that ' " (p. 184). And the boys respond. They become again normal and decent schoolboys. But of course the reader, warned off by the upper-class jargon, if by nothing else, can draw no comfort from this ending. The officer and the other adults are in the middle of a war with nuclear weapons, which is hardly a better show.

Golding insists on our seeing that there is no security in adulthood. "The theme," he spells out, "is an attempt to trace the defects of society back to the defects of human nature. The moral is that the shape of society must depend on the ethical nature of the individual. . . . [A]dult life appears, dignified and capable, but in reality enmeshed in the same evil as the symbolic life of the children on the island. The officer, having interrupted a man-hunt, prepares to take the children off the island, in a cruiser which will presently be hunting its enemy in the same implacable way. And who will rescue the adult and his cruiser?" (p. 186).

During the war, Golding was in command of a rocket ship, and he describes the war as having been a cold-blooded genocide. Before that experience, he says, he believed in perfectibility. That is to say, he believed in what Piggy believed in, and to some degree in what the officer believes in—the Enlightenment ethos—like Ballantyne, Defoe, and the Robinson story. But *Lord of the Flies,* like Spark's *Robinson,* is an attack on that faith.

In 1989 Marianne Wiggins published a revision of Golding's story with a female cast of characters, titled *John Dollar.* Her story begins in 1917, when Charlotte Lewes, a war widow, went to Burma to teach the daughters of Raj officials and took as lover a sea captain called John Dollar. To celebrate a King's Birthday, three English ships sailed to an unclaimed Andaman Island to name it as King George's. A tsunami wrecks the ships, the boys die, the parents are captured by savages, Charlotte disappears, but the girls live on. They see their parents canni-balized, and some of them learn the lesson too well. They find and look after Dollar, who is paralyzed from the waist down but can give them some instructions about survival. But the two leaders, who alone minis-ter to him directly, begin cutting off flesh from his covered-up legs and eating it, unknown to their friends. When Charlotte finds them, she kills the girls. The story is embellished with quotations from Defoe and Kipling, but also from Cavafy and Leonardo da Vinci.

Since we are likely to assume that this version of the myth (the Golding/Spark/Wiggins version) is the only one to be found in the modern world, it is worth calling attention to an autobiography published in 1966 by Tom Neale. This is a New Zealander's account of how he chose to live alone on a South Seas island (one of the Cook chain, named after the famous explorer) for a number of years. By his own account, which is confirmed by the testimony of those who finally took him off the island, he maintained his self-respect and his engagement in the social contract, in dignifying the human condition, throughout his solitude, as successfully as Defoe's hero is said to do. But the world of letters has found more authority in Golding's fable of atavism, because it fits their preconceptions, and their doctrine of disillusion.

14

Vendredi: ou Les limbes du Pacifique (1967)

s we have seen in discussing Giraudoux and Psichari, France has long been a home to playful and ironic treatments of the Robinson material. One could examine other cases, like Paul Valéry's revision of the story as one of his *Histoires brisées,* or Jules Supervielle's "Robinson ou l'Amour vient du loin" of 1952 (published together with "La belle au bois dormant," which suggests its fantasy character). But then in the 1960s came a treatment that was both more thoroughgoing and more clearly in touch with contemporary ideas, and so in some sense more serious—though also in another sense the most "decadent" of all. This was Michel Tournier's *Vendredi,* and to call it decadent is not to make a moral judgment against it, but to acknowledge what the author meant in calling himself the Huysmans of his generation.

The book can be read as a satiric response to Rousseau and *Emile* almost as much as to Defoe. One of Tournier's main targets is manhood, and humanity defined through manhood, which was of course evoked most eloquently by Rousseau. Let me recall a familiar passage from *Emile:* "Before his parents chose a calling for him, nature called him to be a man. Life is the trade I would teach him. When he leaves me, I grant you, he will be neither a magistrate, a soldier, nor a priest; he will be a man."[1] It is just that proud confidence that Tournier works to undermine, seeing it as implicit propaganda for an imperialist worldview. He undermines that philosophy by reinterpreting the story to take the advantage away from Robinson and give it to Friday. The cult of manliness (implicitly masterful, implicitly white) seems to have been more tied to the Robinson Crusoe story in France than elsewhere; the word "man" was one of the keynotes of Verne's rhetoric also, so it makes sense for Tournier to focus his attack there.

In his book of autobiographical essays, *Le vent paraclet,* Tournier makes several attacks on *Emile.* For instance, he blames the book for its Protestant stress on conscience as an instinct to be cultivated, a cult that, during the Enlightenment, undermined the older idea of Sophia, *sagesse,* wisdom. Conscience is the moral motor that drives man in his manliness, while Sophia lifts one above gender. And he blames the whole Enlightenment theory of education for concentrating on instruction or information and undermining the older idea of initiation. The latter idea allowed for different kinds of humanness, appropriate at different life states and for different genders. The former is built on a dangerously narrow and single idea of man.

Thus the Enlightenment theory of education (for instance, Rousseau's or Campe's) assumes that a child is already "human," whereas aristocratic and primitive theorists more wisely assume that the child is animal until initiated. Tournier speaks often in defense of children and against our too high and "antiseptic" expectations of them. "Their distress is the invention of a society ferociously anti-physical, mutilating, and castrating, and no-one can make us doubt that certain character problems, explosions of violence, even juvenile drug-addiction, are sequels to the physical desert to which our habits exile the child and the adolescent."[2]

Tournier is thus an ally of Michel Foucault and Roland Barthes in their attacks on "man," "humanity," and "humanism." Like them, he is looking for an escape from these self-flattering and self-falsifying generalizations. He was born in 1924 and lived through the war and the Occupation in Paris. The experience was especially painful, and perhaps ambiguous to him, because his parents came from Alsace and spoke

---

1. See note 1 to chapter 3.
2. Tournier, *Vendredi,* 26.

German. Immediately after the war, he spent three years in Germany, and he has written often about German literature. He and Giraudoux are two of the French men of letters most influenced by German writers and thinkers, and, as we have seen, this seems to be connected with a profound ambivalence in them about issues of patriotism, and therefore of manliness. It is ultimately connected with their ironic attitude to the Robinson myth.

Tournier has a lot to say about myth. "A myth is both a beautiful and profound story embodying one of mankind's essential adventures, and a miserable lie produced by a mental deficient, a 'mythomaniac' in the true sense."[3] This doubleness of face guarantees myth's vitality and authenticity. Thus Tournier says it is misleading to distinguish between the truth and the fictionality of myths. They celebrate man's inability to adapt to society; they are a celebration of the outcast (p. 132). The great examples he cites, besides Robinson, are Don Quixote, Tristan and Iseult, Faust, and Don Juan. Thus he is more responsive to the Robinson story than others who have satirized it. He grants it the dignity of myth. But he is just as hostile to what the founding fathers of that story, like Rousseau and Defoe, made of it. Indeed, we are bound to note, reading that list of mythic heroes, that Robinson is quite unlike the other examples he cites, in his fictional realism as well as in his rational consciousness; and that to assimilate him to them is to attenuate his factual presence as much as to glorify his fictional or legendary quality.

Tournier has been described as a middlebrow writer, but he sees himself as a surrealist, though he says he interprets surrealism the way painters rather than writers have understood it. In other words, his writing subverts the idea of reality by means of an overpolished, and "academic," surface realism. He has also been said to write nineteenth-century novels about twentieth-century themes. But, as that epigram indeed suggests, his is a characteristically twentieth-century—late twentieth-century—mind. The poststructuralist critic Gilles Deleuze is a longtime friend of his and wrote an essay on *Vendredi,* which was published with that novel. Indeed, Tournier was a student of philosophy, and in his early years read the same books, and in the same way as Foucault, Derrida, Barthes, and so on—the generation after Lévi-Strauss. One reviewer said that *Vendredi* was Defoe rewritten by Freud, Lévi-Strauss, and Walt Disney. He himself said that he put into the book all

---

3. Tournier, *Le vol du vampire,* 12.

he learned from years of study at the Musée de l'Homme, and especially from Lévi-Strauss. (He had hoped, he said, to be the Hegel of his generation but is now resigned to being the Huysmans.) This link with the avant-garde shows itself in his profound social skepticism but also in his sexual doctrine.

In *Vendredi* sexual regression turns out to be a form of growth, and the best form of sex is polymorphous perversity.[4] His later novel, *Le roi des Aulnes,* is described on the flyleaf as offering a new model of nongenital sex. Tournier thus takes a place in the band of crusaders against genitality and that earlier bogy of sexual liberation, sublimation. In *L'Anti-Oedipe* Deleuze and Guattari say that sublimation is completely anal, and that it is the anal personality that always sublimates. They associate this with the biblical figure of Abel, the nomadic hunter, and the enmity between him and Cain is a myth also dear to Tournier. Cain is the hero now. Abel says, "Me, Me, Me, I am a powerful nature, an irritated and aggressive nature" (p. 52). To be engaged in contradictions, even self-contradictions, is what energizes such natures. Robinson Crusoe is another of those.

Tournier won a prize from the Académie française for this version of the Crusoe story, and he has returned to the same material in other books. Since he is a member of the generation of intellectuals now dominating France's intellectual life, and also one of its best-regarded contemporary novelists, his book forms a temporary climax to our story, showing the power of the Crusoe story still to attract around it the resentments and anxieties of the contemporary literary mind.

Tournier's Version

Tournier's main innovation in, or adaptation of, the Robinson story is sexual. His version is heterodox simply for *being* sexual, but also for describing a nonheterosexual and even nongenital sexuality. In two of the most vivid episodes in the book, his Robinson has sex with the island. He first glides down into a little rock cave and (having previously

4. Cloonan, *Michael Tournier,* 29.

coated himself with milk) curls up there.[5] And later he embraces and fecundates a patch of pinkish swamp, generating mandragoras (p. 137). (An example of what Tournier means by his careful surrealism is perhaps that he first made sure that mandragoras do in fact grow on Juan Fernández.)

What has been said so far might suggest the wholly rose-colored frivolity of Giraudoux, but Tournier's reader is bound to feel a sharper unease than that, and in other episodes that unease is unequivocal. In conscious decadence, Robinson wallows in another, mosquito-haunted swamp, which is also a manure pit for peccavis, until "a crust of dry excrement covered his back, his sides, and his thighs. . . . His nose in the dirt, he ate unspeakable things" (pp. 37–38). There is, moreover, a horrible malice in Tournier's nature, quite unlike Giraudoux's. We meet a squid that squirts poison in Robinson's face, termites who eat away his boat, crabs who use their pincers as saws. This is of course emotionally black, but the book's moral philosophy prizes the light, if in no traditional fashion. Toward the end Robinson addresses a prayer to the sun. But the sun is for him not only the source of light but of lightness, of superficiality, of an escape from reality. "Sun, deliver me from gravity. Wash my blood free from its thick humours . . . which spoil the surge of my youth and snuff out my joy in living" (p. 217). He believes in grace, but that is something that—in the Pacific—comes in physical as much as spiritual form. "Instruct me in irony. Teach me lightness, the laughing acceptance of this day's immediate gifts. . . . Sun, make me like Friday" (ibid.).

This declaration is, as the book's title suggests, its climax in terms of ideas. Robinson now wants to learn how to be Friday. Defoe's assumption that the white man is superior to the black, and has everything to teach him, is defeated and reversed. However, this proposition is less likely to strike or startle the reader than the erotic suggestions. For a good fifty years, readers have been taught to take for granted the aspiration of white men to be—partially and playfully—black. There are hints of this in earlier Robinsons, for instance, in Psichari and Giraudoux. A concentrated expression of the idea is D. H. Lawrence's poem "Tropic," written at the same moment as those novels.

5. Tournier, *Vendredi*, 105.

> Sun, dark sun . . .
> Behold my hair twisting and going black.
> Behold my eyes turn tawny yellow
> Negroid;
> See the milk of northern spume
> Coagulating and going black in my veins
> Aromatic as frankincense . . .[6]

Tournier has nothing really new to say on this topic, which has been cultivated by the Western imagination for quite a long time.

Tournier's analysis of Robinson's character begins in the book's first scene, before the storm and the wreck, when Crusoe sits smoking with the ship's (Dutch) captain, who is described as "a solvent intelligence and cynical epicureanism."[7] Captain van Deyssel, in his judgment on Robinson, in some sense represents the author. He shows Robinson a pack of Tarot cards, which includes the Demiurge, who struggles against the disorder in the universe, and Mars, whom van Deyssel calls "King Robinson" (p. 7).

Robinson is presented as being twenty-two (much younger than Defoe's hero) and as having a wife and children at home in York. He has a shaven head and a square red beard. He is a Roundhead in seventeenth-century terms, a square in twentieth-century terms. His glance is described by the captain: "Your clear gaze, very direct, but with a something fixed and limited in it. . . . You are pious, miserly, and pure" (p. 8). Purity, as we would have guessed, turns out to be no good thing from this author's point of view, any more than from the captain's. It is another sign of moral and emotional avarice. Any place of which Robinson was king, says the captain, would become a store-cupboard, which is of course what Defoe's island did become.

Other Tarot cards with a symbolic significance for Tournier are the Hermit, Chaos, Saturn (who hangs upside down), Jupiter, the Solar City, and finally Gemini. The last depicted two children, hand in hand, and attached to a bisexual angel, the emblem of a "circular," intransitive sexuality. These cards suggest the themes of the story Tournier is going to tell. Indeed, they announce other books by Tournier too. And taken not individually but as the Tarot pack, they announce his taste for the

6. *Complete Poems of D. H. Lawrence*, 301.
7. Tournier, *Vendredi*, 9.

occult, for the anti-Enlightenment strains in our culture. (In Spark's *Robinson,* one of the men wrecked on the island has a salesman's sample case of lucky charms, which function somewhat similarly in her plot.)

The captain says to Robinson, "Crusoe, listen to me carefully; beware of purity. It is the vitriol of the soul" (p. 14). This announces the dominant theme in Tournier's attack on the traditional Robinson and his ethos. Such a man is doomed to produce and accumulate, at any cost to his psyche. Robinson reflects that the same is true of his compatriots founding the American colonies (p. 61). History is always made by just such "disinterested" men, who bring fire and death with them. In this version the wreck takes place off Juan Fernández, but in the year 1759, roughly a century later than Defoe's. This change enables Tournier to refer to later developments of Enlightenment thinking. For instance, his Robinson knows the works of Benjamin Franklin, one of Defoe's closest heirs, and in fact inscribes Franklin's moral slogans all over his island. The reader thus gets some sense of the whole Enlightenment as being indicted in the course of the indictment of Robinson.

The first actions of Tournier's Robinson follow the Defoe pattern quite closely. The first thing he sees on the island is a goat, which he kills. The island is recognizably the same island. He quotes severe biblical texts; his mother is said to have been a Quaker. And like Defoe's hero he passes through the stages of civilized development. "Like the humanity of earlier times, he had passed from the stage of gathering and hunting to that of agriculture and crops" (p. 47). But he is, as this quotation reminds us, more conceptually self-conscious than Defoe's Robinson. He writes in his logbook, "My situation tells me to put the *most* into virtue and the *least* into vice, and to call virtue courage, force, the affirmation of myself, domination over things" (p. 81). His language is obviously close to Tournier's own. "The island was thus criss-crossed by a network of interpolations and extrapolations which differentiated it and endowed it with intelligibility" (p. 54).

These developments, however, are all true to Defoe's idea of his story, however different the tone. But we should note that Tournier is not really interested in the techniques of survival. For instance, Crusoe carries a tinderbox with him when he gets ashore, so the crucial anxiety about fire, so important to early Robinsons, has no place. How to make fire is a theme, a reality theme, which anti-Robinsons cannot afford to sound. In this way Tournier resembles Giraudoux and Psichari. What makes him different, and weightier, is the quality in his mind represented by the hardness and harshness of Crusoe's natural environment. The "reality" this Crusoe defies and flouts is more dangerous than Suzanne's or Yanni's—more like reality.

His Crusoe, moreover, alternates between realistic perceptions and mythical or fantastic ones, between regular work and hallucinatory idleness. The latter draws him to the swamp and the cave-womb and self-degradation. The author divides Robinson's time on the island into three periods, and associates the first with the swamp, *la souille*. This is followed by a period in which he regains control of himself and subdues nature to his purposes. The associated name or idea is administration—*l'Ile administrée*. Afraid of living "out of time," Robinson dresses to dine, admired by his dog, and issues a charter forbidding defecation except at appointed places (p. 72). Of course the reader thinks of British colonial officers and the legend of their dressing for dinner in the tropics. When Friday arrives on the island, Robinson makes him his paid valet and worries about his spiritual inertia.

Friday is a fifteen-year-old black boy who laughs a lot. He dresses the cacti in fashionable European clothes, as if he were a surrealist artist (p. 154). He plants trees upside down and hides himself, his naked body disguised as a tree trunk, in clumps of flowers. Delighting in the flight of his arrows, he refuses to think they must fall to earth somewhere. Robinson is disconcerted by such nonseriousness, but gradually he learns to appreciate Friday's beauty and life wisdom. He comes to realize that Friday is not, like himself, a will, but something better—a nature (p. 181). And when Friday accidentally blows up Robinson's fortifications, Robinson suddenly gives up all he has worked to achieve and decides to learn from Friday how to live (p. 183). Now begins the third period of the story, associated by Tournier with the sun and ecstasy, *l'extase solaire*.

Robinson lets his hair grow long and becomes bronzed and strong, like Psichari's Robinson. "Give me Friday's face," he begs the sun, "opened up by laughter, entirely shaped by laughter. . . . but if my Aeolian comrade draws me to him, is it not to turn me towards you? Sun, are you pleased with me? Look at me" (p. 221). When he sees Friday coming toward him, "Here he is. Shall I ever be able to walk with such natural majesty? . . . He carries his flesh with sovereign ostentation." (p. 228). Friday becomes Robinson's twin, in Gemini. He is not the object of Robinson's desire but the other pole in the circuit of their joint desire, and they energize each other. In a sort of apotheosis we see

Robinson perfectly suntanned. "The tawny light dressed him in an implacable armour, in which his diamond eyes sparkled. . . . His chest curved out like a buckler of bronze" (p. 255).

Such images are familiar enough to contemporary readers from travel and holiday advertising, but they are given a dignifying intellectuality here by means of certain theories of "the other." Each individual's awareness of others shapes and limits his or her perceptions of everything else, including him- or herself. This is what Psichari called "synanthropie." "The other is a potent distraction factor. . . . [His presence] throws a vague light on a universe of objects situated on the edge of our attention" (p. 36). We become distracted from ourselves. Deleuze's essay on *Vendredi* is entitled "Michel Tournier and the World without Others."

Deleuze's argument is that this absence of others is a "perversity" (in the enthusiastic sense these thinkers give to that term: de Sade has taught them all to be interested in perversity). Tournier's Robinson becomes dehumanized and elemental by means of this "deviation." The "implacable armour," the bronze-statue look his days on the beach give him, is the outward sign of his escape from ordinary human fleshliness. The presence of the other is a prerequisite of humanity or normality. Robinson escapes from that identity and from all its drives and dimensions. He discovers superficiality and discards the illusions of depth and weight. Those moral qualities, so suggestive of nineteenth-century humanism as a whole, have been the bêtes noires of dandy and avant-garde writers for a century. Friday was already superficial, and that is why he could be a twin to Robinson, a double and not an other.

Deleuze points out that Defoe's Robinson was determined (limited) to become again on his island what he had been before in England. Tournier's Robinson, on the other hand, is becoming something new and different. That is the formula of triumph: the new—it is implicit— is not merely different from the old; it is real, while the other was fake. And it was because of his determination to stay the same that Defoe excluded sex from his story. Sex is a principle of fantasy strong enough to upset the economic order, the economic reality principle. That is why sex is given so large a part in Tournier's version. Its playfulness is the same thing as its seriousness.

We are probably safe to connect this idea of eliminating the other with another idea less explicit in the story but equally fashionable with the same thinkers. This is the idea of "dissemination," with its suggestions of masturbatory rather than generative sex. Tournier's Robinson realizes that within civilization desire is usually directed by society and imprisoned in a will. But his is now unchanneled. "It overflows in every direction and spreads out like a star" (p. 119). Desire is fulfilled in its own feeling and separated from its "object." The connection between this idea and that about the elimination of the other is that both have the aim of breaking the chains of reciprocity that constitute society and therewith traditional humanity, and of exploding the complementary firm ego. It is a part of "deconstruction" to undermine all traditional notions of individual responsibility and "heroic" posture, which have their ultimate source in sublimated or genital sex. At his story's end, Tournier tells us, "Robinson has seen the ruin of the social constructs to which he owed, notably, his patriarchal sexuality."[8]

This aspiration can be called post-Freudian in that many of its advocates have pointed to Freud's stress on the ambivalence of all emotions, their readiness to switch to their own opposites, and then have pointed to the distrust of moral aggression that that perspective should bring. In America Norman O. Brown, in *Life Against Death,* and Philip Rieff, in *The Triumph of the Therapeutic,* advanced similar ideas. By making the outlines of the ego vague and fluid, and by destroying the dramatic and rhetorical self-definition of the emotions, this mode of analysis promises to save man from his self-righteous (and bloodstained) history. That righteous history is celebrated, though in mythic and idyllic disguise, in *Robinson Crusoe,* so this post-Freudianism can be another weapon in the battery attacking Defoe's story.

It is notable how much of an epitome or anthology of anti-Robinson devices we find in Tournier: devices used by Spark, Golding, Lawrence, Psichari, and Giraudoux. His book is a reverse image of Verne's *L'Ile mystérieuse,* with its anthology of Robinsonisms. Tournier also speaks in harmony with the whole cosmetic, film, and holiday industries. We are told, and it is appropriate, that the author conceived the idea of his book while on a Club Méditerranée holiday. His relation to the contemporary reading audience is as close as Defoe's was to his, despite his fashionable intellectual vocabulary.

So great was Tournier's success that he was able to publish a child's version of his book, and this too was translated into English, as *Friday and Robinson: Life on Speranza Island.* From this, however, the bolder

8. Tournier, *Le vent paraclet,* 118.

and grosser sexual fantasies that gave *Vendredi* its character have been eliminated. So have the Tarot cards and the images of nature's malice. What is preserved is the nowadays orthodox stress on the importance of Friday; plus a new appreciation of Robinson's virtues, which are of course the virtues of Defoe's Robinson. In other words, in most ways, it is a faithful rewrite and modernization of *Robinson Crusoe*. Thus Defoe triumphed over Tournier, and the story triumphed over the teller (as it had done over Swift long before), because when we are thinking of our children and the heritage we bequeath them, we still prefer Defoe. As parents we believe, it seems, in those "virtues" that we mock in our role as readers.

Tournier has said he would have liked to dedicate the book to the migrant workers in contemporary France: to "all these Fridays sent to us by the third world, these three million Algerians, Moroccans, Tunisians, Senegalese, Portuguese, on whom our society rests, and whom one never sees. . . . [O]ur society is seated upon them. . . . [T]hey have nothing to say. . . . [T]he only real proletariat that exists in France."[9]

This gesture of orthodox political orientation, were it developed in the novel, would make *Vendredi* a political story of a modernist kind. But in fact Tournier is postmodernist. The major ideological thrust of his story is toward deconstruction, and thus away from ordinary seriousness. Its attack on our culture is philosophical and imaginative, and for that reason is appropriately aimed at that culture's founding myths, such as *Robinson Crusoe*.

9. Ibid., 230.

15

Conclusion

I have traced a line running for two hundred and fifty years, from Defoe in 1719 to Tournier in 1967, a line of the interpretations of the Robinson story, from being, at its origin, a proclamation of progressive values, to being, at its conclusion, a repudiation of them. But this line would be, if I left it unmodified, a fiction. It links together a number of famous versions of the story, but takes for granted that these are the ones that deserve attention. I have constructed it by arranging the evidence; or rather I have allowed the world of letters to establish the authors' reputations, and so to select which cases I was to examine and how much weight to give to each. A different selection could be made and would tell quite a different story.

It is almost inevitable, in literary studies, that the scholar allows "tradition" to preselect the authors and books from which he takes his topics. This is not so much a practical convenience, reducing his labors, as an acknowledgment of his immediate audience, the community of scholars. They want to test the speaker by his treatment of *their* topics; and so the familiar items keep recurring and always outweigh the unfamiliar. Moreover, there is no clear advantage to refusing that

collaboration. If one turned away from the canon and—in this case—
read all the Robinsons that ever got into print, one still would not know
how many more had perished in manuscript (publishers perform the first
preselection) and how many were elaborated just orally. (How many
*Swiss Family Robinson*s remained just family entertainments?)

And suppose one read the thousands that did get into print. How in
practice would one choose which ones to write about? Should it be "the
best by literary standards"? Surely "those most read" have as many
claims for an inquiry of this kind. No doubt one would discover some
jewels—little known versions that are better than the famous ones. That
has certainly been my experience. But most, almost certainly, would
come, as mine did, out of the old list. That is because the criteria of the
genre have been established, step by step, by the famous ones, by *fame*.
Surely the most any scholar can do is to renew, reanimate, tradition by
adding or subtracting a few items or a principle or a method? The
tradition in itself we may as well accept, mixed blessing as it is in
concept, and mistaken as it is in particular cases.

Perhaps it is a more important criticism that I have simplified my data
and produced a pattern in it by choosing this organizing scheme of a
series of versions of the story, advancing through time. I have looked for
a steady sequence in dates of publication. This is a fiction insofar as it
implies that over two hundred and fifty years there has been a steady
diminution of faith in progressive values (and so in the Robinson story)
and a steady growth of skeptical wisdom. We could never prove anything
like that in general. All of society does not march in step. To make even
a plausible proposition, we must name the groups in whom that faith
died or diminished.

For instance, in 1955 a book was published in London called *The
Gospel of Robinson Crusoe*. This is a collection of sermons by a
Methodist minister, built around the Robinson story, which he called
the throbbing record of a spiritual pilgrimage. According to the historical
scheme I have traced, that book was simply out of date. It was a mere
oddity. Any audience it may have had in 1955 must have belonged to a
special group, out of step with the majority. This still seems to me an
acceptable assumption; but it is definitely an assumption, which dis-
counts a book that after all did appear and may have been read, for all I
know, by many thousands of people, all responding deeply to it.
(Another example is that New Zealand story of a happy and successful
Robinson experience that came out in the 1960s.) My assumption

derives ultimately from the consensus (or what I think is the consensus) of the group I belong to—men and women of letters.

Thus the group to which my historical generalizations aspire to apply can be specified as "the world of letters." But even if I restrict to that group my proposition about the development of the Robinson story— from a faith in progress to a doubt—it is not wholly true. For the first decade after *Robinson Crusoe* was published offers us a mocking dissent from the story's message, just as knowing as Tournier's. Men of letters of Swift's kind did not need two hundred and fifty years to realize or to express the strength of their dislike for Defoe's story and its ideology. The pro-and-con dialectic we have seen in the various versions of the story is a matter of a permanent opposition between sets of contemporary cultural interests as much as of any conflict of eighteenth-century values with twentieth-century ones. (This is the synchronic, in a sense structuralist, view of the matter.)

Indeed there were, as I have said, versions of the story written before Defoe wrote his, and some of those were just as skeptical as any of the twentieth-century retellings about the ability of a shipwrecked man to survive, or at least to triumph, alone on an island. The most lurid of those known to me is by Garcilaso de la Vega, about Central America in the time of the conquistadores. There was also, within *Simplicissimus,* a version of the story as full of moral anxiety and the fear of sin as the tale Golding told. And there was, in *The Isle of Pines,* a version as lighthearted as Giraudoux's.

We might indeed see Defoe's story as the exception rather than the rule—as a bold, temporary defiance of the traditional ways of imagining this story. His version expressed the extraordinary hopes and confidence of the English merchants and adventurers of his day—a group in a very favorable situation—when the capitalist ethos was first establishing itself. Swift's story, on the other hand, expressed the doubts and anxiety of the English clerisy, those who guarded the "values" of their society. Values in this sense are always defensive and backward-looking, defensive about new modes of action and new expansions of pride. To put it another way, Defoe spoke for the expanding civilization of his time, Swift for the contracting and critical culture; for the saving remnant, those who stand back from the battlefield, the marketplace, and the hustings to criticize the men of action and the way they justify themselves. The conflict over the Robinson story therefore is a conflict between two groups always to be found in the world of letters, whom I have called the pharisees and the Galileans. And the conflict has consequences in literary status as well as in ideology. Defoe was one of those consigned to Grub Street, and refused entry to Parnassus, by Swift and his friends.

But before we examine this literary conflict further, let me make the point of how many meanings Defoe's story can have, and how many ideological affiliations. The major drive we have attributed to it was a furthering of British imperial expansion and of the socioeconomic forces that built it up. But we see that connection partly because of the way history has gone since. Perhaps we see that connection also because those forces needed imaginative and ideological forms (stories, images, concepts, theories) to explain them. They in a sense seized on the Robinson story to serve their purposes. We can see Rousseau's editing of the story as an example of that. (Of course it is also true that Defoe himself was personally committed to capitalist institutions and ideas, but even if he had not been, Rousseau and his followers might have given the story that meaning.)

The story in itself has other and almost opposite meanings. For instance, it is about a man tapping hidden resources in himself, and expanding personally when the support systems of his culture are withdrawn, to replace them by his own wit and willpower. This is not necessarily an imperialist or capitalist story. It can be felt as profoundly egalitarian. Defoe saw all the forces he thought of as imperialist, like the empire of Spain and the Roman Catholic Church, as being the enemies of men like Crusoe.

In the years since 1719, moreover, many people have drawn anti-imperialist inspiration from the story, including nonwhite people. One example is Gandhi in South Africa, where in 1909 he set up a farm for *satyagrahis* and their families, with everyone making and doing everything for himself. Gandhi thought of this as living the Robinson life and described *satyagraha* as adventure. In our own day, if we ask where we find the Robinson story being retold most interestingly, the answer seems to be in stories of postnuclear survival. When an individual or a small group has to pick up the pieces of our shattered civilization and tries to make use of them in radically new circumstances, it is the myth of Robinson that carries the writer and the reader through the horrors and promises some satisfactions and some rewards.

Along with Defoe, however, his story was exiled from "literature," and it is a subject that ambitious writers have largely avoided, except in mockery or in nostalgia. We do not find the great novelists of England, from Richardson through Jane Austen, George Eliot, and Henry Fielding to D. H. Lawrence, writing Robinson stories. It is not part of the Great Tradition and is only a peripheral part of the main history of literature. On the other hand, it is not entirely absent from that history, as this study makes clear. Because Western civilization demanded, indeed consumed and paid for, so many versions of the tale, men of letters were constantly drawn back to it, as readers if not as writers, feeling a mixture of responses—nostalgia for their childhood reading, indignation against a dangerous myth, boredom with the "unimaginative" virtues of Crusoe, or a romantic longing for islands and solitude.

So, to sum up, some other lines connect these stories with each other and with certain large cultural forces that cut across what I have called the main line—that which runs from Defoe's naïveté to Tournier's sophistication. For instance, there are the lines opposing culture to civilization, and those opposing literature to popular reading. These lines of force mesh, some almost at right angles to others. Nevertheless, the main line seems to be justified in its fictive preeminence. The story *does* develop from naive faith to doubt and satire. The proof of that does not lie in the number of satiric versions in the twentieth century— numbers are hard to use convincingly in literary arguments. But we are surely bound to see each writer as likely to be learning from his predecessors, and so as becoming more sophisticated in his treatment of the story. We are bound to do so, for one reason, because the writers so often tell us that that is happening. Nearly all of them claim to be correcting a precursor. Moreover, there is no question that all these writers were deeply affected by Defoe's story, and most of them by post-Defoe versions also.

Thus we are bound to see the story as developing historically as it is retold, and the direction of that development is bound to seem to be toward greater truth. We can deconstruct that truth, which is indeed an illusion created by "culture"; but as long as we continue to operate within the circle of culture, it is an illusion, or a hypothesis, an assumption, we have to return to, to act as if it were true. We have to if we are to deal in history at all. For instance, many events in the history of empire and literature correspond to this idea of gradual disillusionment. Certainly the general reputation of imperialism today is very bad. And clearly anti-Robinson writers have felt freer to mock and subvert the story in the twentieth century. How could we possibly think about the sequence of these stories (as distinct from the stories in themselves) except in these terms of growth and decay? In the late nineteenth century, for example, the story clearly had a period of decadence. We have marked that in Ballantyne and Barrie, seeing the story dissolved in the general topic, adventure, and so surrounded with indulgent laughter and nostalgia that it could no longer be taken seriously.

This does not necessarily mean decay of literary quality. Barrie cannot be dismissed by any such formula, nor can Richard Jefferies. One of the most striking cases in which we see the story dissolving is Jefferies's *Bevis* of 1882. This is an extraordinary piece of writing and a precursor for both Kipling and Lawrence. But Bevis, Jefferies's autobiographical hero, who plays at being Robinson, among another things, appeals to the reader all the time as a figure of sensual charm—and that charm circumscribes the adventure. The subtitle is *The Story of a Boy,* and Bevis is always shouting with delight, running like the wind, bathing in the nude. "The sunlight poured upon them, the light air came along; they bathed in air and sunshine, and gathered years of health like flowers from the field."[1] The story expresses a powerful narcissism.

In other of Jefferies's books this vein of feeling is made more explicit. In *Story of My Heart* (1883), "I held my hand so that I could see the sunlight gleam on the surface of the skin. The earth and the sun were to me like my flesh and blood, and the air of the sea, life."[2] One finds the same idea, slightly later, in W. H. Hudson (*Far Away and Long Ago*) and Ernest Seton Thompson (*Two Little Savages*), not to mention Barrie and Stevenson. The reader is invited to admire boys playing Crusoe, but surrounding them and modifying the admiration is this halo of sensual appreciation, unimaginable in Defoe, Campe, and Marryat and extraneous to the Crusoe story. It is the aesthetic movement that captures the story briefly and makes some quite dazzling things out of it.

Then the story, having fallen into "decay," in the twentieth century fell into the hands of its enemies—men and women of letters of the type who had shown themselves hostile to it since 1726 and *Gulliver's Travels.* Exponents of moral anxiety or sardonic skepticism, like Golding and Spark, wrote versions of the story that sometimes attracted mass audiences. In the nineteenth century the *Robinsonaden* were popular and the anti-Robinsons appealed only to the few. In the twentieth century the reverse was true.

1. Jefferies, *Bevis,* 91.
2. Jefferies, *The Story of My Heart,* 48.

These episodes will make no sense unless we use the scheme of historical development. What we must do, surely, is to retain that scheme but add to it these other patterns, some of which challenge it. Besides the secondary patterns already mentioned, for instance, there is that of national difference. The versions of Crusoe written in French will naturally relate to each other in ways they do not relate to English and German versions, even when the latter are closer in date. More important, they will relate to, or resemble, the "serious literature" of France. Rousseau is after all one of the greatest names in that literature, and so Tournier is bound to address himself to Rousseau more than the English Crusoe writers do.

I have found it interesting to stress the counter-truth—that this tradition is international. Though Robinson is a very English name, French and German writers have absorbed it into their versions of the story. Though *Swiss Family Robinson* was written in German, it was immensely popular in nineteenth-century France. But it remains true that Rousseau's editing and endorsement of Defoe's book was a gesture within the Rousseau oeuvre, which is part of a long series of gestures called French literature. Thus as well as a single, many-stranded cable of connections running from 1719 to 1967 upon which one can mark continual changes in the story's significance, which run more or less in one direction, we have also a complex grid with lines running in different directions. This grid generates innumerable spaces, which correspond to more versions of the story than actually exist, or at least have come to my attention. (Among the missing versions are those that were not written in nineteenth-century Australia and America.) To change the metaphor, historical forces acting upon literature play upon this topic, this story; it has been for hundreds of years, and is likely to remain, fascinating to writers. Those forces push it to the forefront in their minds recurrently, though from a variety of angles and charged with a number of meanings.

One place one sees it emerging in contemporary writing is in the literatures of nonwhite societies. Thus Maxine Hong Kingston in her *China Men* tells the story of Lo Bun Sun, a Sinified version of Robinson. Her telling mockingly reflects the meaning of the myth for the Chinese in America. In science fiction the Robinson character often continues his earliest career, with uninhabited planets replacing uninhabited islands. There is a science-fiction movie called *Robinson Crusoe on Mars,* and the novels of Robert Heinlein transfer the traits and virtues of Robinson, along with those of other Western heroes, into space.

To conclude, let me mention three contemporary Crusoe books that lie somewhat to one side of the main line. One is Jane Gardam's *Crusoe's Daughter* of 1985, about a girl and woman called Polly Flint, born in 1898. The story begins in 1904, when Polly goes to live in rather a grim environment on the north coast of England, near the Iron Works, to be brought up by her aunts. Her father had been a sea captain, and she, as she grows up a solitary reader, identifies with Robinson and calls herself his daughter, aiming to acquire his virtues of courage and self-respect in adversity. She sees him as a model especially useful to women. He was "stuck," she declares, as women are, and you have to call that situation of being stuck "God's will."

This affiliation of course distinguishes Polly, and her author, from earlier novel heroines with lonely childhoods, like Rosamond Lehmann's in *Dusty Answer,* who finds that her happiness is promised by poetry and by writers of sensibility. Gardam stresses this difference by having Polly meet a literary circle (which includes Virginia Woolf, unnamed but unmistakable). The members of this circle condemn Defoe as lacking imagination, poetry, and form, and Polly has to separate herself from them. Clearly, this book is not a version of Defoe's story. But it is, as much as Golding's or Spark's, a book about the place of the Robinson myth in English culture. This one is doubly interesting because basically it is friendly to the story and perceptive of its many-sidedness, for instance, its usefulness to women as well as men.

The second is the South African novelist J. M. Coetzee's *Foe* of 1986. This is not exactly a retelling, but it is a historical fantasy about Crusoe and Defoe (and other of Defoe's stories and characters) set in the eighteenth century. The narrator is a woman, Susan Barton, and the first part of the book begins *in medias res,* with the island, Crusoe, and Friday, when she is wrecked there with them. The second part is her journal letter to Defoe in London, written from another part of the city, where she lives with Friday. She wants Defoe to write the Crusoe story. And the third part is her first-person narration of her dealings with Defoe after they meet.

The major symbol of Coetzee's story is Friday, as he is in Tournier's story. But this is a much more somber and agonized image. Coetzee's Friday has had his tongue cut out and cannot speak. He is a dumb victim, around whom Susan Barton's, and the reader's, guilts and anxieties circle. Though coming some twenty years after Tournier's, this could be called a modernist version of the story, while the other is postmodernist.

Finally, there is the American *Mosquito Coast* by Paul Theroux, published in 1982. This in effect is a version of *The Swiss Family Robinson,* for it tells of an all-knowing father who uproots his family from contemporary Massachusetts and takes them to Central America to save them from modern decadence. He there displays a technical genius that recalls Verne's hero rather than Wyss's, before his overweening pride and ambition bring them all to disaster. This novel is interesting above all because Theroux takes the excitements of technical ingenuity and its manifold connections to the old Anglo-Saxon virtues quite seriously. He therefore makes a contribution to the tradition that is in this way superior to Tournier's. He is of course on the thetic side of the dialectic as far as this aspect of the story goes. (The ending of his version, however, is modernist.) What he shows is that the story, even with its original themes, can continue to attract the storyteller in more than satiric ways.

The form in which the Robinson story is most likely to continue to attract writers is the survival story. As the Western mind becomes increasingly preoccupied with the prospect of a nuclear holocaust, the figure of a single figure picking his way over the rubble, learning to cope with a hostile environment, and trying to reconstitute, out of his memory and a few machines, the rich and splendid civilization from which he has suddenly been ejected, which has suddenly shattered around him, is bound to remain a potent symbol and narrative device. Examples are Walter M. Miller's *A Canticle for Leibowitz* (1959), Doris Lessing's *Four-Gated City* (1969), and Russell Hoban's *Riddley Walker* (1980).

It is fitting that this treatment should have an emotional character as ambivalent in its relations to empire as the original. I mean, the story thus sketched makes the civilization that will then be destroyed, the civilization in which we are now still enmeshed, both wonderful and terrible. And just so, Defoe's story had its anti-imperialist as well as its imperialist character. It was the nineteenth century that overwhelmed the story's ambivalence with the surge of Anglo-Saxon success. Now the tide of events has turned, and the story can again evoke a strongly mixed response of strong emotions.

Bibliography

Alekseev, M. P. *Mezhdunarozhnie Svyazi Ruskoi Literaturi*. Moscow, 1963.
Atwood, Margaret. *Survival*, Toronto, 1972.
Bacon, Francis. *Bacon's Essays*. Oxford, 1890.
Ballantyne, Robert Michael. *The Coral Island*. Edinburgh, 1949.
Barrie, James M. *Margaret Ogilvie and Others*. New York, 1930.
———. *Peter Pan*. New York, 1928.
———. *Plays and Stories*. London, 1961.
Beaglehole, J. C. *The Journals of Captain James Cook*. London, 1974.
Birkin, Andrew. *J. M. Barrie and the Lost Boys*. New York, 1979.
Borrow, George. *Lavengro*. London, 1907.
Calder, Jenni. *Heroes*. London, 1977.
———. *Stevenson and Victorian Scotland*. Edinburgh, 1981.
Campe, Joachim Heinrich. *Columbus or the Discovery of America*. London, 1799.
———. *The New Robinson Crusoe*, London, 1788.
———. *Robinson der Juengere*. Hamburg, 1779.
Carlyle, Thomas. *Past and Present*. London, 1912.
Chesneaux, Jules. *The Political and Social Ideas of Jules Verne*. London, 1972.
Cloonan, William. *Michel Tournier*. Boston, 1985.
Commager, Henry Steele. *The Empire of Reason*. New York, 1977.
Cooper, James Fenimore. *The Crater*. Cambridge, Mass., 1962.
Costello, Peter. *Jules Verne*. London, 1978.
Cowper, William. *Poetical Works*. London, 1905.
Craig, David. *Scottish Literature and the Scottish People*. London, 1961.
Dampier, William. *A Voyage to New Holland*. London, 1939.
Daws, Gavin. *A Dream of Islands*. New York, 1980.

de la Mare, Walter. *Desert Islands and Robinson Crusoe.* London, 1930.

Dell, Floyd, *Intellectual Vagabondage.* New York, 1926.

Dottin, Paul. *Daniel Defoe et ses romans.* Paris, 1924.

Downs, Robert M. *In Search of New Horizons.* Chicago, 1978.

Dutton, G. *The Literature of Australia.* London, 1964.

Edgeworth, Richard and Maria. *Practical Education.* New York, 1835.

Eggoff, Sheila, L. F. Ashley, and S. T. Stubbs. *Only Connect.* Toronto, 1969.

Fenn, G. Manville. *G. A. Henty: The Story of an Active Life.* London, 1907.

Fisher, R., and H. Johnston. *Captain James Cook and His Times.* Seattle, 1979.

Frye, Northrop. *The Bush Garden.* Toronto, 1971.

Giraudoux, Jean, trans. Ben R. Redmond. *Suzanne and the Pacific.* New York, 1923.

Golding, William. *Lord of the Flies.* New York, 1962.

Gove, Philip Babcock. *The Imaginary Voyage in Prose Fiction.* New York, 1941.

Grattan. C. H. *The South Pacific to 1900.* Ann Arbor, Mich., 1963.

Green, F. C. *Eighteenth-Century France: Six Essays.* New York, 1964.

Gregg, Pauline. *Modern Britain.* New York, 1965.

Grivel, Guillaume. *L'Ile Inconnue.* Paris, 1784.

Heidenreich, Helmut. *Pikarische Welt.* Darmstadt, 1969.

Huet, Marie-Hélène. *L'Histoire des voyages extraordinaires.* Paris, 1973.

Jefferies, Richard. *Bevis.* London, 1882.

———. *The Story of My Heart.* London, 1883.

Jelavich, Peter. *Munich and Theatrical Modernism.* Cambridge, Mass., 1985.

Johnson, Samuel. *The Letters of Samuel Johnson.* London, 1952.

Kingsford, M. R. *The Life of W. H. G. Kingston.* Toronto, 1947.

Lawrence, D. H. *Complete Poems of D. H. Lawrence.* New York, 1964.

Liebs, Elke. *Die Paedagogische Insel.* Stuttgart, 1977.

Lloyd, Christopher. *William Dampier.* London, 1956.

Lukács, Georg. *Studies in European Realism.* London, 1950.

Maixner, Paul. *Robert Louis Stevenson: The Critical Heritage.* London, 1981.

Mallery, R. H. *Masterworks of Travel and Exploration.* New York, 1948.

Marryat, Frederick. *Frank Mildmay.* London, 1896.

———. *The Little Savage.* London, 1848–49.

———. *Masterman Ready.* London, 1970.

Marx, Karl. *Economic and Philosophical Manuscripts.* Moscow, 1966.

Moore, George. *Avowals.* New York, 1923.

Mott, Frank Luther. *Golden Multitudes.* New York, 1947.

Muir, Edwin. *Scott and Scotland.* London, 1936.

Nordhoff, C., and J. Hall. *The Mutiny on the Bounty.* Boston, 1932.

O'Neill, Kevin. *André Gide and the roman d'aventure.* Sydney, 1969.

Orwell, George. *Collected Essays.* London, 1961.

Pratt, E. J. *E. J. Pratt on His Life and Poetry.* Toronto, 1983.

Psichari, Jean. *Le solitaire du Pacifique.* Paris, 1922.

Pupin, Michael. *From Immigrant to Inventor; an Example for Young Americans.* New York, 1923.

Quayle, Eric. *Ballantyne the Brave.* London, 1967.

Reallexikon der deutschen Literaturgeschichte. Berlin, 1958–84.

Reilly, John H. *Jean Giraudoux.* Boston, 1978.

Rousseau, Jean-Jacques. *Emile.* Paris, n.d. (before 1912).

———. *Emile,* trans. Barbara Foxley. London, 1914.

Slocum, Joshua. *Sailing Alone Around the World.* New York, 1900.

Smith, Janet Adam. *Henry James and Robert Louis Stevenson*. London, 1948.
Stevenson, Robert Louis. *Treasure Island*. London, 1905.
――――. *Works*. Edinburgh, 1907.
Texte, Joseph. *Jean Jacques Rousseau and the Cosmopolitan Spirit in Literature*. London, 1929.
Tournier, Michel. *Vendredi*. Paris, 1972.
――――. *Le vent du paraclet*. Paris, 1977.
――――. *Le vol du vampire*. Paris, 1982.
Ullrich, Hermann. *Robinson und Robinsonaden*. Weimar, 1898.
Van Orman, R. A. *The Explorers*. Albuquerque, N.M., 1984.
Verne, Jules. *The Works of Jules Verne*. intro. Charles F. Horne. New York, 1911.
――――. *The Adventures of Captain Hatteras*. New York, 1911.
――――. *The Exploration of the World*. New York, 1911.
――――. *Five Weeks in a Balloon*. New York, 1911.
――――. *L'Ile mystérieuse*. Paris, 1960.
――――. *The Long Vacation*. New York, 1976.
――――. *Textes oubliés*. Paris, 1979.
――――. *A Trip from the Earth to the Moon*. New York, 1911.
Vierne, Simone. *L'Ile mystérieuse de Jules Verne*. Paris, 1973.
Watson, Harold F. *The Coasts of Treasure Island*. San Antonio, Tex., 1969.
Wells, H. G. *The History of Mr. Polly*. Cambridge, Mass., 1960.
Wyss, Johann David. *The Family Robinson Crusoe*. London, 1814.
――――. *Le Robinson Suisse*. Paris, 1824.
――――. *Le Robinson Suisse*, trans. Henri de Suchau. London, 1869.
――――. *Der Schweizerische Robinson*. Zurich, 1812.
――――. *The Swiss Family Robinson*, trans. W.H.D.A., intro. Charles Nodier, London, 1870.
――――. *The Swiss Family Robinson*, ed. W. H. G. Kingston. London, 187 ?.

Index